This innovative study presents an account of the interaction of people from different ethnic backgrounds who live in Southall, the most densely populated multi-ethnic ghetto of London. Breaking with the tradition of studying a single ethnic community, Gerd Baumann treats Southall as a single social field in which various immigrant groups come to terms both with one another and with the dominant culture of England. The people of Southall affirm ethnic distinctiveness in some contexts, but they are also engaged in rethinking their identities and in debating the meanings of their cultural heritage. This book is at once a vivid ethnographic account of an aspect of contemporary British life, and a challenge to the conventional discourse of community studies.

Cambridge Studies in Social and Cultural Anthropology

100

CONTESTING CULTURE

Cambridge Studies in Social and Cultural Anthropology

The monograph series *Cambridge Studies in Social and Cultural Anthropology* publishes analytical ethnographies, comparative works and contributions to theory. All combine an expert and critical command of ethnography and a sophisticated engagement with current theoretical debates.

A list of books in the series will be found at the end of the volume.

CONTESTING CULTURE

Discourses of identity in multi-ethnic London

GERD BAUMANN
University of Amsterdam

CAMBRIDGE
UNIVERSITY PRESS

Published by the Press Syndicate of the University of Cambridge
The Pitt Building, Trumpington Street, Cambridge CB2 1RP
40 West 20th Street, New York, NY 10011–4211, USA
10 Stamford Road, Oakleigh, Melbourne 3166, Australia

First published 1996

Printed in Great Britain at the University Press, Cambridge

A catalogue record for this book is available from the British Library

Library of Congress cataloguing in publication data

Baumann, Gerd.
    Contesting culture: discourses of identity in multi-ethnic London / Gerd
Baumann.
        p.   cm. – (Cambridge studies in social and cultural
anthropology; 100)
    Includes bibliographical references.
    ISBN 0 521 55482 9 (hb). – ISBN 0 521 55554 X (pb)
    1. Ethnicity – England – Southall (London)   2. Ethnic neighborhoods –
England – Southall (London)   3. Community life – England – Southall
(London)   4. Multiculturalism – England – Southall (London)
5. Southall (London, England) – Ethnic relations.   6. Southall
(London, England) – Social conditions.   I. Title.   II. Series.
GN585.G8B38   1996
305.8′009421′84 – dc20   95-34576 CIP

ISBN 0 521 55482 9 hardback
ISBN 0 521 55554 X paperback

KS

Contents

List of illustrations

Figures

Plates

Between pages 50 and 51
All photographs by Peter Seglow, Department of Human Sciences, Brunel,
The University of West London

1 Punjabi dancers and London police
2 Telephone engineer at work
3 Conversation at the bus stop
4 Muslim refugee outside an 'off-licence' liquor store
5 Policeman, undertaker, and temple official leading a funeral
   cortege
6 Stopping for a chat on the Broadway: men
7 Stopping for a chat on the Broadway: women
8 Sikh ladies passing a public house
9 'Danceasia presents': Ghazal, Bhangra and Rap for Valentine's
   Day
10 Children at a middle school

Tables

Acknowledgements

'Doing ethnography', as it is sometimes called, is not, of course, one process, but at least two. Fieldwork one lives, ethnographies are written. I re-state the obvious here, both to remark on its strange absence in some literary critiques of ethnographic texts, and to help me pull out at least some threads from a fabric of favours so dense that it resists narrative ordering.

First, one settles *on* a place, and it was Adam Kuper who, knowing my intention to 'work among (other) immigrants', pointed me to Southall and suggested that I move there. I might have settled for something less complicated and quicker without him. Throughout the next seven years, Adam Kuper has encouraged my research with a commitment, trust, and critical support that defy any written expression of thanks.

Then, one settles *into* the place. It was Southallians like Narinder Ghattoura and 'Uncle Syd', Balbir Nandra and Floyd Wilson, my neighbours Shiv and Ram Singhji and their families, who made me feel at home and involved in Southall. Along with Kirpal Marwaha, Graham Jimpson, David Baldwin, and many of their friends, they made the difference between living fieldwork and doing some piece of research. The research, however, needed more time than I initially had, and it was the Leverhulme Trust that bailed me out. After two years of fieldwork alongside work, the Leverhulme Trust awarded me a nine months' grant that, effectively, took me out of teaching for fifteen months, and allowed three final-year students to supplement my fieldwork with their own. Hazel Yabsley, Barbara Hawkes, and Teresa McGarry are quoted as ethnographic authorities in this book, for that is what they became. So is Richard Hundleby, a student and friend who had worked with me before, when the going was toughest. Their contributions, and the ways in which I have drawn on them, are detailed in the Introduction on 'the process of research'.

At about the same time, I met Marie Gillespie, then engaged in her own research about Southallians' uses of the media (Gillespie 1995). To acknowledge academic co-operation would, in this case, be a private joke. Between the synergy of sharing fieldworks and the love of friends, I can think of nothing that has not, then or since, enhanced our lives. One of our joint madnesses, a qualitatively conceived mass survey among young Southallians, came near to spelling disaster: 350 young people volunteered 5 million bytes of data. What little of this untapped resource the book can present, I owe to the tireless exertions of Lynette Clarke and Mozzy Hajian. We would have given up on the data without them.

When it came to writing, it was again Adam Kuper who arranged an almost care-free year for me through a reciprocal teaching exchange with the University of New Mexico. The resulting first draft was read closely by colleagues and friends. I thank especially Marie and Tom Cheesman, Rick Hundleby, and Hazel Yabsley. The second draft, written when back in Southall again, was improved with the generous and painstaking help of Peter Seglow and Charles Stewart. Steven Vertovec, who also read this second draft, continued to point me to crucial further reading. An incisive revision was inspired by Chris Fuller and produced a third draft, followed by a fourth which took account of further criticisms by Readers for the Press. This last stage was the hardest, and I could not have coped with it but for the reassuring support of my new colleagues at Amsterdam, Peter van der Veer, Patricia Spyer, and Peter van Rooden. Finally, I owe thanks to Rick Hundleby who put enormous effort and skill into a last round of editing the text, and to Peter Seglow who went out of his way to take the photographs for all the plates.

I dedicate the book to my three teachers: John Blacking who made me an anthropologist; Godfrey Lienhardt, who taught me that data can argue; and Adam Kuper who has made this possible, and made it a thrill to try.

Note on the text

As usual in ethnographies, vernacular terms are printed in *italics*. This applies not only to words taken from Punjabi, Urdu or Hindi, but, more importantly, to two English key words.

The terms *culture* and *community* form part of the Southall vernacular. Wherever they are cited to reflect local meanings and usages, they thus appear *italicized*.

In other places, they appear in quotation marks or with qualifiers such as 'putative', 'assumed', or 'ascribed'. This is when they are quoted or paraphrased from what I have called the dominant discourse about 'ethnic' minorities. This discourse envisages minorities as forming homogeneous 'communities' defined by an inherited 'culture' thought, in a circular fashion, to be based on their 'ethnic' identity. Since 'ethnic' is the crucial cipher of the dominant discourse, it, too, should appear in quotation marks throughout. In order not to annoy the reader with unnecessary 'stumbling blocks', however, I have used quotation marks only in cases of possible doubt.

A distinction between the dominant discourse and the vernacular usages, which in some contexts endorse it and in others deny it, is essential to the argument that the book puts forth.

1

Introduction: the process of research

The ethnographic data presented in this book are arranged in the form of an argument that might be called theoretical. But my involvement and interest in the research were driven by personal motives. After twelve years of study and work as an Africanist anthropologist, I was faced with the choice between a teaching job in New York and another at Brunel, The University of West London. To stay in Britain would make sense, I thought, if I could engage in research among so-called immigrants. Having myself migrated to Britain at the age of twenty-one, I had been puzzled for a long time by the way in which immigrants were portrayed in the British media, in political rhetoric, and, not least, in the academic literature. Among Africanist anthropologists, it had become a common-place that it was wrong to 'tribalize' people. It was wrong both politically and academically to say that what Africans did, they did *because* they were Maasai or Kikuyu, Luo or some other ethnic group. 'An African miner is a miner' was a neat phrase that, lifted from the work of Max Gluckman, served as a slogan against reducing people's culture to their tribal or ethnic identity. Yet, in Britain this ethnic reductionism seemed to reign supreme, and the greater number even of academic community studies I read seemed to echo it. Whatever any 'Asian' infor-mant was reported to have said or done was interpreted with stunning regularity as a consequence of their 'Asianness', their 'ethnic identity', or the 'culture' of their 'community'. All agency seemed to be absent, and culture an imprisoning cocoon or a determining force. Even their children, born, raised, and educated in Britain, appeared in print as 'second-generation immigrants' or 'second-generation Asians', and, unlike the children of white migrants like me, were thought to be precar-iously suspended 'between two cultures'.

This latter commonplace in particular I failed to understand. I could not work out why they should be suspended between, rather than be seen to reach across, two cultures. More importantly, which two cultures were involved? Was there a homogeneous British culture on the one hand, perhaps regardless of class or of region, and on the other hand some other culture, perhaps one which was shared with their parents? If so, how were these parental cultures defined: was it on the basis of regional origin or religion, caste or language, migratory path or nationality? Each of these could define a community, a culture, and an ethnic identity in the same breath, it seemed. So between which two cultures was any young Southallian suspended?

The answers to my confusion could, I thought, be found only by field-work: I rented a house in the centre of Southall, where I lived for the next six years, and from there involved myself in the life of the suburb. My agenda, as in all fieldwork, was open: live locally, socialize locally, find local things to do, and let yourself in for whatever comes. At the same time, keep a daily research diary, write fieldwork notes, and, not least, keep a personal diary in order not to confuse private concerns with the documentation of other people's doings and sayings. I first focused my research on youths in their teens for several reasons. All these young people had been born in the town, went to the same three schools, watched the same four television channels, and spoke the same language, a West London dialect of English interspersed with various American-isms and Indianisms. Their shared circumstances of upbringing would allow me to abstain from tribalizing them: 'a Southallian Sikh is a Southallian', and whether or not I had to refer to their 'Sikhness' or their caste to understand what they did would be a matter of finding out, rather than knowing in advance. Their shared language would allow me to start fieldwork before attending classes in Hindi, Punjabi, or Urdu.

During the first year of living in Southall, I made myself known, and useful as far as I could. What I could draw on, and drew on with great personal pleasure, were my interests as a musician; what skills I had acquired in teaching creative writing; my ability to take minutes at meet-ings and deal with bureaucracies; and, most importantly, my personal desire to make friends and enjoy life to the full in a new place. Fieldwork and the curiosity for local knowledge began to imprint their own stamp on my daily routines. Gradually, the 'Railway Tavern' turned into a living-room away from home, and the grotty living-room of my house into a place where Narinder and Balbir, Joshua, Sukhbir, and Syd would drop in to have an illicit cigarette after school or a drink after work.

'What do you actually do here? I mean, what's this research thing you do for the College?', Narinder once asked me during a get-together with his friends. By then, the first phase of research had become full-time: the Leverhulme Trust, London, had awarded me a grant which effectively relieved me from teaching duties for fifteen months. My project had a neat title now, which I explained to Narinder and his friends. 'Cross-Community Peer Orientations in the Youth Culture of a Multi-Ethnic Suburb of London' had become the focus of my research. That Southall was a multi-ethnic suburb of the capital was clear. That peer orientations concerned the mutual influences, cross-overs, and cultural fusions among young Southallians, was easily confirmed. But what was this 'cross-community' bit? The core of what I had promised the Leverhulme Trust to clarify was deconstructed by a few young Southallians that afternoon.

'It depends what community you mean', was their collective verdict on my research. When the cross-community orientation concerned music, clearly there was Rap, a music of the *Black community* eagerly taken up by *the Asians*. Conversely, there was Bhangra, the Punjabi dance turned disco-music which was performed best, at a recent prize contest, by a *Caribbean* kid who combined it with body-popping and breakdancing. When the cross-community orientation concerned the two notorious gangs that sometimes clashed on Southall's streets and terrified local shopkeepers, the division was between young Sikhs of the Jat or farmers' caste and, probably, everybody else, including 'a few Blacks and whites that got themselves involved'. When it came to 'going out', cross-community would be the right word to describe a young *Asian* flirting with a young *Caribbean* or *white*, or it might apply to a young Sikh flirting with a young Hindu, or indeed a Sikh of East African Asian parentage flirting with a fellow Sikh of Punjabi parentage. Then again, some parents would not consider such a match to go across *community* boundaries since both were Sikh. 'It'd also depend on how many daughters you've got, whether people call it "cross-community" to your face.' If a household had four daughters to provide a dowry for, people would not gossip, I was told, if one of the daughters were to marry across one *community* boundary or another. But if you had four sons to bring in dowry, your only daughter would have to be 'married off ever-so-pure'.

'So what counts as "cross-community" depends on all sorts of stuff [read: sociological variables], including what other people actually know, or think they know?', I enquired after three hours of debate which fulfilled every ethnographer's dream: to see his research agenda torn to shreds and reassembled again. Yes, of course it did: but hadn't I known that all along, living in Southall, and didn't the people at College know that already?

If what counted as cross-community depended on such a variety of factors, recognized as mutually independent variables even by young-sters, the same had surely to apply to what counted as *community* in the first place. The idea did not please me. For one thing, it made my research look stupid: what was the point of calling activities cross-community or community if Southallians half my age knew that the divi-sion depended on context and contingency? Secondly, I did not like the idea because all this awareness of shifting identities seemed to jar with Southallians' predilection for instant categorization or 'telling'. Just as I had learned to 'tell' Catholics from Protestants over seven years' living in Belfast, so I had learned, in Southall, to tell an East African Sikh from a Punjabi one by the fold of his turban, and to deduce on sight the 'community' of the woman ahead of me in the greengrocer's check-out queue. One of these young friends, who now demolished my research plan, had once brought me a list of family names and castes: a concor-dance he had asked his grandmother to help him with, so that I should know the caste of each kid in class when I took up auxiliary teaching in a Southall school. So *community* was a concept to be used and redefined contextually, but certainly it could not be written off as an irrelevancy. The same went for *culture* in its reified form. 'In my culture we do', and 'in our culture we don't' were ever-available phrases to 'explain' why people did or did not do as had been expected of them. Young Southallians seemed at once to reify their *cultures* and *communities*, and to deny their own reifications.

During the second phase of research, I looked to adult Southallians to help throw light on my accumulated bafflements. It seemed to be they who best knew which *community* was which, and what *culture* it stood for. The shift happened gradually as young Southallians invited me to meet their parents, neighbours invited me to weddings and birthday parties, and I pursued the adult contacts I had made in community centres and temples, churches and schools, tandoori shops and pubs. I felt more confident now in talking to adults, despite the fact that my lessons in Punjabi and Urdu had borne little fruit. I had discovered that all but a few Southallians mastered English with a fluency I would never achieve in any of the 'community languages', and I had therefore changed my language strategy to learning extensive glossaries of vernac-ular key words that had no easy equivalent in English, such as kinship, religious, and various normative terms. It remained a source of constant amazement to me how the tone of a conversation changed when, being told of, say, an uncle who had said this or that, I enquired whether this was the *chacha*, the *thaia*, or the *mama*. People would not hesitate, after such an intervention, to use whatever other vernacular terms they thought untranslatable; and if I did not know one at first, I made sure I would know it next time. 'The most important thing about the first interview is the second interview' became my motto in pursuing research with adults who, unlike youths, often expected the researcher to interview them, rather than to sit around waiting to see what the chat or 'lark' might come to focus on.

Adult Southallians were no less relativist than their children in discussing *culture* and *community*. Even assuming that community was a matter of birthplace, as the dominant discourse so often does, some Southallians could, among friends, squeeze a laugh out of the absurdities of ethnic classification. 'See me friend Jas here', said Phil, an Englishman, and pointed to his drinking-mate at the Railway Tavern bar, 'he's an Asian, but he's born in Africa, so I'd say he's an African. And me, I was born in Burma, so I'm the Asian here, aren't I. And Winston here, you think he's a West Indian: he's the only one of us born in this town, so he's the Englishman born and bred!' Attributions of culture and community can clearly not be reduced to one factor alone. Rather, all but the most single-minded of adult Southallians, it turned out, regarded themselves as members of several *communities* at once, each with its own *culture*. Making one's life meant ranging across them. I did find a few people who said: 'I am a Muslim and nothing else', 'I am a Christian and have no other community', or 'I am an African from the Caribbean, but as African as the people born in Africa'. I have tried not to discount their positions in the body of the book, and have mentioned them wherever the ethnographic context allowed it. Nevertheless, the vast majority of all adult Southallians saw themselves as members of several *communities*, each with its own *culture*. The same person could speak and act as a member of the Muslim *community* in one context, in another take sides against other Muslims as a member of the Pakistani *community*, and in a third count himself part of the Punjabi *community* that excluded other Muslims but included Hindus, Sikhs, and even Christians. In this way, they echoed the awareness of shifting identities that young Southallians had alerted me to. Matters got more confusing, however, as fieldwork progressed. Some Hindu parents would claim that 'all Sikhs are Hindus'; some Sikh parents would dissociate themselves from the Sikh *community* and describe their culture as

'British-Asian, basically, whatever the religion you're from'; and Muslim friends would argue with pride that the local mosque was in itself a *multicultural community*. Clearly, all these utterances could be discounted as if they were mere figures of speech. But when an ethnographer collects more of them by the week, should one not ask what makes these usages any less important, authentic, or truthful than the usages that equate culture with community; community with ethnic identity; and ethnic identity with the 'cause' of a person's doings or sayings?

The equation of culture with community was cast in doubt by more adult Southallians as time went on. Fundamental though it was in some contexts, it seemed self-defeatingly simple in others. Sometimes, Sikh Southallians would subdivide their *community* into *communities* of caste, although at other times they would insist that Sikhism entailed a denial of caste altogether. Many Hindu Southallians, though certainly not all, could endorse a Hindu culture that encompassed not only sections of the Sikh *community*, but other *cultures* too. At other times, the same people would blame 'Untouchables' for taking such an 'impure' stance. Irish Southallians were sure that they formed part of an Irish *culture*, but denied the existence of an Irish *community*; English Southallians were unsure how to apply either term to themselves or their neighbours, unless their neighbours were 'coloured', that is, 'people of ethnicity' as certified by the dominant discourse. Afro-Caribbean Southallians spoke of a *community* that had, as yet, not 'found its own *culture*'. Again, none of these further statements should be taken at face value. Yet they cannot be written off either, and what they add up to, I shall argue, is an alternative to the dominant discourse. It does not replace that dominant discourse. But in many contexts this demotic discourse counteracts the dominant one by drawing attention to the daily process of 'making culture', rather than 'having a culture'.

The dominant discourse relies on equating community, culture, and ethnic identity, and its protagonists can easily reduce anybody's behaviour to a symptom of this equation. So long as its human objects can be logged under some ethnic identity other than, say, British, German, or American, it can even claim to speak 'for' them, 'represent' them, explain them to others. The ways in which Southallians spoke about each other and about themselves added up to a very different message: *culture* and *community* could be equated in some contexts, but were not the same in others. What the word 'identity' might mean in any one context, was a question of context. Fortunately, I had not yet worked out these ideas when I set out, with new friends, on the third phase of research.

This was to achieve two independent aims: on the one hand, it was to check up on the qualitative insights I had gathered by pitching them against quantitative data to confirm or contradict the results. On the other hand, it was to supplement my own efforts with qualitative research done independently by trained students.

The transformation of qualitative work into quantitative research had been started already. My colleague and friend Marie Gillespie and I had devised a questionnaire which addressed both her research concerns and my own and was based on the data each of us had gathered independently. Dr Gillespie wanted to collect statistical data on young Southallians' uses and views of the media, having given the subject some five years of ethnographic attention (Gillespie 1989, 1995). I wanted to find statistical confirmation or counter-evidence for the hunches I had formulated on 'cross-community peer influences' among Southall youths. Our combined questionnaire made a point of asking locally relevant questions in local terms, language, and style. It was piloted several times, and in the end we managed to administer it to some 350 young Southallians. Portions of this bulky survey of ninety-odd detailed questions were also to serve as a means of entry into the ethnographic field for three further researchers on whose work this book draws. Each of the three went through their own process of research.

I had previously enjoyed the co-operation of two interested students who joined me in Southall to conduct their own fieldwork. Richard Hundleby had researched a subtle and insightful case-study of local stereotypes about Afro-Caribbean youth; Bryn Williams had pointed to the 'West London culture' shared among a wide variety of Southall youths observed during a drama summer school. Now, the Leverhulme Trust had generously granted me some additional funds to pay for three more fellow researchers. These researchers were outstanding final-year students at Brunel University, specializing in Anthropology and Sociology. They had three tasks. The first was to further their own academic growth by involving themselves in real-life research, pursued not as a methodological exercise, but as a full-time preoccupation for five months of fieldwork and a year's unrelenting work in writing their BSc dissertations about it. I wanted these dissertations to be of the highest quality, so as to have a secondary literature with which to compare, and by which to judge my own results. I cannot pretend, of course, that I never influenced their approaches to the work in hand; but nor would they, or indeed I, accept that I did more than alert them to two essential caveats: firstly, social groups should be distinguished from social categories, whether these be called tribes or communties, races, generations, or castes. All of these terms designated categories that Southallians might, or might not, use in one context or another. The task was to document their uses, rather than take the words at face value and then peddle them as self-evident analytical concepts. Secondly, by stereotyping informants as 'belonging to' or even 'speaking for' a pre-defined 'community', one runs the risk of tribalizing people, instead of listening to them, and might end up studying communities of the researcher's own making.

Whether these caveats were an intrusion upon their independence of thinking or a precaution against commissioning three more studies that would replicate the dominant discourse, readers of their ethnographies can decide for themselves. Hazel Yabsley's dissertation (1990) explored 'Processes [*sic*] of ethnicity and community' on the most deprived of Southall's multi-ethnic housing estates, and drew attention to conceptions of spatial proximity, something I have not made enough of in this book. Barbara Hawkes' (1990a) 'Southall, An Ethnography of Change' analysed the self-understandings and selective cross-*community* alliances current among 'English' Southallians, and Teresa McGarry (1990) examined notions of *culture* and *community* among the three cohorts of Irish Southallians she was able to discern.

Their combined work produced a body of documentation as good as any that an ethnographer of 'communities' in Britain could draw upon. I have therefore used Hundleby (1987) and Hawkes (1990), McGarry (1990) and Yabsley (1990) as one would use any body of secondary literature gathered by others in the same field: quoting from it where it is relevant to the argument, spelling out agreements and disagreements where they arise, and drawing on transcripts of informants' statements where they could help to substantiate or qualify the argument. In the latter case, I have sometimes included the questions posed alongside the statements elicited. This is to allow readers to locate the context of informants' utterances, as well as to reassure themselves of the fieldwork rapport and high ethnographic standards that all four of the authors have brought to their work. In case it needs saying, all their contributions have been acknowledged by name and my uses of their materials checked with them. Moving the matter beyond attributional ethics, I must add that their findings have been invaluable in contextualizing, correcting, delimiting, and refining the argument put forth in the following pages. This argument will seek its strength from data, rather than deduction, but it needs first to be situated in its anthropological and political contexts.

2

The argument: identifying a dominant discourse

The reification of culture
The discourse of 'community' on the basis of ethnicity
The dominant discourse in Britain
Presentation of the data

The reification of culture

No idea is as fundamental to an anthropological understanding of social life as the concept of culture. At the same time, no anthropological term has spread into public parlance and political discourse as this word has done over the past twenty years. Together with the word community, it has become the cornerstone of public discourse about ethnic minorities. Thus, whether the people concerned be immigrants in Europe, native or hyphenated Americans, or warring 'ethnic groups' in the Third World and the post-socialist Second, political discourse is couched in the language of separate communities defined by their cultures that demand collective recognition and rights. An almost global range of contestations and conflicts thus appears to rely upon a vocabulary developed by anthropologists. Yet the word culture need not mean the same in political rhetoric or informants' usages as it does in anthropological analysis. To distinguish these meanings, though also to see where they overlap, is the chief task of this book.

Its ethnographic focus is Southall, a multi-ethnic town on the outskirts of London. Southall numbers some 60,000 people of internally highly diverse South Asian, Afro-Caribbean, Irish, English, and various other ethnic or national backgrounds. The obvious starting-point for fieldwork in such an 'immigrant ghetto' would have been to concentrate on a 'community study': to select one community, preferably national, religious or ethnic, and to describe it as an autonomous culture. Some of these community studies I had read, but the recipe seemed uncomfortably predictable: page one isolated some community of culture that the author had pre-defined, and the final page concluded that it, or they, were 'encapsulated'. The author's conclusion, in other words, seemed predetermined by the fieldworker's starting-point. Yet in Southall there seemed to be communities within communities, as well as cultures across communities. The equation between community and culture, dominant as it is in much public discourse about ethnic minorities, disintegrated the more I got to know Southallians. As I have indicated, Southallians indeed replicated the equation between a *community* and its *culture* in a number of contexts. But in others, the same Southallians could dissolve the dominant equation by statements such as: 'In our *community*, we don't have a *culture*'; 'Of course we have a *culture*, but we're not a *community*'; or 'That [other] *community* is really part of our *culture*.'

The words *culture* and *community* were thus used in two systematically different ways among Southallians themselves. One range of usages reflected the dominant discourse as emphasized by many experts in 'community relations', many community studies and also, remarkably, by their political opponents who blamed 'ethnic minorities' and their reified 'cultures' for the 'social problems' facing 'the nation'. Besides engaging this dominant discourse, however, local usages established an alternative discourse which I have called demotic (lit. 'of the people'), and which denied the congruence between *culture* and *community* that was the hallmark of the dominant discourse.

In using the word 'discourse' to gloss these two ranges, I am aware, of course, that the term has assumed a bewildering vagueness as it has spread from the humanities to the social sciences. Yet I share Lutz and Abu-Lughod's (1990) view that 'rather than being alarmed by its spread ..., it might be better to ask ... what theoretical work ... [one] want[s] the term to do' (Lutz and Abu-Lughod 1990, 7). Of the uses they delineate, I subscribe to two in particular. One is to help focus the analysis of language and other social practices on pragmatics, rather than semantics, and the other is to relate these 'large-scale pragmatics' to the efficacy of power relations (Lutz and Abu-Lughod 1990, 9–10). Arrestingly, the very spread of the term 'discourse' may be related to what I have here called the reification of culture:

For many, ... the term [culture] seems to connote a certain coherence, uniformity and timelessness in the meaning systems of a given group, and to operate rather like the earlier concept of 'race' in identifying fundamentally different, essentialized, and homogenous social units (as when we speak about 'a culture').

Because of these associations, ... [it] falsely fixes the boundaries between groups in an absolute and artificial way.   (*Lutz and Abu-Lughod 1990, 9, my italics*)

This false fixing of boundaries is a direct consequence of the reified version of culture, and this reification is the very cornerstone that holds the dominant discourse together across all political divides. In order to distance myself from this reified understanding of 'culture', I shall sometimes use quotation marks when paraphrasing its meaning in the dominant discourse. This seems preferable to sacrificing a good, if complicated, word altogether.

What the notion of culture might signify has been debated by anthropologists for over a century. Sometimes these debates have indulged in purely definitional argy-bargy. Definitions, of course, are not judged by their truth value, but by their usefulness. This should be stressed in order to prevent an otherwise fatal misreading of the argument: to point out that a word carries different meanings in different discourses is not to call one discourse true and the other one false. Southallians, after all, use both of them: engaging one, they endorse the dominant equation between culture and community, engaging the other they dissolve it. The question thus raised concerns two understandings of culture.

Ethnographers' uses of the word culture have established one essential point of consensus: culture is not a real thing, but an abstract and purely analytical notion. It does not cause behaviour, but summarizes an abstraction from it, and is thus neither normative nor predictive. As a deliberate abstraction it is there to help anthropologists conceptualize that ever-changing 'complex whole' (Tylor 1871) through which people engage in the continual process of accounting, in a mutually meaningful manner, for what they do, say, and might think. Culture thus exists only insofar as it is performed, and even then its ontological status is that of a pointedly analytical abstraction. This ethnographic insight has been clarified, and enshrined even against the Boasian heritage of American anthropology, by a new consensus against essentialist approaches to culture (Barth 1994; Keesing 1994; Sahlins 1994; Vayda 1994).

Outside anthropology, however, the word was borrowed and assigned a new, and far more concrete, meaning in the discourse of what Rothschild has described as 'ethnopolitics'. The term is used to describe the process of 'mobilizing ethnicity from a psychological or cultural or social datum into political leverage for the purpose of altering *or reinforcing* ... systems of structured inequality between and among ethnic categories' (Rothschild 1981, 2, my italics). In this process, ethnopolitics 'stresses, ideologizes, reifies, modifies, and sometimes virtually re-creates the putatively distinctive and unique cultural heritages of the ethnic groups that it mobilizes' (Rothschild 1981, 3).

Ethnic categories are thus validated as forming ethnic groups, and these 'groups' are defined with reference to a 'culture' they are assumed, *ex hypothesi,* to share. An early example of this new public and political use of 'culture' can be seen in the Black Consciousness Movement of the United States. Whereas the Civil Rights Movement demanded equal individual rights for all citizens regardless of who they were, the Black Consciousness Movement addressed its constituents, not as citizens, but as a distinctive community with its own culture. In the new political discourse of ethnic and culture-based political rights, the anthropologist's abstraction of a perpetually changing process of meaning-making is replaced by a reified entity that has a definite substantive content and assumes the status of a thing that people 'have' or 'are members of'.

In this new context, the word culture can no longer function as a purely analytical abstract; it has to be filled with standardized meanings, that is, specified as a substantive heritage that is normative, predictive of individuals' behaviour, and ultimately a cause of social action. Kapferer (1988) has described such processes of 'the reification of culture, the production of culture as an object in itself' (1988, 97) and shown how selected established patterns and traits are 'systematically removed from their embeddedness in the flow of daily life, fashioned into symbolic things, and placed in a stable, dominant, and determinate relation to action' (1988, 210). Keesing (1994) has suggested that this 'conception of culture [which] almost irresistibly leads us into reification and essentialism' (1994, 302) is based on an ethnocentric construction of 'radical alterity – a culturally constructed Other radically different from Us' (1994, 301). He seems to forget, though, that people may reify their own *culture* as readily as they reify 'other' *cultures.* Van der Veer (1994) indeed traces Indian communalist conflicts to 'the basic ... fallacy of both sociological and [non-academic] communalist versions ... [This] is that it portrays Muslim and Hindu values as reified systems' (1994, 29). In working through the Southall data, I was blissfully unaware of these recent sources on reification, and culpably forgetful even of Berger and Luckmann (1967) who so cogently theorized the term for use in the social sciences:

Reification is the apprehension of human phenomena as if they were things, that is, ... the apprehension of the products of human activity as if they were something other than human products – such as facts of nature ... Man, the producer

of a world, is apprehended as its product, and human activity as an epiphenomenon of non-human processes. It must be emphasized that reification is a
modality of consciousness, more precisely, a modality of man's objectification of
the human world. Even while apprehending the world in reified terms, man
continues to produce it.   *(Berger and Luckmann 1967, 106–7)*

That Southallians indeed continue to produce culture, rather than
being produced by it, will be obvious throughout the book. Yet they also
share in what Clifford has called a 'powerful structure of feeling' which
sees *culture* as:

a body that lives and dies. Culture is enduring, traditional, structural (rather than
contingent, syncretic, historical). Culture is a process of ordering, not of disrup-
tion. It changes and develops like a living organism. It does not normally
'survive' abrupt alterations.   *(Clifford 1988, 235)*

Such a statement would find ready endorsement among many Southallians, and not only those who have direct experience of the abrupt
alterations that mark a transcontinental migration. The very process of
enculturating children entails the necessity of isolating elements, traits,
and norms that stick out as distinctive and which are thought, in the
widest sense, proper to a cultural 'us'. It may well seem plausible to most
anthropologists that, in Rosaldo's words, 'the notion of an authentic
culture as an autonomous internally coherent universe no longer seems
tenable, except perhaps as a "useful fiction" or a revealing distortion'
(Rosaldo 1989, 217). I shall return to this contention later. Meanwhile,
the fact remains that Southallians, and probably other people elsewhere,
subscribe to this useful fiction when they see fit. In tune with the dominant discourse, Southallians find it useful and plausible, in some
contexts, to reify *culture* at the same time as making, remaking, and thus
changing it.

Such a reification of culture must appear necessary, moreover, if the
word is to serve in the contestation of a new kind of rights: a category
of rights more collective in conception than the traditionally individualist
Civil Rights, but far more exclusive in character than generally Human
Rights. They are claimed, or indeed denied, on the basis of people's
membership in a collective defined by 'its culture'. Vertovec rightly
stresses the element of political contestation when he describes how
'Trinidad Hindu culture was made an object in itself so as to articulate
a shared ethnic identity in the face of potentially intensified patterns of
ethnic inequality and resource competition' (Vertovec, in press). With
regard to Britain, I have already mentioned a condensed example of this

reified view of culture in the phrase 'between two cultures'. The image it evokes is not of young people performing culture as a process of making sense of each other and of others, but of a culture-less flock lost between two immovable objects named cultures. Again, to note reification in a public discourse is not to call that discourse false. For analytical purposes, of course, reification makes no sense. In Whitehead's well-worn phrase, it involves the fallacy of misplaced concreteness. In a discourse of political contestation, however, reification may be desirable, and even seem necessary, to effect mobilization. This mobilization of all that are deemed to 'have the same culture' is helped by the call, reassuring or challenging, to form part of a pre-defined community.

The discourse of 'community' on the basis of ethnicity

Unlike the word culture, 'community' has never held a privileged place in the vocabulary of social scientists. On the contrary, among academics it has had a decidedly bad press. It is usually traced to the German sociologist Tönnies (1887), who tried to use it as an analytical abstraction in an essentially evolutionist account. Hillery (1955) researched a grand total of ninety-four meanings attributed to the term by sociologists, and the word appears quite clearly as a common-sense term with no theoretical potential for analytic use. Macfarlane (1977) has forcefully advocated that it be abandoned altogether. More recently, the anthropologist Anthony Cohen (1985) has, in one brilliant short treatise, stripped away whatever substantive meaning one might have attributed to the word, and shown community to be a contextually contingent 'symbolic construction'.

Even plain common sense would, in any case, suffice to warn one off the word as used in public rhetoric. In Northern Ireland, the 'Catholic community' and the 'Protestant community' are exhorted to make peace for the sake of 'the community'; the BBC speaks of stockbrokers as 'Britain's financial community'; and a British government, during my fieldwork, labelled a poll- or head-tax as a 'community charge'. Closer to the ethnographic concern of this book, one of Britain's most widely read commentators on current affairs avows that '"community" is a dishonest word ... It is invariably a party to pious fraud. Ethnic minorities are called "communities" either because it makes them feel better, or because it makes the white majority feel more secure' (Ignatieff 1992). Strikingly, Ignatieff goes back to a contestation that took place during my fieldwork and shows that constructions of a community may not, in fact, make people identified as minorities feel good at all:

One of the ironies of the Salman Rushdie affair was that the only thing on which anti-Islamic liberals and their fundamentalist opposite numbers agreed was that there was such a thing as a 'Muslim community'. 'It' was either a threat to liberal civilisation as we know it, or 'it' was a resurgent faith on the march. At the height of the affair, Muslims in Britain could be forgiven for wishing no one had ever thought them a community at all.   *(Ignatieff 1992)*

The stylized confrontation between a seemingly monolithic Muslim community and the British political establishment may indeed have more to do with white fears about 'British identity' than with an all-Muslim consensus, as Asad (1990) suggests. I shall offer some local data below. Here, however, it is more important to enquire why community in general might be thought an intrinsically dishonest word. Raymond Williams (1976) included the word among his famous 'Keywords' precisely 'because the problems of its meanings seemed to me inextricably bound up with the problems it was being used to discuss' (Williams 1976, 14):

It was when I suddenly realised that no-one ever used 'community' in a hostile sense that I saw how dangerous it was ... Community can be the warmly persuasive word to describe an *existing* set of relationships, or the warmly persuasive word to describe an *alternative* set of relationships ... What is most important, perhaps, is that unlike all other types of social organisation (state, nation, society, etc.) it seems never to be used unfavourably, and never to be given any ... opposing or distinguishing term.   *(Williams 1976, 66, my italics)*

The invariably positive connotations of the word no longer apply in Britain since it has become a polite term for 'ethnic minority'. Ignatieff implies as much. Yet the word retains connotations of interpersonal warmth, shared interests, and loyalty. To Gilroy (1987), for example, it 'signifies ... a particular set of values and norms in everyday life: mutuality, co-operation, identification and symbiosis' (Gilroy 1987, 234). Yet the question remains whether the word is chosen to describe a collectivity one willingly participates in oneself, or a stereotype of uniform commonality projected upon others on the sole basis of their ascribed ethnic identity. It makes a difference, after all, whether one postulates communities defined by some ethnic culture or one discerns different *cultures* within a *community*, as Pryce (1979) has so subtly done among the West Indian population of Bristol.

To make general statements about 'the Asians', 'the Jews', or 'the Irish' reeks of disrespect, ignorance, and even prejudice. Yet the same statements can be made to sound respectful and even solidary when uttered about the Asian, Jewish, or Irish 'community'. The word is so attractive, even to the detractors of ethnic minorities, because it appears to value people as members of a special collective. What is special about this collective is, in the case of ethnic minorities, that they are readily presumed to share a culture in its reified form.

In this dominant discourse, 'community' can function as the conceptual bridge that connects culture with ethnos. It can lend a spurious plausibility to the assumption that ethnic minorities must share the same culture by necessity of their ethnic bond itself. This is all the easier since culture appears as a reified entity already, and it is a general propensity of reifying thought that 'through reification, the world of institutions appears to merge with the world of nature' (Berger and Luckmann 1967, 108). Thus culture, and especially ethnic culture, can indeed appear as 'a universal mandate of natural laws, as the necessary consequence of biological ... forces' (ibid. 1967, 108). Not all public discourse about minority communities defined by their reified cultures needs to invoke this explicitly. It can be observed, nevertheless, in innumerable examples, for it offers two strategic advantages: substantively, it appeals to a popular biological reductionism; formally, it allows for discursive closure.

An appeal to biological reductionism is not surprising, of course, when examining a dominant discourse used about ethnic minorities. It is still a popular assumption, found as easily among anthropology students as in mass media across the globe, that ethnos, much like tribe, and indeed like the scientifically discredited notion of race, designates a biological fact. These purportedly natural cleavages between humans are easily and widely associated with cleavages of 'culture'. The tenacity with which even the term 'race' continues to dominate many informants' ideas of biology as the foundation of cultural diversity is evidence, if any were needed, of the persistent appeal of common-sense biologism: the expectation that cultural differences are founded in natural ones. This biologism is understandable, and the ethnographic record of pre-colonial times, too, is replete with peoples who regarded their own kinship systems, incest prohibitions, family structures, political, economic, and religious conventions as natural. It is thus not surprising that even notional collectives such as ethnic minorities should be credited with that reassuring quality of being both natural and cultural entities at once. From the stylization of ethnic categories into communities defined by a reified culture, the dominant discourse can thus progress to a portrayal of minorities as forming ethnic-cum-cultural 'communities'.

At this point of circular argument, discursive closure is complete. The two key terms mutually reinforce each other, for those defined as ethnic minorities must form a community based on their reified culture; and their culture must appear in reified form, because they are, after all, identified as a community. In cases where a reified minority culture can be equated with a particular ethnic group, the circular discourse can seek added plausibility from popular forms of biological reductionism. It can thus reduce all social complexities, both within communities and across whole plural societies, to an astonishingly simple equation: 'Culture = community = ethnic identity = nature = culture.'

Again, not all protagonists of the dominant discourse who turn ethnic categories into ethnic groups depict these as natural collectivities. It makes no sense, for instance, to call Muslims in Britain an ethnic group, although they are widely called a 'community' defined by a shared 'Muslim culture', as the dominant discourse would suggest. Many Muslims in Britain indeed do likewise, for the dominant discourse is not the exclusive preserve of majorities, however defined, or of politicians, activists, or mass media. Yet ethnic implications are discernible even in the dominant discourse about Muslims as observed among white Southallians: since few Muslims in Britain are white, the 'Muslim community' is certainly associated with being an ethnic minority, however heterogeneous on purportedly ethnic criteria, rather than simply a religious community. The same is not true, for example, of Jehovah's Witnesses or Latter-Day Saints, either of whom would be called a religious community, but hardly a culture and certainly not an ethnic community. The example makes clear that the dominant discourse is a discourse about purportedly ethnic minorities, rather than minorities in general. It makes clear also that the word 'ethnic' cannot be taken at face value as a descriptive term.

The word 'ethnic' is inescapably a relational term in at least two respects. The first concerns the criteria of distinction that are used to tell one ethnic category from another. On the face of it, ethnic criteria appear grounded in the biological criteria sometimes called 'descent' or 'race'. But this biological basis disappears as soon as it is scrutinized: anthropologists have known for a century that descent is a social construction, not a biological fact. All serious social scientists agree that differences of 'race' are biologistic reductions of differences which mask a plethora of non-biological criteria and would readily endorse Gilroy's 'reminder that "race" is a relational concept which does not have fixed referents. The naturalization of social phenomena and the suppression of the historical process which are introduced by its appeal to the biological realm can articulate a variety of different political antagonisms' (Gilroy 1987, 229). Biologists, too, agree that any distinction of human races is but an approximate shorthand for statistical tendencies, or clines, in the distribution frequencies of some 4 per cent of human genes over very large population samples. Needless to say, these genes are irrelevant in all cultural respects; even if they were not, race would still remain the weakest contender for any explanation of the criteria that 'ethnic' distinctions might 'really' be based upon. That they are not based on biological criteria is clear to every first-year biology student. It was already clear to Weber who wrote in the early years of this century:

All in all, the notion of 'ethnically' determined social action subsumes phenomena that a rigorous sociological analysis ... would have to distinguish carefully ... It is certain that in this process [of examination] the collective term 'ethnic' would be abandoned, for it is unsuitable for a really rigorous analysis.

(Weber 1978, 395)

Ethnic divisions are indeed based upon a proliferation of distinctions, all of them mutually independent. Social scientists and proverbial men-on-streets speak of ethnic groups on the basis of a shared language or a common homeland; a common nationality or an, often transnational, religion; a caste, however delineated, or a political axiom as, for instance, in the pan-Africanist case. Which criterion is stressed to draw an ethnic boundary is a matter of context, and Fredrik Barth (1969) has been influential for over twenty years in drawing anthropologists' attention to 'the interconnection between the diacritica that are chosen for emphasis, the [ethnic] boundaries that are [thus] defined, and the differentiating values that are espoused' in the process (Barth 1969, 35). Clyde Mitchell's (1956) pioneering analysis of the urban creation of a Bisa ethnic boundary in Zambia remains a classic of the field, and Haaland (1969) has given a paradigmatic case-study of how, in the Western Sudan, individuals and families exchange a Fur ethnic identity for a Baggara one. In a similar vein, Kandre (1967) has described how Chinese and other strangers are incorporated into the Yao ethnic category, and Barth (1969, 117–34) himself documented the process of Southern Pathans becoming recognized as 'ethnic' Baluch. Van den Berghe (1975, 73), writing about Highland Peru, likewise observes how ethnic boundaries are defined 'subjectively, relatively, and situationally, rather than objectively and absolutely ... The same [ethnic] terms can be used with a wide variety of meanings and referents.' Studies such as these have established time and again that ethnic boundaries, far from adumbrating biological distinctions, are socially constructed on a variety of criteria. Even in preindustrial societies, each of them is manipulated and re-evaluated according to context. In plural societies, moreover, the very multiplicity of purportedly ethnic criteria, be they language, national loyalty, or even caste, gives almost everyone singled out as 'ethnic' a whole range of 'ethnic' labels that are declared, or can be rendered, socially relevant.

This touches upon the second reason why 'ethnic' is inevitably a relational term. Its use depends not only on the criteria chosen in any one definitional context, but also on the criteria that determine whether it is used at all. Living in England as a German national, I was not assigned to a German 'ethnic group'. Most white English people would be upset if they found themselves designated as an 'ethnic group', rather than 'the population', 'the locals', 'the host society', or any such formula that sets them apart from the 'ethnic' character of 'others'. In Belize or Australia, they would, of course, expect otherwise, for who is thought ethnic and who is not is relational also in this sense. Writing as an anthropologist, my use of the term 'ethnic' must thus always be a matter of quoting. It reflects current English distinctions between 'ethnic' identities and those other identities that are deemed distinctive but not ethnic. The reader is asked to 'see' the word in quotation marks throughout and to remember that some distinctions based on national, linguistic, religious or caste criteria are thought to mark 'ethnic' differences, while others of precisely the same sort are not so evaluated. Yet, irredeemably relational and thus analytically impotent as the term must be, it cannot be ignored in the ethnographic description. The widespread belief that some social distinctions are ethnic by nature can take on its own social momentum as ethnicity, too, is subjected to reification. This process must be related to structures of power and inequality, as Comaroff and Comaroff (1992, 61) have stressed: 'in systems where "ascribed" cultural differences rationalize structures of inequality, ethnicity takes on a cogent existential reality. It is this process of reification ... that gives it the appearance of being an autonomous factor in the ordering of the social world.' This reificatory double bind applies even to the emancipatory movements of what Rothschild (1981) termed 'ethnopolitics', that is, those movements that seek to counteract civil discrimination by appealing to 'ethnic' commonalities:

For any activity aimed at the reversal of 'ascribed' inequalities may reinforce the [purported] primacy of ethnicity as a principle of social differentiation: the very fact that such activity is conducted by and for groupings marked by their cultural identities confirms the perception that these identities *do* provide the only available basis of collective self-definition and action.

(Comaroff and Comaroff 1992, 62–3)

As ethnopolitical movements turn their attention from such civil entitlements as housing, schooling or jobs to matters of 'cultural' entitlement or empowerment, the reification of ethnicity and the reification of culture can reinforce each other to the point of synonymy. Thus Turner (1993) has observed how in the United States:

> *multiculturalism* tends to become a form of identity politics, in which the concept of *culture* becomes merged with that of ethnic identity. From an anthropological standpoint, this move, at least in its more simplistic ideological forms, is fraught with dangers both theoretical and practical. It risks essentializing the idea of culture as the property of an ethnic group or race; it risks reifying cultures as separate entities by overemphasizing their boundedness and mutual distinctness; it risks overemphasizing the internal homogeneity of cultures in terms that potentially legitimize repressive demands for communal conformity.
>
> *(Turner 1993, 411–12, italics in original)*

It seems important, in this light, to recognize that so-called ethnic problems show one thing in common that reaches right across state and national boundaries: the presence, and the social efficacy, of a dominant discourse that reifies culture and traces it to ethnicity, and that reifies ethnicity and postulates 'communities' of 'culture' based on purportedly ethnic categorizations. This discourse is neither good nor bad in itself, and it is not the point of this book to censure it or its users. Southallians, after all, use it selectively, too, and it may even reflect a 'chronic anthropological tendency, born as much from the practice of intensive fieldwork as from theory, to focus on cultures as discrete units in isolation' (Turner 1993, 415). What matters for the ethnography, though, is to show that it is not the only discourse about culture that Southallians speak, and not the only discourse that anthropologists should document. Given its prevalence in many community studies, the task seems worth doing, and given its importance beyond Southall, it needs to be placed in a framework of more appropriate, in this case nation-wide, scale.

The dominant discourse in Britain

The tendencies to reify the 'cultures' of ethnic minorities, to stylize pseudo-biological categories into communities, and to appeal to popular biological conceptions of culture are not difficult to substantiate in British politics and media. Almost any copy of a daily newspaper will contain mentions of 'the Muslim community', 'the culture of Afro-Caribbeans', or 'the Asian community' and 'its culture'. There have been detailed analyses of the representation of ethnic minorities in the media (van Dijk 1991), in common parlance (Dummett 1984), and in public political discourse (Reeves 1983). Astute as these analyses are at identifying biologistic assumptions and racist stereotypes behind examples of the dominant discourse, Brah (1987) was, to my knowledge, the first author to have remarked on the reification of culture that it involves. Speaking of the representation of women of South Asian background, she notes how 'many of the contemporary academic, political and popular discourses ... operate within a totally reified concept of culture as some kind of baggage to be carried around'. To escape from this conceptual cage, Brah stresses culture as 'a dynamic, and potentially oppositional, force which stands in a complex relationship with the material conditions of society' (Brah 1987, 44). Regarding academic studies of originally Afro-Caribbean people in Britain, Phoenix (1988, 153) points in much the same direction: 'concentration on cultural differences between black people and white people has frequently obscured the fact that ... culture itself is dynamic rather than static'. Trenchantly, her assessment draws attention to the way in which such an approach 'frequently confuses colour and culture. White people are treated as if they were culturally homogeneous and British whatever their ancestry ... Black people are treated as similar to other black people whose ancestry lies roughly in the same region, but not as British' (Phoenix 1988, 159). One might wonder indeed whether such translations of stereotyped 'colour' traits into reified 'culture' traits is not part of the 'strategic discursive deracialization of discourse' that Reeves (1983) has observed:

Whereas a general racialisation of practice and ideology could be said to have occurred in the nineteenth and early twentieth centuries ... the contrary process of general deracialisation might be regarded as characteristic of the post-Second-World-War era ... Since the Second World War, however, ... a practical racialisation within Britain has come about as black migrants have ... met with widespread discrimination and rejection. ... that animosity has failed to find much direct expression in specialist political discourse. As a result, the deracialised feature of British [public] ideology has become increasingly apparent.

(Reeves 1983, 179)

This is possible, though it does not fully account, of course, for the fact that the dominant, strategically deracialized, discourse of communities defined by shared cultures is also engaged among ethnic minorities themselves in suitable contexts. Gilroy (1992) has addressed this salient overlap in his courageous critique of the 1980s 'anti-racism' movement. He notes the elaboration of 'new forms of racism [which] ... are distinguished by the extent to which they identify race with the terms "culture" and "identity" ...' (Gilroy 1992, 53). In other words, and if I understand Gilroy rightly, the terms culture and identity may function as surreptitious code words for 'race'. Gilroy indeed pursues his argument down to the meaning of culture. The argument is that both the New Right and the anti-racist movement have converged on 'a belief in the absolute nature of ethnic categories ... compounded firstly by a reductive conception of culture and secondly by a culturalist conception of race and ethnic identity' (Gilroy 1992, 50).

In Britain, too, one can thus observe a dominant discourse that envisages 'cultures supposedly sealed from one another forever by ethnic lines' (Gilroy 1987, 55). On the other hand, Britain is not the only country where simplistic equations between ethnic identity, culture, and community have congealed into a hegemonic discourse about any and all 'ethnic minorities'. To understand its dominance in British 'race relations' or 'community politics', there will thus be general reasons, related to the discourse as such, and specific ones, relating to Britain in particular. For a discourse to be recognized as dominant, one would expect it to show five features that are, in practice, interdependent: its conceptual make-up should be economical, not to say simple; its communicative resources should border on monopoly; it should be flexible of application and should allow for the greatest ideological plasticity; finally, it should lend itself to established institutional purposes.

On the count of conceptual economy, the dominant discourse proposes several equations between terms that in any creditable analysis would have to be considered mutually independent variables: whether ethnic categories correspond to ethnic groups; whether ethnic groups must by necessity share the same culture; whether even a shared culture establishes community; and in what sense of the word. All these are, to a researching anthropologist, empirical questions, not foregone conclusions. Yet by equating ethnic minorities with social groups, equating these with reified cultures, equating these in turn with communities, and, where at all plausible, associating these with supposedly natural groups, the dominant discourse achieves a conceptual economy that would defy Ockham himself.

Such an economical, indeed hermetically closed, discourse is well placed when it comes to competing for communicative monopoly. In Britain, as perhaps elsewhere, its protagonists command communicative resources that guarantee it unrivalled access to the general public. Its chief protagonists are, on one side, politicians claiming to represent the interests of 'communities'; and on the other, politicians claiming to speak for some wider 'national' interest, or indeed 'the majority'. Multiplication of their dialogue is the business of the popular media, which beside television include national and community press, national and community radio stations, and, sometimes as importantly, national or community artists, authors, comedians, musicians, and poets. In Britain, the dominant discourse is reflected by virtually all voices that shape public opinion.

This hegemony requires a highly flexible applicability of its key terms. The range of cases that the dominant discourse is used to encompass is indeed remarkable. At its most schematic, and harking back to the idea of race as the foundation of culture, it postulates two large 'communities': an Afro-Caribbean and an Asian one. The latter designates people of all South Asian backgrounds and credits them with a shared 'Asian culture'. Where race is not seen as the relevant marker of cultural difference, protagonists of the discourse may appeal to criteria of national origin. Thus, one can speak of a Jamaican as opposed to, say, a Barbadan community, or an Indian as opposed to a Pakistani, each with their reified culture.

In other contexts, this proliferation will go further still. The putative basis of culture may be sought in language, so that there are transnational 'communities' such as the Arab, the Armenian or the Punjabi. Cutting across ethnic, national, and linguistic criteria alike, communities with reified cultures are postulated on the basis of some religions. Thus 'Muslim culture' is thought to establish a community despite the greatest ethnic, national, and linguistic diversity. In yet other contexts, followers of different faiths may be stylized into communities based on regional origin or migratory history. In this way, the discourse can recognize a Gujarati community tying together Hindus and Muslims, or an East African Asian one that unites Hindus, Muslims, and Sikhs. It stands to reason that the same person can thus be classified as a member of half a dozen communities, each credited with its own reified culture. An individual may thus 'have' almost as many communities and cultures as a sociologist may distinguish roles.

The fact that different social cleavages cut across each other is constitutive, of course, of any plural society. Yet the dominant discourse thrives, rather than falters, on ascribing community status to any one cleavage that is considered relevant in any one context. Its very multiplicity of empirically overlapping communities, each credited with its distinctive culture, lends it pragmatic flexibility, and renders it applicable in virtually any contestation over collective rights.

Most remarkably, the dominant discourse can be engaged to serve the greatest range of ideological positions and interests. Ethnopolitics is a field of striking ideological variety, and the postulation of communities defined by reified cultures is as useful to right-wing as it is to liberal and left-wing political agendas. The right-wing version of the dominant discourse envisages people from the former colonies who migrated to Britain for a better life. Yet their ethnic and cultural distinctiveness sets them apart from an equally reified British or English culture. They thus live in disadvantaged communities which, viewed almost as societies within society, create 'social problems'. Classic recent examples are 'the black community' and its putatively problematic family structure and 'the Asian community' and its 'problem of arranged marriages'. Classic examples among migrants of the past are 'the Irish' and their supposed collective drinking problem. On the recent examples, I shall comment in the body of the book. The historic example should here suffice to indicate the absurdity of this right-wing version of equating migrants with communities, communities with a reified culture, and that culture with some 'social problem'.

Liberal versions of the dominant discourse shun any reference to problems in a community's culture. Instead, they envisage immigrants, or more politely migrants, who are excluded from full civic equality by social disadvantages. These handicaps, an almost natural consequence of migration, keep them living in their insulated communities, captives of their reified 'cultures', often specified as 'traditional'. The remedies envisaged are gradual, and they need to be directed at both sides in the contestation, 'host population' and migrants alike. Better social services and the eradication of mutual prejudice through education can then promise progress. They will help the processes of acculturation, accommodation, or at least generational change, which will liberate communities from the fetters of their inherited cultures.

The left-wing version of the dominant discourse replaces cultural reform with cultural revolution, yet it, too, endorses the equation between 'communities' and their reified cultures. Rather than judging community cultures as an obstacle to social mobility within the system, it validates them as a necessary and progressive form of resistance against racism and an often reified institutional racism. More radical factions pitch a newly evolving, unitary 'Black community' against the oppression thought inherent in a reified 'white culture'. This 'black community' and its culture are thought to encompass people of South Asian, as well as Afro-Caribbean and African descent. I shall later detail a number of Southallians' views on this postulate of a comprehensive, unified Black community.

The greatest richness in nuances, as well as the most serious ideological contestations occur between the liberal and the left-wing protagonists of the dominant discourse. Thus, communities may be credited with 'special needs' which require 'community provision'. Such 'ethnic targeting' of services and resources may be demanded, in the liberal tradition, to increase social mobility in a 'multi-ethnic society'. Alternatively, they may be demanded to allow communities to follow, maintain, or preserve their 'cultures' and claim their right to difference in a 'multi-cultural society'. Further to the political left, the doctrine of special needs is discredited as a buy-out strategy which stands in the way of black unity: the foundation of an anti-racist, rather than a multiculturalist stand. The multiple shades, strands, and sects within each ideological camp would warrant their own study. What matters here is the observation that the dominant discourse can easily encompass the entire political spectrum from the far-right to the far-left, and is as serviceable to minority bashers as to minority advocates.

The institutional efficacy of the dominant discourse might be documented by scores of local instances of the municipal 'politicization of ethnicity', as Kalka (1991) has described it. Studies like Kalka's are rare, however, for several reasons. For one thing, they require fieldwork among 'ethnic activists', which in turn depends upon the goodwill of these activists themselves. Few anthropologists publish accounts that might alienate or anger their one-time key informants who were indeed, in many cases, gatekeepers. Secondly, the dominant discourse has been established in institutional structures and political expectations for so long that most researchers simply take it for granted. Nor does the genre of the community study do much to help throw it into critical relief. Given this long-standing and taken-for-granted practice, it is rare to find, as Kalka has done, a local area where the dominant discourse is institutionalized, so to speak, from one year to the next. It will be helpful, therefore, to summarize and quote Kalka's observations in more detail than usual.

The London borough in question had been settled by South Asian expellees from East Africa and had, over the 1970s, seen the foundation of overlapping voluntary associations based variously on national loyalties, regional origins, religion, language, and caste. For a decade or so, only one, however, 'was active in raising issues that concerned Asians as residents of the borough of Harrow. This was also the period when these newly arrived Asians were establishing themselves financially, and this partly accounts for what appeared to be their lack of interest in the local political arena' (Kalka 1991, 219). This was to change dramatically when the Borough Council saw itself forced to act upon new guidelines aimed at improved consultation with, representation of, and services and employment for, 'ethnic' residents. A structure of consultative committees, positions of influence, paid posts, and liaison groups was set up and cranked into motion. The consequences were dramatic in several ways:

> Activists who previously had had to articulate their own tactics on how to approach the council, now had direct access to both the council and its employees. Moreover, since committeee meetings were open to the public, people who were *not involved* in the *locally* based ethnic associations could now put forward their own opinions. They were not impelled first to become 'internal leaders', though this was a safer way to exert influence. That, is, only participants who were delegates could claim to represent at least a certain segment of the Asian population. Nevertheless, since the majority of Asian residents in the borough were totally unaware of the struggle conducted presumably on their behalf, activists did not wish to risk their authority as representatives being challenged from within. Delegates of small associations [e.g. with *ca.* fifty members] could thus act with the same amount of assertiveness as those of larger ones.
>
> *(Kalka 1991, 219, my italics)*

In the acrimonious debates over political analyses and local policies, and more particularly about honorary or paid positions in the Borough's budding 'race relations' field itself, overlapping regional, national, religious, and caste associations were pitched against each other in structural rivalries, factional enmities, tactical allegiances, and sometimes 'sectarian interests' (Kalka 1991, 220). This may well be as it should be, and factionalism, intrigue, and even ideologizing are of the stuff of local politics. Yet the deliberate creation of ethnic community politics in the image of the dominant discourse was a mixed blessing in several ways. Locally, it pitched Pakistani associations against their more numerous Gujarati counterparts in a battle for public resources to be fought under ethnic banners. These ethnic banners, moreover, were not nearly as distinct as protagonists of the dominant discourse had assumed them to be.

> The people concerned had a 'stock' of overlapping ethnic allegiances at their disposal, to reinforce various claims. They evidently entertained multiple ethnic identities, oscillating between those arising from regional loyalties, those connected with the Indian sub-continent, and those which emerged as a result of their disadvantageous position in British society. ... The segmentary nature of roles, the multiplicity of ethnic identities an individual may claim, all these seem to have permeated the public arena, regularly leading to seemingly contradictory claims of ethnic affiliation and conflicting demands.   *(Kalka 1991, 220)*

Kalka's insistence on multiple ethnic identities and her reminder of Barth's well-known argument about the permeability and contextual definition of all ethnic boundaries are fully in keeping with the intentions of this book. In attending to these, Kalka implicitly moves from describing to critiquing the dominant discourse. It was enacted institutionally to provide for ethnic minorities, yet it failed to produce the simplistic and clear-cut ethnic identities that its reificatory logic would require. Once set into motion, its institutional infrastructure kept ticking on like a *perpetuum mobile*. No one seems to have paused to reconsider its assumptions even when most 'ethnic' residents were 'unaware of the ongoing debate in the town hall and activists often complained about the apathy and the difficulties involved in "organising" Gujaratis. Perhaps this very apathy has allowed a new ethnic elite to emerge in such a short space of time' (Kalka 1991, 221). The connection raises interesting questions:

This elite is composed of well-educated people who have taken it upon themselves to study subjects related to racism, colonialism, and so on. They hold numerous conferences and repeatedly debate these issues. The same people who now write speeches, manifestos, and pamphlets were, only a few years back, to use their own phrase, 'collaborators' with the establishment.   *(Kalka 1991, 221)*

One might well wonder whether the new converts to the dominant discourse may not be collaborating more fully with the establishment than they had done before. But the question is too value-laden to be answerable here. Suffice it to consider Kalka's own assessment of the dominant discourse put into policy action:

In such a situation the rewards offered by the state in exchange for relegating people to 'minority' status will always be insufficient in two respects: they will never satisfy individual ambitions and will never contribute adequately either to welfare provisions or to institutions which are managed by ethnic residents. Presumably, if more funding became available, more contenders for power would come forward ... Activists who are incorporated into the so-called white establishment are being 'neutralised' in this process, only to be replaced by new activists.   *(Kalka 1991, 221)*

Given such observations, one cannot but ask why the dominant discourse of discrete and bounded ethnic minorities should enjoy such uncritical endorsement in Britain. I have tried to establish five general reasons that would contribute to a discourse gaining such a hegemonic dominance. Yet there may also be specific historical reasons that apply more particularly to the British case. In tracing the ancestry of the dominant discourse, I have already referred to the United States and the Black Consciousness Movement. At a critical juncture, it turned from a campaign for individual Civil Rights regardless of 'race' to a campaign for collective rights as a community based on a shared culture. In doing so, it inspired and helped to shape many other ethnic liberation movements. In Britain, however, the community discourse has a second line of ancestry, one that is rooted in the colonial administration of ethnic groups in East Africa. In tracing this second line of ancestry, I do not intend to prove an unbroken line of historical continuity. I suspect that it could be discerned, and I certainly agree with Bhachu's (1985) finding that 'the maintenance of a separate East African[-Asian] identity in Britain is also linked to the establishment of a clear-cut group status in East Africa' (Bhachu 1985: 12). The same seems to apply among Kalka's (1991) informants. Yet this is not the prime reason why I cite the colonial precedent. Rather, I do so in order to highlight how the dominant discourse is based upon, and reinforces, a denial of the cross-cutting social cleavages that characterize plural societies, even colonial ones.

British policy in the East African colonies entailed the recruitment of skilled manual labour from the Indian subcontinent, followed by an influx of merchant and trading families. Many of these 'East African Asians' came, over the first half of this century, to form a middle stratum between the British colonial rulers or settlers and the African population at large. The colonial administration of African affairs largely followed the doctrine of Indirect Rule and dealt in the currency of tribes. For the South Asian migrants, however, administration could not follow the tribal model, but had to invent a new political discourse. Its up-dated currency was the idea of South Asian communities. It is significant that, as Morris' (1968) ethnography of 'the Indians in Uganda' recalls, South Asians employed the term 'community' with the greatest ease, but 'usually in its English form, whatever the language actually spoken' (1968, 25). Morris documents its emergence from three requirements of colonial government. The first concerned the need to allocate plots for worship and burial to South Asians who were legally barred from buying land. Thus from 1910, 'any group of people who wished to ... hold property was required to incorporate itself by registration ... [and to] elect annually a committee of management with a stipulated number of officers' (Morris 1968, 28–9). As 'places in schools became scarce, ... members of larger [South Asian] castes and sects began to make provision for their own children and to seek assistance as separate communities' (Morris 1968, 35). Politically, too, the unrepresentative government found that 'Indians were needed to sit on advisory committees' (Morris 1968, 27–8) and could best be recruited and proportioned on community lines. The requirements of the colonial administration could be met more easily as East African Asians themselves stood to benefit from being parcelled up into communities with officially recognized collective rights. The success of the Ismaili community in particular inspired many other religious and caste interests to seek incorporation as recognized communities. The resulting classification of overlapping social networks into discrete communities showed the same flexibility of criteria as is evident in Britain today:

In East African usage the English term 'community' was considerably over-worked. It might, for example, signify people in *'racial'* categories: the African, the Asian or the European communities. One also heard of the Arab community, which was not regarded as part of the Asian community. The Goan community, whose members came from the former territory of *Portuguese* India, even more surprisingly, was not always of the Asian community either ... The *Muslim* community ... [however] included Arabs, Africans, Indians, and others; or [the Asian community] might be divided into smaller categories such as the Hindu or the Sikh communities, which were neither castes (*varna*) nor sub-castes (*jati*) ... Finally one also heard of such *occupational* categories as the 'trading community', the 'farming community', and so forth.   *(Morris 1968, 25, my italics)*

Such semantic mayhem, or polysemy of the word community, indeed prefigures current British usages, although no historical precedent can prove a causal connection. The comparison, however, is remarkable enough, not only as a historical precedent, but also as the background to the differentiation into *caste communities* among Sikh Southallians which I shall discuss later. Morris traces the East African developments to the very vagueness of the word, and was admirably clear in recognizing 'community' as a colonial construct, rather than a basis of sociological analysis:

The word community ... covered almost any category of people with an easily recognised common identity ... The word community is also technically used in sociological writing for the aggregates of people within which all an individual's social relationships may be found. In this sense neither castes, nor sub-castes, nor sects, neither Hindus nor Muslims, nor the Indians as a whole constituted communities in East Africa.   *(Morris 1968, 26)*

Three things seem important about Morris' evidence. Firstly, the division of people-to-be-governed into communities is a time-honoured colonial strategy. This may help to account for the appeal of the community discourse among those Britons who associate ethnic minorities with social problems. Secondly, what a political discourse calls communities may not be communities at all in a sociological or descriptive sense, however vague. The fact that a public discourse uses terms also current in anthropology or sociology should invite scrutiny as to whether they are actually used to mean the same thing. Thirdly, the reason why the communities postulated in the colonial discourse did not constitute communities in any sociological sense, was that the South Asian ethnic minorities – even in East Africa – lived in a society characterized by cross-cutting cultural, economic, political, and other social cleavages. In the colonial context, the community discourse itself can be seen as a denial of these cross-cutting cleavages in the interests of a ruling elite. Those who were not meant to belong to it were conveniently parcelled up into communities, there to mind their own business under community supervision. In the context of present-day Britain, one must wonder whether the dominant discourse may not, unintentionally perhaps, follow its precursor along the same path.

The discourse about ethnic minorities as communities defined by a reified culture bears all the hallmarks of dominance: it is conceptually simple, enjoys a communicative monopoly, offers enormous flexibility of application, encompasses great ideological plasticity, and is serviceable for established institutional purposes. Yet each of these features raises doubt in its own way. The conceptual economy of the discourse relies on equations that no researching anthropologist can take at face value. In discussing its flexible applicability, it has been seen that communities may be defined on half-a-dozen mutually independent criteria that cut across each other in many ways, just as they are likely to cut across many other cleavages characteristic of a plural society. Its ideological plasticity, as indeed its serviceability to established institutional purposes, may be related, in part, to its colonial roots. The dominant discourse, in other words, needs to be questioned. Hegemonic though it may be, its reifications, its circularity, and its tell-tale ideological plasticity make it a misleading guide to understanding the culture of any 'ethnic' minority.

Saying this, however, does not render it any less dominant for the people whose culture one wants to understand. Southallians, too, use the dominant discourse whenever their judgements of context or purpose make it seem appropriate. It would be naive to pitch a Southall demotic discourse against the dominant one, and presumptuous to adjudicate their relative merits. The ethnography argues only one thing: the dominant discourse is not the only one that Southallians engage in, and therefore does not capture the wealth of meanings that they create and live.

Local usage and practice sometimes affirm and sometimes deny the dominant discourse. What Southallians say and do cannot simply deny the dominant reification of culture. Who indeed can claim freedom from reifications, even if such freedom were desirable or possible? Berger and

Luckmann (1967) have pointed their sociological fingers at 'the reifying propensities of theoretical thought in general and sociological thought in particular'. At the same time, they warn that 'it would be an error to limit the concept of reification to the mental constructions of intellectuals. Reification exists in the consciousness of the man in the street and, indeed, the latter presence is more practically significant' (Berger and Luckmann 1967, 107). They reason their assertion by reference to the objectivation of 'the social world' as a whole; in the present context, one might as plausibly replace 'social world' with the word 'culture':

as soon as a [putatively] objective social world is established, the possibility of reification is never far away. The objectivity of the social world means that it confronts man as something outside of himself. The decisive question is whether he still retains the awareness that, however objectivated, the social world was made by men – and, therefore, can be remade by them.

(Berger and Luckmann 1967, 106)

That culture is made by humans taking into account, rather than being taken over by, their ascribed or perceived ethnic identities, is obvious as soon as the word culture is allowed to signify something more than a reification of 'ethnic' distinctions. Cultures, however easily reified, are the products of human volition, desires, and powers.

Yet cultures, even in their most individualized practices, result also from validations of a past. Culture-making is not an *ex tempore* improvisation, but a project of social continuity placed within, and contending with, moments of social change. Southallians engage the dominant discourse as well as the demotic one. They reify *cultures* while at the same time making culture. Even when they explicitly engage the demotic discourse, the faultlines of the dominant one are effective and, moreover, empirically visible. Thus, the patterns by which, say, Sikh or Afro-Caribbean, Muslim or white Southallians re-map their *cultures* and *communities* are, and remain, distinctive from each other, not only along sociological criteria but also by their tone. The presentation of the data has had to take account of this.

Presentation of the Data
All the following chapters ask the same ethnographic question, namely: 'what is Southall culture?' But they do this from four different analytic angles. The first, guided by the premise that Southallians should not be tribalized, approaches their town as a whole and enquires how a 'Southall culture' might be described. It finds a culture based upon competition among *communities* as defined by the dominant discourse.

Chapter 4 therefore introduces these *communities* one by one. It briefly traces the dominant discourse about each and then localizes it in relation to each *community*'s migratory history and relative position in town. The descriptions raise empirical doubts about the adequacy of the dominant discourse and its equation of 'culture' with 'community'. These doubts are pursued in chapter 5.

This chapter again focuses on each *community* in turn, but with a new analytical intention. It wants to show how, within each *community*, the dominant equation between culture and community is disengaged by Southallians themselves. To do this *community* by *community* is useful for two reasons. Methodologically, an orthodoxy like the dominant discourse can be challenged best if one sticks to its own premises, that is, 'self-evident' *community* divisions. Ethnographically speaking, the dominant equation is challenged differently in different *communities*. At the end of this chapter, there are thus two ways of thinking about *communities*: each could be described in the terms of the dominant discourse, yet each of them also harbours internal dynamics that question it, push it aside, or put it to unexpected uses.

The more that chapter 5 has attended to the demotic discourse within each *community*, the more questions are raised about the relationship between community and culture, as between one local *culture* and another. My submission is that the relationship of culture to community, and indeed the meanings of these words themselves, are matters of continual contestation in the culture that Southallians share. To show this, chapter 6 reviews how these contestations proceed across *community* boundaries. Cases in point can be seen in relation to ideas of an *Asian culture* across religious divides, a comprehensive *Black community* across ethnic divides, and a religious *community* across doctrinal divides. While the relevant questions tend first to be raised by the less established, such as young people or political or religious avant-gardes, the ensuing contestations involve far wider circles of people. In taking these up, and in pitching the dominant discourse against the demotic, Southallians debate and create a Southall culture which revolves around the terms *culture* and *community* themselves.

The words can thus no longer appear as self-evident analytical concepts to be applied to ethnic minorities. Rather, their meanings in different contexts are the pivotal points of Southallians' 'multi-cultural' culture. In the remainder of this section I shall flesh out the general itinerary with a brief synopsis of findings and propositions.

Introducing Southall as a single town, it can be approached as a bounded space that people of whatever *community* happen to share and cannot but cultivate. The cultivation of public spaces appears shaped most distinctively by South Asian Southallians; yet Southallians of all *communities* share a culture of privacy even in the busiest of the densely populated areas. Linguistic convergence can be seen in some adult greeting conventions and in the West London dialect of English shared among all youth. Many adults of all *communities* agree in their deprecation of the town as a 'grotty' place, and often equate moving out physically with moving up socially. An examination of data from the British National Census will help to juxtapose the ethnic variety of Southallians with their economic commonalities. Among these, unemployment figures and women's employment patterns show the town to be worse off than the rest of the London Borough to which it belongs. The figures (given in tables 1–4) will show why the ideas of 'moving out' and 'moving up' are equated by so many Southallians of all *communities*.

Social mobility involves competition, as does access to the scarce public resources which, ironically, political rhetoric calls 'community' facilities. In this highly competitive environment, which shows a dearth of comprehensively civic institutions, appeals to the needs of *communities* come to be the chief resource in the competition for other resources. These *communities* are defined on the ethnic and religious criteria familiar from the dominant discourse. Since Southall local politics are shaped largely by the discourse of *community* needs, a case study will show how a municipal 'community centre' sparked controversy as to which particular ethnic *community* it was to serve. The town's public culture, I conclude, is predicated on civic competition thought to run along *community* lines. Chapter 4 therefore turns from exploring the town as a whole to focusing on each *community* in turn.

In most general and descriptive contexts, Southallians identify five *communities*, and their logic reflects the dominant discourse. It is based on the 'racial' divisions between Asians, Caribbeans, and whites which are readily taken for granted in Britain. Among the large numbers of local Asians, however, most Southallians draw a distinction on religious criteria, and thus speak of a Sikh, a Hindu, and a Muslim *community*. Religion by itself is not thought sufficient, however, to forge a *community* of Christian Southallians. Rather, Afro-Caribbean Southallians are deemed to form a community of their own; and Irish and English Southallians are said to form a *white community* by others, though many of the putative members are deeply equivocal about their *community* status.

The delineations of *communities* and their *cultures* are pervasive and familiar even to children below the age of functional literacy. Among these, I shall speak of a veritable 'culture consciousness' (*Kulturbewusstsein*) that is highly articulate in stressing religious, political-sociological, or individualist conceptions of *culture*. Children, like adults, tend to endorse the view of *cultures* as the stable, collective, and distinctive possessions of *communities*, to think of the two as co-extensive, and indeed to equate one with the other. However, this equation between *community* seen as a self-evident entity and *culture* seen as its co-extensive, exclusive, and collective possession requires greater scrutiny. Even the summary portrayal of each *community* will have raised ethnographic doubts. Chapter 5 therefore re-examines each with a view to its dynamics of self-definition.

Processes of cultural and class differentiation have led to the formation of several Sikh *communities* based upon congregational criteria subtly articulated with the idiom of caste. Among Hindu Southallians, remarkably undivided by caste norms, it is the discourse of Hindu universalism and of encompassing other faiths that now serves to disengage the equation between Hindu *culture* and the Hindu *community*. Muslim Southallians see themselves as members of a *community* of the faithful that is pointedly multi-cultural not only on the global scale, but locally, too. In the newly forged Afro-Caribbean *community*, one can discern four different approaches to 'finding' and 'building' an Afro-Caribbean *culture*, which thus appears not as a given possession, but as a deliberate and highly dynamic process of creation. White Southallians, unusually equivocal about their cultures as well as their putative *community* or *communities*, often rely upon forging bonds, sharing loyalties, and even endorsing personal identification with 'other' *communities*.

The re-examination of each *community* in turn will thus show how Southallians disengage the equation between *culture* and *community* that underpins the dominant discourse. While *culture* can still be seen as the possession of an ethnic or religious *community*, it can also be appreciated as a dynamic process which relies upon personal agency, the renegotiation of *community* boundaries, and the possibility of redefining what *community* is to mean in any one context. Southallians thus engage not only in the dominant discourse about ethnic minorities, but also in an alternative, non-dominant or demotic, discourse about culture as a continuous process and community as a conscious creation. In this way, they command, and make use of, a dual discursive competence. Depending upon their judgements of context and purpose, they will affirm the dominant discourse or engage the demotic, and in pitching one against the other, the very meanings of '*culture*' and '*community*' become the objects of social contestation. Some of the most momentous contestations indeed concern the reaffirmation or the redefinition of the meaning of '*community*'.

To illustrate how these work in practice, chapter 6 draws on three sets of evidence. Among juveniles of South Asian backgrounds, one sees a growing awareness of the commonalities of an *Asian culture* which reaches across the religious divides as emphasized by children. This is helped by the fact that juveniles socialize quite freely across religious *community* boundaries and begin to distinguish their own divisions from those pertaining among their parents. 'Traditional' institutions like caste and arranged marriage are thought of as 'Asian', and they give rise to assessments that are greatly varied and often equivocal. The idea of a new *Asian culture* finds enthusiastic support, however, when it promises a sometimes political unity and the forging of comprehensive cross-*community* convergence, as associated with the new 'all-Asian' music of Bhangra.

Other important contestations about the meaning and relationship of *culture* and *community* occur in the political and the religious spheres. The disputes, as well as the language in which they are debated, tend to be shaped by particular networks, even quite small ones, which are committed to special public agenda. Thus, local socialists and feminists have questioned the merits of *Asian culture* and proposed the political unity of all former migrants in a comprehensive *Black community*. Southallians at large took up this 'Black or Asian?' debate with a variety of approaches that did not cleave along ethnic *community* lines. Local and ecumenical Interfaith networks have questioned the boundaries of 'religious *communities*' and posited an overarching *community* of all 'people of faith'. Southallians were confronted with this agenda when educational reforms challenged them to discuss the future of religious instruction in schools. The negotiation of religious *community* boundaries will show up processes, and local ideas, of religious convergence which can be neutralized by claims of encompassment or reference to a widely shared multicultural discourse of equal respect and equal representation for each *community*. In all these debates, it is the contestation of *culture* and *community*, their meanings and their interrelations, that I argue lie at the heart of a shared Southall culture.

The Conclusion addresses some further general questions that the data have raised. It notes the result, strange at first sight, that the demotic discourse itself shows a patterning along *community* cleavages. To understand this, it can help to distinguish legitimacies of the past from legitimacies of the future. Southallians need and use both of these to legitimate their *communities*, be they long-standing or recent. In this way, the dominant discourse remains a part of Southallians' discursive competence, and it can even put limits on the use of the word culture in much, though not all, of the demotic discourse. Having examined the relationship between the two discourses, I shall try to apply the findings to current policy debates. The old juxtaposition between individualist civil rights and the rights of communities has been revived in the United States and has there reshaped the public debate about social, or welfare, policy. The same has happened in Britain, but under different premises. One may thus ask, in the end, what the pursuit of ethnographic knowledge can contribute to these debates.

3

A shared Southall culture?

'Town' : a cultivated space
Ethnic distinctions, economic commonalities
Some local history: migration and the 'white backlash',
community building and 'The Southall Riots'
Local politics as *community* competition

'Town': a cultivated space

A densely populated area, Southall is situated amidst the more spacious
western suburbs of London, not far from Heathrow Airport. Its name
does not describe a culture or even a community in any established sense
of the word. As a geographic area, however, it is delineated by unusually clear boundaries. To approach what shared 'Southall culture' there
may be, the area can be surveyed as a cultivated space. This space is not
neutral, since present-day Southallians have found houses, roads, ameni-
ties, and other defined spaces already laid out. The physical environment
sets limits to any new cultivation of the space, yet these limits are often
elusive. A description of the area as a cultivated space will introduce
readers to what they are likely to see first, and in the process it shows
evidence of how far the space is cultivated jointly or separately by
Southallians of different *communities*.

Southall is called a 'town' by most of its 60,000 inhabitants, although
it lost its status as a metropolitan borough in the 1960s. Politically and
administratively, it now forms part of the London Borough of Ealing
which numbers some 300,000 residents. Traffic connections to Ealing are
tolerable; those to the centre of the capital are inadequate, and to 'go to
London', as locals call it, requires at least an hour's drive on congested
roads, a train journey that may involve changing, or reliance on what
must be London's worst-run bus route: 'the 207s always come in packs
of six, just after the drivers have met for a tea-break'. Southall is

by-passed by two lines of the London Underground system, but there is no 'Tube' station to tie it into the capital's infrastructure or make people feel part of the metropolis. Southallians who work in central London may spend between two and six hours each day in getting to work and back. Bus connections to work are most regular to nearby Heathrow Airport, which is a major employer, and to the light-industrial and food-processing plants strung along the arteries that connect London to the western Home Counties.

The sense of a discrete town may also owe something to the local topography. Natural boundaries surround Southall on three sides: to reach it, one will cross a hump bridge over the Brentford–Birmingham Canal if coming from the south, another hump bridge over the Grand Union Canal if coming from the west, and the meads of the River Brent if coming from London. Only the northern approach into town appears nondescript: coming from Greenford, a vast expanse of inexpensive housing, one passes the municipal rubbish tip and the deprived Golf Links Estate to join the inevitable traffic jam on the town's Broadway. The Broadway is one of the two arteries of town, runs east to west, and was known, until the early years of this century, as the Oxford Road. Topographically, it is a continuation of London's Oxford Street; and around the Christmas and Diwali Season it is second only to that 'real' Oxford Street in the turnover per square yard of its commercial premises. For Southall, 'ghetto' town though it may be, is a capital in its own right: the capital town of South Asians in Britain, a point to which I shall return shortly.

The other commercial thoroughfare runs from north to south and looks much like the Broadway: an unbroken double file of vegetable shops, butchers, saree shops and jewellers, virtually all owned by South Asians. The bridge spans the Great Western Railway line by which Isambard Kingdom Brunel expedited London's nineteenth-century poor to the emigration port of Bristol and, in the process, cut the budding town in two. The railway line, and its wasteland belt of disused gas- and water-works, has come to separate 'Old Southall', a maze of Late Victorian terraced houses, from 'New Southall', a meticulously surveyed area of terraced and semi-detached houses built between the 1920s and 50s. The rivalry between the 'Old' and the 'New' part of Southall dates back to the 1920s, when the town was populated by English and Irish labourers; it lives on in the rivalry between two notorious 'Asian gangs', the Holy Smokes and the Tooti Nungs. The physical lay-out of the town is sketched in figure 1, which also contains ward and census boundaries that will be relevant later on.

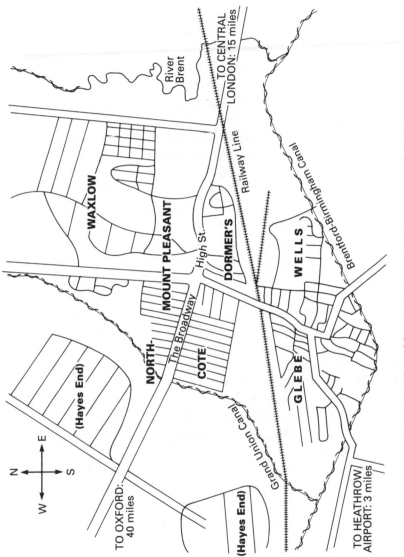

Figure 1   Map of Southall: electoral and census wards, 1989

The inherited physical fabric of the town is adequately maintained in the public sector and widely enhanced in the private. There are some two miles of busy, bustling shopping streets and a few hundred miles' worth of quieter streets of terraced and semi-detached houses. Three-quarters of these show signs of recent improvements, such as new roofs, extensions, or patios; continuous files of parked cars give an impression of modest but sustained prosperity.

Among the civic spaces, there is an ill-repaired former Town Hall, built around the turn of the century and now used as an advice centre, a restored Tudor manor house now owned by the local Council, and the mandatory War Memorial of every English town. Another relic of 'Olde England' is the country's busiest surviving market for horses, poultry, and goats, established in 1698 and still attracting breeders' and hobbyists' custom on Wednesdays. On Saturdays, it sells Asian textiles to locals. Emblems of 1970s England can be found in a shopping mall converted from an Edwardian cinema designed in a quaint 'Chinesey' style, and in a few purpose-built estates for small and medium-sized enterprises. Opposite the ruins of pre-war industrial plants, including the one-time largest margarine factory in the world, there is a community centre, converted from a solid Edwardian 'Workers' Institute', once endowed by the Danish philanthropist whose Southall margarine helped Britain win the First World War. Another community centre, conspicuous by its elegant, some say posh, 1980s design, offers adult evening classes and hires out its space for conferences and wedding receptions. A few parish halls double up as smaller community centres, each with its own programme of education, entertainment, or advice.

Among the other public spaces, there are the vast suburban pubs and churches that Edwardian planners provided for 'their' working class. The pubs, half of them still run by Irish landlords, half by South Asians, do not do well any longer: many Punjabi Southallians, mindful of their respectability, are reluctant to drink in public. There are pubs where Irish and Afro-Caribbeans, English and South Asians mix freely or even prop up the bar in daily cliquish companionship. Other pubs are favoured by some clienteles more than others. On the whole, an impression of segregation, or at least separateness, is inescapable in most pubs. The same applies to the few venues of Southall's sparse night-life: the town's two music clubs attract a clientele predominantly of Afro-Caribbean West Londoners from Southall and beyond.

The best places to encounter 'mixed crowds' are the churches scattered around town. Most of them serve small congregations, but St John's, an

Anglican church of evangelical bent, and St Anselm's, the Roman Catholic church, often see large assemblies comprising white, Afro-Caribbean, and South Asian Southallians in equal numbers. The majority of Southallians, though, worship in the large, often impressive, temples and mosques. On the drive of less than two miles from the southern hump bridge to the centre of town, one passes the gilt-domed temple of the Ravidasi *community* of 'untouchables', the marble-clad minaret of the central mosque, a brick-faced gurdwara frequented mainly by Jat Sikhs, a pretty church hall converted into a Hindu mandir, a spacious disused warehouse serving as a further temple mainly for Jat Sikhs, a turret-fronted, elaborate second mandir, and a representative, purpose-built gurdwara mainly for Sikhs of the Ramgarhia castes. In sidestreets, one finds at least thirty-five further small temples, mosques, prayer halls, and private houses where Sikhs, Hindus, Muslims, and other Southallians meet for regular prayer. Southall teems with religious activity, and the crowds that leave after Sunday worship pour out into the main shopping street, the Broadway. At weekends, this thoroughfare is jammed with shoppers and strollers, not only from the town but from South Asian settlements throughout the Home Counties. Then, the commonplace fabric of Southall takes on the air of a capital: England's centre of South Asian life.

Despite its marginal position in the infrastructure of Greater London, Southall is uniquely well connected to the English cities that have attracted settlers from South Asia. Express coaches owned by local South Asian entrepreneurs leave several times daily for East Ham, Barking, Catford and Gravesend in England's south-east; to Coventry, Birmingham, Wolverhampton, and Leicester in the industrial Midlands; and to Derby, Sheffield, Leeds, Huddersfield, and Bradford in the north of the country. Their fares are the most competitive in Britain, and South Asian Southallians can be seen every day at the coach stops outside the town's football stadium and in front of several temples, waiting for kin to get off the coach, or queuing to get on it and enjoy the Hindi movies shown during the journey.

Southall is not inhabited exclusively by South Asians, yet on its central thoroughfares one could well think so. Youngsters from the neighbouring suburbs who ride through town on the top of a double-decker bus sometimes play 'Spot the White Man': the first to spot five Caucasians is bought a can of beer or a pack of cigarettes by his or her mates. Southall's street culture certainly bears the imprint of its South Asian majority. Their conventions on the use of space are shared, willingly or otherwise, by all. The pavements of the Broadway are not walk-ways, but elongated plazas: shopkeepers and freelancers open wildcat stalls; here one can buy vegetables and fresh tropical fruit at half their London prices; batteries in German and Swedish wrappers at two-thirds of the British-packed price; Indian and Pakistani spices, medicines, cosmetics, and trinkets; South Asian-styled gold jewellery from the devo-tional through the chic to the ostentatious; sarees in abundance and the loose-fitting *salwar-kameez* preferred by many women to European dress; for menswear the uncollared *kurta* smocks and baggy *salwar* preferred usually by Muslim men or, for their Sikh neighbours, pantaloons in their pleated *pajami* daywear or narrow *pajama* nightwear varieties. Groups of men, and less often women, recognize each other, shake hands in an elab-orate round, and stand chatting, gossiping, or negotiating. Determined shoppers weave their way round them without much visible irritation. One is more polite on the Broadway than on Oxford Street: the throng of people on foot and in cars gives rise to little impatience or aggrava-tion. Should it seem to, one can step aside and, from a Delhi-style counter in a *Tandoori*, select an East African Asian *Chaat* or some Punjabi *somose* or *karhai*, some sweet *barfi* or a green leaf of *pan* rolled to envelop a dozen spices and essences selected to order.

Weekend and rush-hour traffic on the Broadway is notorious; some-times a driver can move only with the co-operation of two or three others. Yet emerging from a side street one is allowed without fail to join the gridlock. One is waved in by the most widespread gesture of indul-gence, which is not of the polite 'After you' variety; it resembles a resigned, almost dismissive wave of the hand that says: 'I bestow on you my right of way: you see, I can't use it anyway.'

Outsiders dread driving through the Southall jam; yet there are insiders who like nothing more. Young men in their twenties, virtually all of South Asian parentage, get together to cruise on the Broadway. This requires the right make of car, most commonly a Ford Capri with conspicuous extras and, indispensably, a sound system which can blast music at deafening volumes. The preferred genres are the disco adapta-tions of a Punjabi folk dance known as Bhangra Beat and Bhangra Rock, or for those who want to project a 'harder' image, Reggae music of Afro-Caribbean origin or Black American Rap. The cruisers' satis-faction grows with the number of heads that are turned and with the whispers that identify one or the other as a 'big guy' in one of Southall's two well-known 'gangs'. He who is bored on the Broadway is beyond entertainment.

Yet for a town so distinctive among London's drab Western suburbs, there is surprisingly little civic pride expressed by its adult inhabitants. Young people who have grown up there and know their way around sometimes express their affection: 'Southall is like your mother and father', one of them told me, 'you grow up with it, and it – sort of, makes you what you are.' Adults, too, will on occasion express an appreciation of the security that living in Southall brings with it. Most prejudiced neighbours have long moved out of town, and many householders have, of course, built up networks of neighbourly support and trust that they appreciate. Yet most adult Southallians I know profess a desire to move out and, in a euphemism for social advancement, move 'up the road'. To move out geographically and move up socially are synonymous in all but a few cases. The electoral ward surrounding the Broadway lost nearly 20 per cent of its residents between 1971 and 1981 (Ealing 1982, Census 1/10), and many more wish to escape its persisting high population density, the lack of parking spaces, and what they call its dirtiness.

Southallians complain that their town is 'dirty', 'grotty', or 'tatty' as other Londoners complain of the weather: as a matter of course. I still do not understand this. Having lived in a road off the Broadway often littered with packing refuse from the Broadway shops and with discarded cigarette boxes and drinks cans, I still find even the busiest parts of Southall as well-kept as any of London's commercially active areas. To understand this common deprecation of the town one lives in, one probably has to appeal to the class system that in England is applied not only to households, but to whole areas. An English Southallian, aged sixty, details the 1930s class hierarchy of London suburbs in retrospect:

You see, at one time, if you were a Southall, – – Southall was that little bit above Hanwell, a little bit above, above Hayes: 'Southall, ah well, you come from Southall, well, of course ...' The next place above Southall was Ealing. I mean, at one time, if you say you come from Southall, they'd say: 'Oh!', you know, 'a posh place !' But now – you don't mention Southall. Southall's got a really bad name now ... 'Ooh, that grotty place?' ... the tattiness of it!   *(Hawkes 1990, 4)*

Such oral memory cannot be taken as historical fact, of course. Like all oral recollection, it is made up and remade after the event, continues to be encoded and standardized, and always serves the purposes of today, much as it does in illiterate cultures (Goody and Watt 1963, Goody 1968). In the present case, the speaker is a Southall-born Englishwoman whose husband's job took the family to Kent in the 1950s.

The provenance of the quotation does not, however, invalidate its significance. The topos of a dirty, tatty, or grotty Southall is common among Southallians of all *communities*, and as widespread among the young as the old. The variables that appear to affect this judgement are related not to local or ethnic origin, but to perceived mobility. Those who can realistically consider moving out voice it more readily than those who cannot. This is partly a matter of financial resources and, in the vaguest sense, class. Thus, tenants of Ealing Council and of housing associations, who are seldom able to exchange a Southall flat for one elsewhere in the borough, may echo the criticism during their first few months, but do so less often as they get used to their lack of mobility. House owners who, by selling up, would risk higher mortgages or financial losses, are again more reluctant to voice this commonplace. Those who have greater mobility, or perhaps wish to project greater confidence, are often adamant in their distaste for 'this grotty town'. Geographical mobility is perceived by vast numbers of Southallians as a sign of upward social mobility.

This recurring motive strikes home both to common sense and to anthropological reasoning. Using common sense, few people can be expected publicly to put down what personally they cannot escape. Anthropologically, it stands to reason that there is more to the loss of class associated with Southall's tatty image than is contained in the Registrar General's classification of socio-economic groups. The conceptualization of class is, in England, and not only among the English, anything but colour-blind. The pervasive connection between notions of class and 'race' is also acknowledged by another locally born Englishwoman, although she herself regards it as rubbish:

You get a lot of people say, 'Oh, the Indians have overrun Southall', when all the white families moved out. It really makes me laugh to think about them, they're saying 'how can you? there's a community of Indians!' I say, well, there wouldn't be so many: they bought their houses off white families. They moved out because – I was talking to some security men, and they came from up North, and they were saying that – because when you get a family of a different colour, that brings down the value of the house prices. Yeah, that as well: it brings down the – it makes it a lower class area. I said rubbish – that is rubbish … So they start moving out because they want to be in a better class area!   *(Hawkes 1990b, 40)*

The equation between moving out and moving up is widespread among Southallians. This move into a reputedly 'better-class area' is also a move into suburbia, be it that of Southall's own suburbs or the neighbouring areas of Greenford, Hounslow, or Hayes. The semi-detached and detached houses there offer what is sought by many in Southall's urban parts, but is hard to find for most: the assurance of privacy.

The terraced streets leading off the busy Broadway and King Street can indeed appear to be cultivated as if they were private spaces. In mine, ten seconds' walk from the Broadway throng, a neighbour and I, working on my car, were passed by two young men, busily engaged in a noisy conversation. One of them used a common expletive. In an instant, my neighbour turned, raised himself, and hollered: 'Watch your language, boys!' Unlike the public arena of the Broadway, the sidestreets are considered a private space, the pavements almost part of the residents' property. Such anecdotes prove nothing conclusive, of course, but they may serve to highlight the gulf between the public space of the thoroughfares and the private spaces behind them. 'Living in India is so different, you know', the same neighbour said to me on a hot summer's day: 'Here, people don't use their gardens! In India, people would be sitting outside, and there'd be a dozen radios playing, and, you know, everybody would be perfectly happy, nobody would complain!' 'But why *don't* people play their radios then?' I enquired. 'In England, it's not done, is it?', was the shoulder-shrugging reply. My good-humoured rejoinder that there was no Englishman in sight for a mile and a half received a curt rebuke: 'It's England.' English conventions of privacy indeed influence Southallians' cultivation of space, though they are only one influence among many. Southallians share neither the urban English convention that neighbours are nobody's business, nor the rural conventions of good neighbourliness with anyone, no matter who they are. In the streets most familiar to me, the range of neighbours whom one would greet is, by and large, circumscribed by the trapezoid that includes one's own house, a few to the left and right, and the fewer ones immediately facing.

Across many adjoining streets, however, there are kinship networks that go well beyond these household-centred trapezoids. Whole clusters of kin may reside in close proximity, and a great many households are connected to kin residing elsewhere in Southall or nearby. As the kinship density of a whole town is impossible to establish in such a setting, it may help to consult the results of our survey among young Southallians aged between twelve and eighteen. They were asked to number the relatives 'in or near' Southall whom they counted as 'cousins'. It is immaterial here whether they would be recognized as cousins by a genealogist: what matters are the informants' conceptions of peers, and by implication elders, as kin. Some two-thirds of Sikh youngsters (65 per cent) reported the presence of five cousins or more, and Hindu youths (51 per cent) and Muslim youths (34 per cent), too, counted more 'cousins in or near

Southall' than their white peers (28 per cent). Asked about grandparents nearby, Sikh and Hindu youths reported these in numbers similar (36 per cent, 29 per cent) to those of their white peers (29 per cent). For the offspring of migrants this is remarkable, and the far lower figure registered by Muslim youths (19 per cent) would be much closer to expectations from a post-immigrant population.

The widespread desire to move out of 'tatty' Southall and 'live up the road' may thus be interpreted in more ways than class advancement alone. It may, of course, promise an escape from the town's low rank in the pervasive class hierarchy among whole suburbs, conditioned in part at least by racist equations of class with colour of skin. It may be an escape, further, from neighbours deemed alien by whatever difference of cultural heritage is recognized by householders themselves; but it may also promise escape from the often strict censure of those of the same categorized background. All three interpretations could easily be linked. Each could be seen as an escape from being stereotyped: be it by life in an immigrant 'ghetto', by co-residence with subjectively alien minorities, or by the social control of 'one's own folks' with whom one may share a heritage, but sometimes little more. It is possible, indeed, to surmise that the oft-desired privacy afforded by 'moving up the road' is valued as a kind of household autonomy that life in the central wards of Southall seldom affords. It is also possible that Southallians of Punjabi backgrounds may wish to move out to escape the stereotypes associated with their part of London in the Punjab. I am told that Southall's reputation among Punjabis on the subcontinent is unfavourable, and that a migrant proves success by leaving behind its 'gang warfare', its 'dirtiness', and the proximity of cultural 'others' considered unsavoury or inferior.

Such a link to an escape from being stereotyped is hypothetical; more tangible is the link between social control by one's own network of kin and cultural *community* and the caution advised in 'being friendly with the wrong crowd', however one's own network may define them. The denser a household's network of kin and *community* censure, the more cautious, on the whole, is its engagement with neighbours shunned by this network. Stereotyping and sometimes disdain of neighbours from different *communities* are by no means rare. Yet there is the strictest censure on declared or open enmity. The make-up of the population is varied enough for everyone, on the surface at least, to pretend to 'get on well with everyone'. The public tone is polite. It has, among men at least, developed local conventions that reflect the multi-cultural composition of town. To call neighbours 'mate', as is usual in London's working-class districts, is rare. When greeting other men in English, some South Asians stick to the Indian-English 'Hello Sir!' even for next-door neighbours, while others have borrowed the Irish 'Hello my friend!' A few have made the Afro-American or Caribbean 'Hi man!' their own. Among and toward women, I am not aware of similarly easy conventions newly agreed in a process of daily cross-*community* exchange. Moreover, young Southallians have come to converge on a dialect of English that bears witness to a community of language in various ways. Phonetically, it is clearly recognizable as a West London accent, and its lexis integrates Americanisms ('*bad*' or '*wicked*' for 'good'), Afro-Caribbean usages ('*cool, man*') and Indianisms ('*innit*' for 'isn't it', 'aren't you', 'aren't they', etc.).

To speak of a shared Southall culture, none the less, may still sound a far-fetched idea. The town, considered as a shared space, shows few signs of joint cultivation by different *communities* placed on equal terms. What a commonly shared Southall culture might consist of, cannot be ascertained by observing public behaviour and street life. Yet culturally shared absences, or blank spots, may be as telling as readily recognized positive agreements. The absence of any widely shared appeal to civic pride as Southallians, and the widespread desire to move out and up, are cultural facts in their own right. They are so widely shared as to be taken for granted, and they need thus to be explored. This exploration must concern two factors at once: on the one hand, it should clarify the cultural heterogeneity of Southall's population; on the other, it should account for the equation, professed across this heterogeneity, between moving out and moving up. Southallians, internally differentiated as their cultural heritages are, must have something in common if so many of them think of moving out as social advancement.

Ethnic distinctions, economic commonalities
To begin to shed light on the ethnic heterogeneity that lies behind the still elusive shared culture of Southallians, this section will introduce some basic demographic and economic statistics. In its course, the focus will veer from ethnic differentiation to the economic commonalities shared among all ethnic minorities and indeed by many of its white people, too. The national census of 1991 counted just over 61,000 Southallians living in the five wards of town. Each ward comprised between 11,000 and 13,000 people. It was the first census in British history to ask questions about the respondents' ethnic group, and although one may debate any such categorizations, it allows for a reason-

Table 1. *Major ethnic categories among Southallians*

Category	%
'Indian'	50
'Pakistani'	7
'Other Asian'	3
'White'	30, of whom one in ten was born in Ireland
'Black-Caribbean'	5
Other categories	5, which comprise 'Black-African, Black-Other, Bangladeshi, Chinese, Other-Asian, Other-non-Asian'

Calculated from: 1991 Census Local Base Statistics 02AXFC, Table L 06: Ethnic Group: Residents.

ably clear profile of Southall's ethnic diversity, which is summarized in table 1. These figures must surprise anyone who has strolled along Southall Broadway and failed to see any evidence of a 'white presence'. The reason is simple enough: the 'ethnic spread' of Southall's population is decidedly uneven across its five wards. These wards, which the census takes as its base, are fixed by local politicians for electoral purposes:

When we had to redraw the [ward] boundaries, the Tories came up with this ridiculous map that showed a 'Lady Margaret Ward' or something like that: a huge long hose-pipe all the way up the Lady Margaret Road – sort of three miles long and 500 yards wide. They thought that'd be a safe Tory seat.

The local politician who told me this story was amused at the futility of the Conservative councillors' attempt, rather than surprised at its party-political bias. Given that virtually all local politicians have strong party loyalties, ward boundaries tend to reflect calculations of electoral advantage at least as much as the local topography of class or ethnic profiles. To some extent, this masks the common-sense impression that there are in many ways two Southalls: an urban, post-migration, inner town and a 'leafy', nearly half-white suburban belt. Yet these two interact and even condition each other, much as Anderson (1990) found when his planned study of a 'gentrifying neighborhood' in Chicago had to be broadened into 'a more inclusive study of the relationship between it and the adjacent black ghetto' (Anderson 1990, x). It is useful, therefore, briefly to introduce the five wards. Their differences are traced most easily by moving from west to east, following a gradual decrease in population densities.

Northcote ward comprises the smallest and the most densely populated area. Its housing consists mainly of terraces built between the 1920s and

1950s. It covers the most urban part of 'New Southall'. *Glebe* ward, to its south, covers almost twice as large an area and so is less densely populated. It comprises some very crowded Edwardian terraced streets with inexpensive properties, and many more streets of lower-density housing. It is not 'leafy', however, as much of its space is taken up by industrial estates and post-industrial ruins. *Mount Pleasant* ward was newly carved out in the 1970s, when the safe Labour ward of Northcote was becoming too populous for electoral purposes. It combines a densely populated part of Northcote with an adjoining suburban area in a way that has usually absorbed the 'semi-detached vote'. The ward thus represents a half-way house between urban, and largely post-immigration, Southall and the leafier suburbs of town. Among these, *Waxlow* ward is Southall's northernmost ward and offers mostly semi-detached and detached properties. By and large, it is a well-to-do and mainly white suburban area. *Dormer's Wells* ward, Southall's eastern suburb, covers twice as much ground as any other Southall ward. It comprises most of the town's more affluent avenues, but also includes both of its major housing estates. One of these council estates, called Golf Links, comprises almost a thousand flats and a population of whom half were economically inactive in 1984 (Yabsley 1990, Appendix 5).

Even with the major housing estates counted in, the suburban wards differ markedly from the ethnic profiles of the inner wards. Thus, in the outer wards, the proportion of white residents reaches at least 45 per cent, while in all the inner wards, settlers from the New Commonwealth make for well over 75 per cent of residents. The ethnic differences between outer and inner wards are also reflected in their socio-economic profiles (see table 2).

It is remarkable how occupational class differences continue to distinguish the outer wards from the inner ones. The relative weight of the three non-manual classes and the three manual ones goes through a gradual, but complete, reversal from the central wards to the suburbs. Having started out in Glebe with its six-to-four preponderance of manual occupations, the demographic tour ends in Dormer's Wells with a six-to-four preponderance of the non-manual occupations. The trend is not even dented by the Dormer's Wells housing estates with their large number of unskilled residents. The question must arise, then, whether this stratificatory distinction can indeed be traced to ethnic distinctions. Table 3a details the relationship between ethnic categories and occupational class.

Now it is Black-Caribbean and Indian Southallians, as well as those

Table 2. *Census ward and social class based on occupation*

	Glebe %	Northcote %	Mount Pleasant %	Waxlow %	Dormer's Wells %
1 Professional occupations	2	3	2	3	3
2 Managerial, technical	15	15	21	24	29
3 (N) Skilled non-manual	21	24	24	25	29
All non-manual	38	42	47	52	61
3 (M) Skilled manual	23	17	22	24	16
4 Partly skilled	25	26	23	18	15
5 Unskilled	14	15	8	5	8
All manual	62	58	53	47	39
Total	100	100	100	100	100

Calculated from: 1991 Census Local Base Statistics 02AXFC, Table L 93 SEG: Social class and ethnic group (10 per cent sample): Residents aged 16 and over, employees and self-employed. Percentages are calculated for totals exclusive of 'Armed forces' and 'Occupation inadequately described or not stated'.

born in Ireland, who reverse the proportion of non-manual to manual occupations found among whites at large. None the less, the reversal is not as drastic as that found between wards: an indication of the presence, in the suburbs, of those who have successfully moved out and up into the once all-white suburbia. Yet the table contains troublesome indications. Its most astonishing detail must be the occupational profile of the Pakistani category which alone equals that of the white one. Since in the light of my fieldwork this puzzled me, I have detailed, in table 3b, the unemployment figures for males as reported by the census authorities, and added the best available country-wide figures for comparison. The relative placing of each ethnic category reflects the national averages calculated by the Labour Force Survey of 1988–90 (Jones 1993, 120). Thus, men categorized as Pakistani were most likely to be unemployed, and white males least. Yet the Southall figures are higher throughout than the ethnic averages across the country. Among Pakistani men the local figures amounted to almost a third, when nationally they were less than a quarter. Among white men, they amounted to 14 per cent in Southall, while the national survey had counted 8 per cent (Jones 1993, 120). These high – and in the case of Pakistani men exorbitant –

Plate 1   Punjabi dancers and London police

Plate 2   Telephone engineer at work

Plate 3   Conversation at the bus stop

Plate 4   Muslim refugee outside an 'off-licence' liquor store

Plate 5 Policeman, under-taker, and temple official leading a funeral cortege

Plate 6 Stopping for a chat on the Broadway: men

Plate 7 Stopping for a chat on the Broadway: women

Plate 8   Sikh ladies passing a public house

Plate 9   'Danceasia presents': Ghazal, Bhangra, and Rap for Valentine's Day

Plate 10 Children at a Middle School

TABLE 3. *a. Ethnic category and social class based on occupation*
          b: Ethnic category and male unemployment rate

	White %	(Born in Ireland) %	Black-Caribbean %	Indian %	Pakistani %
3a					
1 Professional occupations	2	4	1	3	1
2 Managerial, technical	28	28	19	16	17
3 (N) Skilled non-manual	23	13	24	24	33
All non-manual	53	45	44	43	51
3 (M) Skilled manual	22	23	21	21	17
4 Partly skilled	16	20	22	26	23
5 Unskilled	9	12	13	10	9
All manual	47	55	56	57	49
(Total)	100	100	100	100	100
3b					
Local male unemployment (Census 1991)	14	18	19	16	32
Country-wide male unemployment	8	N/A	16	11	22
(The Labour Force Survey, 1988–90)					

Calculated from: 1991 Census Local Base Statistics 02AXFC, Table L 93 SEG: Social class and ethnic group (10 per cent sample): Residents aged 16 and over, employees and self-employed, and Table L 09: Economic position and ethnic groups: Residents aged sixteen and over. Percentages are calculated for totals exclusive of 'Armed Forces' and 'Occupation inadequately described or not stated'. People 'born in Ireland' form a sub-sample of the category 'white'. Country-wide unemployment figures from Jones 1993, 120.

unemployment rates must beg some serious questions. Why should men of ethnic minorities be unemployed more often than white men, and why should even white men in Southall be unemployed more often than whites elsewhere?

These questions are all the more urgent because many Southallians are clearly desperate for paid jobs. For a town with one of the highest proportions of youngsters under sixteen in the country, the participation of women in paid employment is altogether staggering. Their largest single field of employment is centred on Heathrow Airport where airlines and other businesses provide some 80,000 jobs. The employment rates

Table 4. *Ethnic category and employment rates of economically active*
women

	White %	(Born in Ireland) %	Black-Caribbean %	Indian %	Pakistani %
Employed full-time	63	63	72	66	51
Employed part-time	25	26	17	16	17
Registered unemployed	8	8	10	13	26
Other, e.g. self-employed or govt. work scheme	4	3	1	5	6
Total	100	100	100	100	100

Calculated from: 1991 Census Local Base Statistics 02AXFC, Table L 09:

and unemployment figures for Southall women are detailed in table 4.
These figures are considerably higher than anything that could have been
expected even from an analysis of the country-wide patterns. Jones'
(1993) country-wide analysis puts the labour force participation rates of
'all ethnic minority' women at 57 per cent. Afro-Caribbean women
exceed this average to reach 76 per cent; Indian women meet it precisely;
and Pakistani women remain furthest below it at 23 per cent (Jones 1993,
88). In Southall, women's employment rates reach 80 to 90 per cent in
four of the five ethnic categories; and even among Pakistani women two-
thirds go to work, while their rate of registered unemployment is as
exceptionally high as it is among their menfolk.

This intense participation of women in earning a family income is fully
congruent not only with the high figures of local male unemployment,
but also with the widely shared desire to move out and up. It appears
even more intense as one puts aside the official statistics and looks
around in the town. In the inner wards, the actual employment rate of
women is certainly higher than the officially registered one, and households are regularly leafleted with fly-sheets such as this:

SEWING MACHINISTS WANTED
in Southall
Apply: ... rear of
72, Western Road.

This backstreet jeans factory turned out, on police inspection, 'to be an
overcrowded Dickensian sweatshop ... and a fire and health risk'
employing some 150 women in toxic conditions (*The Recorder*, 4 May

1990, 2). The case of a Southall seamstress earning just over £1 an hour was due to be brought to a High Court during my fieldwork (*The Gazette*, 3 July 1987, 7). Seamstresses, food packers, part-time shop assistants, and unregistered cleaners bussed every night to commercial premises and even government offices – many of these are neither officially employed nor registered unemployed. Women's labour is drawn upon to an extraordinary degree, and the widespread wish to move out and up appears entirely credible in the light of these exertions. In an area of high dependency ratios and high unemployment, all available human resources seem to have been thrown into the struggle for economic security or upward mobility.

The argument of this brief section has progressed from a preoccupation with ethnic distinctions to an interest in economic commonalities. Local unemployment rates are high, and they are not helped by the town's bad traffic connections to London. I have known Southallians travel three hours each way to a low-paid job in East London. A number of locals, whites as well as former migrants, have described to me their impression that a Southall address by itself is a handicap when looking for work. I have not been able to confirm this impression statistically, but should not be surprised if a better statistician did.

Certainly, most people who can will try to escape what they see as the stigma of a Southall address. Moving out is the obvious possibility, but given the intensive competition it is difficult. Many Southallians living in the Norwood Green area of the Glebe ward insist that they live 'in Norwood Green, which isn't really Southall'. The same is true of many houscholds located in the no-man's-land between Southall's northern suburbs and the largely white, if unattractive, Greenford, and those that, just beyond Southall's western hump bridge, reside in Hayes End. Southall indeed 'has a bad name', as I have heard it expressed in dozens of interviews, even by youngsters quite unaware of the niceties of British class distinctions by area. One way of exploring this reputation which influences the shared culture of Southallians in that they all have to deal with it, is a short survey of the town's local history. I shall use this brief summary for other purposes, too: it will help to clarify aspects of migratory as well as political history which the main chapters will take for granted, and it will give a historical background to the *community* discourse that is so prevalent in Southallians' thinking about their town.

Some local history: migration and the 'white backlash', *community* **building and 'the Southall riots'**

The history of modern Southall begins with a railway line. In the mid-nineteenth century, Brunel's Great Western Railway turned the thousand-year-old hamlet and manor into a Victorian shunting yard ready for industrial investment. Victorian Glebe and Edwardian Northcote grew together to form a metropolitan borough from 1905, and in the 1930s their low-wage industries and speculative housing developments attracted the first 'wave of immigrants' from the depressed coalfields of South Wales and northern England, as well as from Ireland.

The first noticeable influx of labour migrants from the New Commonwealth began in the mid-1950s when a local manufacturer of rubber accessories for cars began to recruit labourers overseas. One of the family owners of this firm, Woolf's Rubber Company, had commanded a unit of Punjabi Sikhs in the previous war. The need for unskilled labour was intense throughout England at the time, and the Punjabi Sikhs so recruited found it easy and useful to spread the word among their friends and kin in India. Employers and workers alike set in motion a process of chain migration from the Punjab, and further local jobs were on offer, especially in the food-processing industries of West London. Nestle, Batchelor's, Kraft, and Lyons were some of the well-known names in search of 'immigrant labour'. While the national census of 1951 had counted a mere 300 Southallians born in the New Commonwealth, ten years later their numbers had risen eightfold to 2,400. Of these, three-quarters were of South Asian birth, and apart from Sikhs they included a small number of Muslims from Pakistan; of the remaining quarter, most were drawn from the smaller Caribbean islands.

By the time of the 1961 census, the erstwhile labour migrants had imperceptibly changed into settlers. The 'myth of return' took its first batterings for both personal and political reasons. The proverbial 'five years abroad' were stretched from one contingency to the next, as an Afro-Caribbean friend recalled in the most tangible way:

When I got here, we all said, it's five years, and we'll go home. But then the wages wasn't ever enough, – you send money home, and then, after a year or two, you want a better place, and – well, till you've got another place, the five years is over, and you can just see that it's going up, not down. And then I said, OK, I'll stay till I'm thirty. And I turned thirty alright, but then I was with Vicky, and – you know, we both wanted to stay together, – I wasn't going off to the West Indies without her. And then, oh well, – it's the brats now. They go to school here, they're British in a way, they're not going now, are they. I mean, 'back'?, – they've never been nowhere but here.

The question of girlfriends and children did not arise in the same way for the vast majority of South Asians, whose marriages were built upon arrangements concluded between the two families and had to follow elaborate norms of 'clan' (*got*) exogamy. But during the late 1950s, British politicians began in public to debate restrictions on immigration and settlement policies. The Commonwealth Immigrants Act (1962) established a system of entry vouchers, and a 1965 Government White Paper effectively ended the granting of such vouchers to unskilled applicants. From the mid-1960s onwards, the reduced influx favoured a higher proportion of skilled people; among Sikhs, they were of the crafts castes of carpenters and builders; among Hindus and Muslims, from a wide variety of castes and social backgrounds. Their numbers, however, were exceeded tenfold by a most vigorous movement of dependants who wished to join relatives already in Britain. The publicized threats of British politicians about closing the door to further immigration had, of course, the opposite effect. As Hawkes summarizes:

Many decided to send for wives, children and dependants immediately to beat the ban. Relatives and others were also encouraged to come now before the door finally shut ... After 1962 the profile of South Asian immigration to the U.K. changed. Whilst in 1960, South Asian and Caribbean children accounted for 1 per cent of the [Southall] school population, by 1964 this was 15 per cent: 1,130 of South Asian origin, 100 West Indian (Institute of Race Relations and Southall Rights 1981, 31). In 1966, whilst only 3,840 immigrants holding Ministry of Labour vouchers entered the U.K. from South Asia, 24,368 dependants were admitted. Thus, 92 per cent of immigrants were women and children.

(Hawkes 1990a, 19–20)

With the arrival of these dependants, two conflicting processes took shape simultaneously. On the one hand, the labour migrants turned settlers began to organize and to build up *community* organizations. An Indian National Association, an Indo-Pakistan Cultural Society, a West Indian, later Caribbean, Association and, most importantly, from 1957 an Indian Workers' Association provided advice, welfare, and educational services. It is important to note the *community*, rather than inclusively civic, basis and bias of these self-help organizations. South Asian Southallians in particular found little welcome or support from the bodies of civil society, whether they were trade unions, residents' associations or social clubs. In 1959, the town saw the establishment of its first Sikh temple which became a focus of religious *community* building.

On the other hand, the local white population began to voice growing resentment at having 'so many foreigners' in their midst and fastened their attention on two issues in particular: the 'overcrowding' of homes and the 'swamping' of schools with 'immigrant children'. Overcrowding had indeed been an issue of concern throughout the 1930s and 1940s, and a forgotten part of Southall's history is a determined resettlement policy effective from 1947, well before the first South Asian settlement. It is described by Kirwan, a local historian:

After the war the most pressing problem was overcrowding. The population exceeded 56,000, and there was little room for new residents as well as those coming back from the services or evacuation ... The declared policy of the county council was to resettle in new towns as many people and industries as possible, and for a time this was in some measure successful. By 1961, after more than ten years' operation of the scheme, the population of Southall had dropped to little more than 50,000. By that time, however, a new wave of immigrants had tended to make the policy unworkable, so in 1962 it was formally abandoned.

(Kirwan 1965, 49)

Speaking in general, this quotation makes it clear that Southall was an area of considerable urban problems, sub-standard housing, insufficient communications, and a weakening industrial infrastructure well before the arrival of its Commonwealth residents. Political rhetoric of the left sometimes blames these on the effects of racism; rhetoric of the political right on the presence of 'immigrants'. The evidence appears clear that if Southall has changed economically, it has changed for the better. Speaking in particular, the above quotation helps to explain how migrants could find cheap, though often poorly maintained, houses in Southall: some were vacated by resettled residents; as importantly, the county authorities of the time were far more reluctant in Southall than in neighbouring parts of Middlesex to exercise their statutory right of overcrowding controls and inspections. For the local whites, on the other hand, the recent memory of their own overcrowded conditions may have contributed to their resentment of the 'newcomers', who often had no choice but to resort to multiple occupancies and even the sharing of beds across shifts at work.

As early as 1959, a small delegation of twenty Southallians had petitioned the Borough Council to 'stop coloured people from buying houses in the area', citing the overcrowding that many of them had only just left behind (Hawkes 1990a, 60). Four years later, the right-wing British National Party gained 27 per cent of Southall votes at council elections, campaigning on the slogan 'Send them Back!', and relegating the Conservative Party to an unprecedented third place. One of the British National candidates founded a Southall Residents' Association which, from 1963, demanded that the Borough Council adopt a compulsory purchase policy, buying up vacated properties and thus keeping them from 'the undesirable elements in our midst' (SR and IRR 1981, 25–6). Yet the British National Party continued to lose votes throughout the 1960s, dropping from 9 per cent in the General Election of 1964 to less than 5 per cent in 1966: 'partly as many of its supporters had moved out of Southall ... and partly because the mainstream political parties had moved 'right' on immigration issues' (Hawkes 1990a, 63). The racist campaigns orchestrated by 1960s extremists are well documented in a locally produced booklet, *Southall: The Birth of a Black Community* (SR and IRR 1981). Among Southallians, however, they are not as widely remembered as a later controversy about white and 'immigrant' children in Southall schools.

'Bussing' or 'coaching' are the well-remembered words for a policy of dispersal of 'immigrant children' to schools outside Southall. At the height of public tensions, in 1963, white residents, particularly from Old Southall, petitioned the borough authorities to prevent 'the swamping of Southall primary schools by immigrant children'. Government guidelines were widely interpreted as recommending that all schools and classes be composed of a majority of English-born students. The local borough thereupon introduced a policy of dispersing South Asian and Afro-Caribbean children to neighbouring schools. From 1966, thousands of young Southallians were thus 'bussed out' every morning, and many now in their thirties and forties remember the practice as a clear sign of discrimination and racism. It was not formally phased out until 1976.

By this time, however, Southall's economic townscape, as well as its political climate, had changed beyond recognition. Economically, it was the arrival of South Asian refugees from Kenya (after 1967) and Uganda (after 1972) which had rejuvenated and 'Asianized' the town's infra-structure. As 'white' shops closed, 'Asian' shops opened to fill the gaps, using capital and business know-how gathered in the East African countries. Southall became a town of 'Asian' shops and three 'Asian' cinemas that showed nothing but Hindi movies. Politically, too, the 'white backlash' of the 1960s had proved ineffective, and the central wards of town had been virtually emptied of all visible white presence. The *community* building of the settlers had progressed at a steady pace, and the Indian Workers' Association (IWA) had grown to be the town's chief broker and pivot of political influence. Factional infighting, however, was rife within its ranks, and its contending leadership networks were suspected of corruption by many elders, and of collaborating with the powers that be by a younger cohort of 'radicals'. The political polarization and the widespread civic crisis of the late 1960s had seen the rise, also in Southall, of a new stratum of young activists who wielded enormous influence over their peers. Drawn largely from the cohort of teenage-migrants, they had grown up in England, yet they saw their life chances diminished by racial prejudice and their *community* politicians locked into factional skirmishes, powerless against job discrimination and even bussing. No less importantly, the 'old guard' seemed oblivious to the country-wide rise, from the mid-1970s, of neo-fascist ideas and racist violence. When the political and racialist polarization of the time was carried into Southall, now a fast-developing 'Asian' enclave amidst the largely hostile suburbs of London, the reaction was dramatic.

In 1976, a young Southallian named Gurdip Singh Chaggar was stabbed to death by a group of white youths right outside the Dominion Cinema and the headquarters of the IWA. Youth activists gathered in the recently founded Southall Youth Movement, a club mainly of young South Asian Southallians, and in Peoples Unite, its analogue among Afro-Caribbean youths. Together, the two networks marched on the police station. Local relations with the police had been in a state of crisis for years, and even the more establishment-minded *community* organizations had petitioned the Home Secretary to set up an independent inquiry into recurrent allegations of police brutality (Pulle 1974). The 1976 demonstrations and arrests, sit-ins and detentions were widely reported in the British press and treated in the terminology of 'race riots' between 'Asian youths' and the police. The Southall Youth Movement and Peoples Unite continued, in the aftermath of these events, to widen their support among local youths, as the Metropolitan Police continued its policies of surveillance by searching premises for stolen goods, as well as persons for the illegal possession of recreational drugs. With relations steadily worsening, the next confrontation must have seemed but a question of time, and it happened on 23 April 1979. This was the day of 'the Southall riots' which made the town famous or infamous in the British media.

A neo-fascist party, called the National Front, had contrived to hire a space in Southall Town Hall for one of its meetings. To hold it in Southall was an obvious affront to all local pride and sensitivity. The day being St George's Day, the borough authorities, moreover, had followed English custom in flying the Union Jack over the building, despite the fact that the National Front had usurped it as its own partisan emblem. As anger rose, crowds gathered and converged on the Town Hall where they encountered more than 2,500 officers of the Metropolitan Police, many in newly introduced riot gear. Police orders were to push back, cordon off, and then disperse several thousand Southallians, in order to protect the freedom of assembly of the sixty or so neo-fascists. In the attempt to clear a whole town centre of its local population, emotions brimmed over, possibly on both sides. The ensuing street battle resulted in the death of a demonstrator, intensive care for several leaders of the Southall youths, and numerous injuries. The name of the dead demonstrator, Blair Peach, would later serve a Labour-led Borough Council to name a Southall school, and would be expunged by a subsequent Conservative local administration. The memory of several hundred Southallians battered by police protecting the civil liberties of a racist group remained a potent political force. Feelings ran high, therefore, when, two years later, neo-fascists planned another local event.

In July 1981, a musical 'gig' in the Hambrough Tavern pub drew three busloads of white skinheads from London's East End. Arriving in Southall, they had already clashed with local youths who had heard – whether rightly or wrongly is uncertain – that other youths and women had been harassed. Extra police were again drafted in to protect the peaceful conduct of a provocative gathering, though this time they knew when to withdraw. The Hambrough Tavern, already sued previously for disbarring 'coloured' patrons, was burnt to the ground on the same night. There was no loss of life, and it has since been rebuilt and welcomes all patrons who pay for their drinks.

Unlike bussing, one cannot say that 'the Southall riots' have left a deep imprint on most Southallians' collective consciousness. While outsiders may still associate the name 'Southall' with 'riots', local people rarely mentioned them without prompting. At the time of my fieldwork they seemed, in many ways, to be battles of a distant past, overtaken by new local concerns. Yet, historically speaking, they served to galvanize a younger cohort of local political activists, and a number of their former leaders went on to achieve prominent positions in established political bodies. Some of them guide Southall's socialist and feminist initiatives, discussed at a later stage; others have begun to exert influence on the more mainstream *community* organizations that shape the town's political processes. It is to these that the account must now turn, in order to continue the search for the culture that Southallians might share.

Local politics as *community* competition
For the purposes of local government and municipal administration, Southall forms the western-most part of the London Borough of Ealing.

A borough is London's smallest unit of local government, usually numbers between 200,000 and 300,000 people, and is run by an elected Borough Council. Southall had been a discrete London borough until 1965, when government reforms created far larger political units, and this loss of local autonomy may have contributed to the crucial lack of comprehensively civic institutions in the town. It certainly led to a fierce competition for public resources. Besides Southall and Ealing proper, the amalgamated Borough of Ealing comprises the relatively prosperous suburb of Hanwell, the suburban sprawl of Greenford and, closest to central London, Acton Town. All these areas are surrounded by vast housing estates which show clear signs of material deprivation and social need. Money is needed everywhere, and Southallians make up little more than a fifth of the borough's population. Borough funds are needed to run voluntary organizations ranging from crèches for the children of working mothers and refuges for battered women to advice centres for the unemployed, support services for handicapped people, and evening classes in music, literacy, sewing, or computer skills. All of these activities, and many more, are run by voluntary or *community* associations, vying with each other for annual grants from the borough's scarce funds.

Shortly before my fieldwork, this competition was exacerbated even further by a second local government reform. There had until then been an intermediate layer of provision between the national government and each London borough. This, the Greater London Council, however, was abolished by the first Thatcher government in a decision that cancelled scheduled elections. At the time, the metropolitan council's majority was formed by Labour politicians, and its policies had gained a reputation for radical approaches to provisions for minorities. The abolition of this metropolitan body had two consequences for Southallians. Firstly, competition for public resources came to focus on the Borough Council alone, and *community* organizations and '*community* leaders' often found themselves pitched one against the other in this highly competitive arena. Secondly, the dissolution meant that the Council's policy makers and Community Relations officials needed new posts. Understandably, the more radical of these gravitated to those London boroughs that were known to endorse their ideas. Ealing was one of these, and it attracted a sizeable number of such policy makers to staff its newly established supervisory bodies concerned with equal opportunities and minority rights. Southallians' views of their Borough Council's policies and public discourse polarized considerably over the years of my fieldwork, the end of which coincided with the election of a Conservative majority.

The electoral defeat, in 1990, of the Labour majority on the Borough Council, however, was not due to the Southall vote. While the Borough of Ealing had been governed by both Labour and Conservative majorities, the Southall vote had for long been solidly and often overwhelmingly Labour. Council seats in the central wards went to Labour politicians almost inevitably, and only the leafier suburbs had been known to return the odd Conservative from time to time. Solid Labour support is not surprising among an electorate of former migrants who have come to Britain from New Commonwealth countries. Conservative policies are associated with restrictive immigration laws and, latterly, a de-regulation of the labour market, while Labour policies profess the values of ensuring public welfare and serving the needs of *communities*. Nor is Labour support surprising if one considers the standard of political argument proposed by the Conservative candidate in the June 1987 General Election. This pamphlet reached my letterbox after my first year of fieldwork:

Vote Conservative! Labour say No to Car Park!

For years the Labour Party have promised Southall that when they were in power they would provide a car park. Now the Labour candidate in the General Election, Syd Bidwell, is trying to STOP THE CAR PARK IN HERBERT RD BEING BUILT.

Your Conservative Candidate ... says
'This car park is vital to Southall ...'

VOTE FOR THE CAR PARK – VOTE CONSERVATIVE ON JUNE 11TH!

The text was neatly translated into Punjabi, yet one wonders whether an English-born electorate would have been offered such an offensively petty argument for electing their sole parliamentary representative for the next five years. Be that as it may, the Conservative Party in Southall had, of course, to contest local elections within the ward boundaries cut out by their Labour opponents.

So far as national, rather than borough, elections are concerned, Southall forms a constituency together with the northern parts of Ealing. This constituency returned the same Labour Member of Parliament from the mid-1960s until after my fieldwork ended. This MP was an Englishman. At first sight, the fact might seem strange, and Southall an obvious area to be represented by an MP of South Asian background. Yet Southall's political arena is characterized by a high degree of factionalism, as well as distrust between different interest groups, as one local councillor explained with some glee:

Labour here isn't a party, you know. Labour is the name for politics. The parties
are inside the Labour Party.
Q.:   You mean like – factions?
A.:   Yes, factions. You take seven people, and you find you've got eight
factions.
Q.:   But how do they get to decide on anything?
A.:   Really, the whole thing is sewn up between five chiefs. There's A.R., and
K. of course, and S.G., and V.S., although he's out now, he's no longer a real
force, and R.P. of course, he's a Brahmin, you know; and really, whatever has
three of them behind it, goes. That's what goes. And whoever's at the helm,
goes with the three against the two, whatever it's about.

The councillor was well aware that this was a simplified model; he was,
after all, a successful local politician. Yet there is little doubt about the
importance of certain key figures and their factions, and the processes of
personal lobbying, strategic realignments, and of the forging of alliances
true, deceitful or ambiguous. There is nothing new in factional politics,
of course, be it in the ethnography of small towns or indeed of the rural
Punjab (see Pettigrew 1975). To the conspicuously 'foreign' fieldworker
they are hard to document, and while I had considered joining the
Labour Party for some time before moving to Southall, I decided not to,
as the conflicting imperatives of the researcher and the party member
would have spelled duplicity sooner or later. One particular episode of
factional politics is, however, worth relating here, because it sheds light
on the co-existence of Southall's *communities* in the public arena.

Most British constituency Labour Parties were involved in a process
of reselecting their prospective parliamentary candidates in the course of
1985. Such reselections were decided in long sequences of ward and
constituency meetings and on several occasions resulted in the deselec-
tion of a sitting Member of Parliament. The Ealing–Southall reselection
was, however, postponed in that year amidst allegations of ballot rigging
directed against 'activist' members who wished to select a South Asian
candidate. The exercise was repeated under the supervision of the Labour
Party's National Executive Committee over the summer of 1986. The
local press published furious allegations of 'cynical manipulation' and
readers' letters accusing politicians of racism if they did endorse the white
MP and inverse racism if they did not. The powerful Indian Workers'
Association forewent its usual stance of neutrality in party-political
matters, and openly endorsed the sitting MP. One by one, four of the five
candidates were endorsed by one electoral ward each. In the end, the
white MP was reselected at a meeting, behind closed doors, of some sixty
constituency delegates. Ethnographically most telling was the published

comment of a Hindu *community leader*: 'Syd Bidwell ... has been a Hindu MP, he has been a Muslim MP, he has been a Christian MP.' (*The Gazette*, 26 September 1986, 5).

This list discreetly fails to mention Sikhs, the vast majority of South Asian Southallians. Representation by an English-born MP seemed to reassure local minorities that no Sikh hegemony would be established in local politics. Seen in this light, it cannot have helped one favoured contender that the local press made him out to be 'bidding to become Britain's first *Sikh* MP' (*The Gazette*, 19 September 1986, 4, my italics). The idea that a white MP was an appropriate choice because of his neutrality was widespread among my informants; none the less it was thought certain that his successor would eventually be a Punjabi, as well as a Sikh, namely the Chairman of the Indian Workers' Association. The prediction was proved correct by the reselection process of 1991.

The local Indian Workers' Association, which claims a membership of 18,000, including 12,000 among Southall residents, was founded in 1957. As its name indicates, it is not a comprehensively civic institution, although Southallians of Pakistani nationality are admitted as associate members. Nonetheless, it is the only organization that could rival the Labour Party for its political influence. Its most prominent members were indeed active in the Party as well, and even the Council of Ealing Borough as a whole would think long and hard before antagonizing the organization. The extraordinary links between the local Labour Party, the Borough Council, and the IWA were well illustrated in the mid-1980s when the Borough Council used part of its own funds, as well as substantial European subsidies, to build an ostentatious new community centre for Southall. It was built on a site immediately adjoining the IWA offices and on a plot that remains the property of the IWA. This resource, known as the Dominion Centre, was completed, after much wrangling, in 1986. Below I shall give a brief case-study of 'stories' told about this community centre, in order to focus on the *community*-orientated discourse of Southallians' political culture. To appreciate the context of these 'stories', it is useful to sketch the parameters that command most of the town's political and civic activity. The two factors that shape it most visibly are the commitments of *community leaders* and the need to relate local requirements to wider policy concerns.

The notion of a *community leader* is no less vague in Southall than elsewhere in Britain. The vagueness of the term is connected, it appears, to the vagueness of *community* as a descriptive term for an ethnic or cultural category of people. Just as *communities* show large areas of overlap depending on the criteria chosen to define them, so *community leaders* may claim to speak for a religious, a regional, a linguistic, or a putatively ethnic *community* depending on context. Alternatively, they may evade clarification and claim to speak for '*the*' *community* at large. Some ambiguity over whom exactly one represents is indeed a political asset for many *community leaders*. It allows them to widen or to focus their search for *community* support and credibility, and it is necessary for co-optation into the mainstream political establishment in which politicians represent not notional *communities*, but territorially discrete constituencies.

To seek recognition as a *community leader* in Southall, there are, broadly speaking, two paths to be followed. The first is epitomized by the successful businessman or, usually male, professional who enhances his social status by gaining a reputation for public-spiritedness. Public service for voluntary associations can be validated by placing it in parallel to the religious duties of rendering 'service' (Punjabi: *seva*), especially when it benefits charitable institutions without an explicitly political agenda. The key resources of these, by and large liberal or conservative, *community leaders* are personal status and respectability; election to the management committee of one or preferably several voluntary organizations; and often also membership of the local Labour Party or the IWA. The second path to claiming recognition as a *community leader* is characteristic of younger men and women with explicitly political commitments. Sometimes known as 'political activists', these personalities may be volunteers or paid employees in a wide range of politically combative organizations. Examples could be seen in an advisory service financed by trade-union funds, and in institutions funded by grants from the borough, such as two law centres, a body to monitor racist attacks and policing practices, or organizations set up on ethnic or national criteria to provide services for one or another *community*. Many who pursue *community leader* status along this 'politically activist' path acquired their political commitments together in the Southall Youth Movement of the 1970s and the later 'Southall riots'. Their political ideas and strategies have diversified since, and their sectional interests can lead to mutual suspicion and rivalry. None the less, the 'activist' path to legitimation as a *community leader* can, on occasion, be rewarded by full co-optation into the institutional bastions of the local Labour Party, the Borough Council, and various 'community relations' bureaucracies.

Within the borough, Southall politicians and *community leaders* must pursue scarce resources in competition with each other, as well as with their counterparts from the neighbouring areas. It is easy to see that creative alliances, factional appeals, and some in-fighting are inevitable strategies in this competition. Furthermore, to make a case for any project or initiative, one must appeal both to ideas of 'ethnic' justice and to the current political or ideological priorities endorsed by the council, the party, or the national government. These priorities are most often prefigured at the centre of the national parties; and to hook one's constituency's interests on to one of these requires special skills. The effort is promising only if one finds allies who 'know the game' and are prepared to engage in a certain amount of the horse-trading that is necessary in such competitive circumstances. An almost ironic example of such horse-trading is the following exchange overheard in a Southall pub. One of the protagonists, here named Dave, was a council administrator, a trade union shop steward, and an active member of the Labour Party; the other, Dick, was employed to run an initiative to alleviate youth unemployment.

DICK: Tell you something: I'm looking for a space about 1,500 square feet, for doing upholstery and furniture and that. With office space as well, – with [*grins*] a nice office for yours sincerely …

DAVE: Yes, I could maybe do something. There's a lot of space coming up.

DICK: Yeah, that'd be great! About 1,500 feet we'd need.

G.B.: 1,500? That's huge!

DICK: It's not when you think about it. This pub's easily – what – 1,000 already!

DAVE: Has it got anything to do with unemployment?

DICK: Yeah, it's all for training actually, training people for jobs and that. – I can also say that – it's – at least half of them's Asian youngsters.

DAVE: Well, that's not so important for me …

DICK: [*interrupts*] No, no, I know.

DAVE: No, but if it's unemployment, that's just my concern.

DICK: [*repeating*] Yeah, I know it isn't...

DAVE: No, if it's unemployed people, we could maybe do something there. Though you know, it can take a bit of time. Maybe two or three months. Have I got your phone number?

DICK: Yeah, there'd also be about half Asian kids on it. Do you have a pen? I'll give you my office number. – Ta! [*writes a phone number on a paper napkin*] – Who was it they say used to sign cheques on napkins – Churchill, wasn't it?

DAVE: [*takes the napkin and folds it*] Yes, I'll see what I can do for the space. 1,500 you say.

DICK: Yep, that'd be good! Thanks a lot, Dave! [*hands back the pen*].

Hurrying to the toilet to take my notes, I wondered if Dick might not better try a political broker with a Council brief for 'Asian kids'. There is, it should be said, nothing corrupt or untoward in this exchange; it shows merely that the search for public resources must be hooked onto one or another recognized political concern, and that the activist must know both which concern might serve the purpose, and which broker of resources should be approached. Success is rarely as effortless as in this example, and I have often marvelled at the painstaking and ceaseless toil that some *community leaders* are prepared to shoulder beside their full-time jobs. Given that competition and scarcity often spell failure rather than success at securing resources, why do they continue; and, as importantly, why do their followers continue to rely on them?

The answer is threefold in both cases. *Community leaders* are often motivated by a strong moral sense of justice for, and service to, their claimed constituencies; they are able to function because the political establishment has co-opted them as representatives of their *communities*; and they gain from their efforts access to more desirable social networks and the respect or gratitude of those they have served. Yet it would be quite wrong to assume that all, or perhaps even most, *community leaders* are representative of their *communities*, let alone able to mobilize them. This is also common outside Southall, as is clear from most of the discussions of 'Black and Ethnic Leaderships' assembled in Werbner and Anwar's (1991) comprehensive collection. Why then do so many people continue to rely on them? The answer again involves at least three factors. People unable to secure the resources due to them on the basis of citizenship alone may follow *community leaders* because they are seen to have been co-opted by the political establishment; they will do so for as long as they see no better or alternative brokerage services offered to them; and they rely on brokerage because what they want is often so strikingly simple, precisely defined, and cheap, that it seems 'only just' out of reach. Many Southallians cannot believe that it could take so much patience, ingenuity, bureaucracy, and rivalry for *community leaders* to secure what is needed.

Yet the competition for resources, and the vagaries of the political or ideological concerns that one needs to hook one's case onto are such that most *community leaders* serve communities full of disappointment and grievances. This is so not only in Southall; here, however, competition between different *communities* is perhaps more starkly defined, and the leaders of one particular *community* feel especially aggrieved at the lack of their own resources and even of access to those secured by others. The marginalization of the Afro-Caribbean population appears marked in many regards and forms the background to the following case-study. It is a study of words proffered, rather than actions observed, and is thus presented as an account of 'stories' told. What matters in re-telling them is not to adjudicate which story is 'true'. Rather, the stories are offered as an illustration, in one case, of how even a civic resource is subject to competition and claims, counterclaims, and denials, all expressed on behalf of *communities*.

Case-study: stories of a community centre

A cinema named the Dominion, one of Southall's three film theatres in the 1960s, was purchased by the Indian Workers' Association in 1967. It then provided showings of Indian films, a highly popular entertainment at the time. Over the 1970s, attendances dropped, however, as South Asian families were quicker than most others in Britain to purchase their own video recorders for the same purpose: to view Indian films and often thus to share with their children a part of their cultural heritage (Gillespie 1989). By the late 1970s, the cinema had lapsed into disuse and disrepair. A group of young Afro-Caribbeans, named Peoples Unite, occupied the semi-derelict building in late 1981. The context of this occupation needs some explanation. Peoples Unite was part of the liberationist political culture of the late 1970s; many of its members were Afro-Caribbeans who had also participated in the formation of the Southall Youth Movement in 1976, responding to the perceived 'sell-out' of older *community leaders* in the face of police harassment and a lack of protection from racial attacks. In 1979, 'Peoples Unite' had leased from the Borough Council a house known as '6 Parkview' and had run in it a drop-in centre mainly used by Afro-Caribbean Southallians. Shortly after the 'Southall riots' in April of that year, this house, situated in close vicinity to Southall police station, was bulldozed without prior announcement and without compensation, in order to make room for a purpose-built old-age-pensioners' home. Finding themselves deprived of their base, the activists turned to the disused Dominion Cinema and installed on its first floor a second-hand pool table and music equipment. One of the organizers described it thus in an interview with Richard Hundleby:

The youth of Southall realised they needed a place to use, and, being pushed by myself, took over the Dominion, – not the running of it *all* – took over the running of what was happening there, and we fixed it up. We gave it a paint job and fumigated the place. We fixed the seats in the cinema etc., so we could use the place as a centre and as basically a place where we could also have functions ... We started off using the Dominion as a drop-in centre for the unemployed – it was not an Afro-Caribbean centre in the Caribbean sense. Those who were using the place were young people of employable age, and this varies. Also a lot of elderly members used the centre; even though they were working, they would still use the place to meet and socialize.   *(Hundleby 1987, 31, italics in original)*

In another activist's account, it was not Afro-Caribbean youths that occupied the Dominion, but an 'Asian' organisation that cynically used the derelict building for its own ends. The story thus told serves as a charter of origin for one of Southall's two principal Afro-Caribbean organizations, named Unity of African Caribbean Peoples or UACP:

The reason the Black Community became so outraged was because there were NO organisations in Southall that could show how IT had helped the Black Community. Yet there was an Asian organisation claiming in the local paper that the 'drop in Centre' which they had established in a derelict cinema was about to be closed and they were looking at ways of getting more grant-aid to run another similar project for the unemployed West Indians.

On investigation into the organisation and its so-called West Indian Centre it was found to be a large empty derelict ballroom above a cinema, with two broken pool tables, one broken tennis table, *no heating*, drinking water etc. The fury of the Black Community was further enraged when it was discovered that this was not the only Asian Organisation in Southall which was receiving grant-aid on behalf of the Afro-Caribbean Community. *Out of this fury U.A.C.P was born.*
(Afro-Caribbean Focus and Beyond 1987, 11, italics in original)

Accordingly, the organization lists as the first of its 'Aims and Objectives: To obtain an Afro-Caribbean Centre in Southall and provide a channel for the voice of the Afro-Caribbean Community in Southall and its surrounding areas' (ibid. 1987, 11). This objective was, ostensibly, to be secured by the demolition of the building and its replacement by a purpose-built community centre. The activist first quoted recalls how:

other organisations started complaining after we'd been in the place only a couple of weeks. Specifically, we got messed about by the I.W.A. who at the beginning were quite prepared to let us use the place. But once our job had been done, showing that the centre was viable to be used as somewhere by the community, they were no longer interested, and they were just looking to get us out as quickly as possible.   *(Hundleby 1987, 32)*

The need for a new community centre was indeed endorsed both by the IWA and by the Borough Council. In the aftermath of the 'Southall riots', and faced with widespread fears of larger-scale 'racial unrest' during the economic recession and political polarization of the early 1980s, politicians of all echelons discovered the 'needs of ethnic minorities'. With extensive financial help from the European Community's Urban Aid programme, Ealing Council took in hand the demolition of the Dominion Cinema, leased the land from the IWA for ninety-nine years, and began with the construction of a purpose-built new community centre.

A consultation process was set in motion to solicit future users' views and wishes. One of the preferences, championed by a number of Afro-Caribbean activists, was for the provision of musical facilities. Acknowledging the importance of music in the youth cultures of both Afro-Caribbeans and South Asians, and the intense activity of local Reggae and Bhangra musicians, the group proposed the provision of soundproofed practice rooms, instruments, equipment, and tuition. Musical provisions were integrated into the centre's official development plan, and there were persistent and credible rumours that £40,000 had been set aside for visual and audio equipment. Yet when the centre opened in November 1986, the room originally proposed as a studio had been turned into a weightlifting gym, and no musical provisions were to be found.

From its official opening in January 1987, the centre got off to a very slow start. The building itself, architecturally by far the most sophisticated in all Southall, was such that I myself, fully initiated into the confidence tricks of a middle-class upbringing, felt intimidated for a long time whenever I entered its cool splendour past the elegant gateway spelling selectness and some reception staff eying all visitors from their haircuts to their shoes. Many others told me that they felt likewise. Its grandly elegant style and staff, however, were not the only problems.

Afro-Caribbean activists judged their *community* excluded on purpose and pressed the point in an anonymous pamphlet circulated in Southall from April 1988: 'Even at this early stage [that is, soon after the opening of the centre three months before] complaints were coming in thick and fast from the Afro-Caribbean community that when they walked into the building they were made to feel unwanted by the majority of staff' (anon. 1988, 1). Some accounts mention that not one of the seventeen places on the centre's Management Committee was offered to an Afro-Caribbean organization or person; another, by a South Asian activist, relates that, in a gesture of solidarity, she passed her own seat to the chair of an Afro-Caribbean organization. The centre's own Annual Report for its second year of operation lists one Afro-Caribbean Southallian among its Management Committee. The report admits that 'the year has been a mixture of success, failure, hard work, trials and tribulations' (Dominion 1989, 4). Among its successes, it lists adult education classes with 240 enrolments between September and April; a pensioners' luncheon club serving food contracted from a South Asian restaurant to a grand average of ten participants; letting its space for recitals and classes of South Asian music organized by a pre-existing and independent foundation; and running a crèche with an average of only five children attending (Dominion 1989, 5–7, 10–12). Among its 'priorities for the future', the first was identified as 'representation from a wider network of women and women's groups in the community' (Dominion 1989, 16).

Laudable and politically correct as this priority must be, it fitted better into the worldview of Ealing Council policy makers than into the local discourse of separate *communities* vying for equal rights of access. The two had already clashed early in 1988, when the centre declared Wednesdays to be 'Women Only' days. As it happened, it was a Wednesday when the chair of the local 'Age Concern' group of pensioners tried to show the newly built centre to a score of, mostly white, retired women and men. In accordance with the new policy, the group was refused access to the building, reportedly empty at the time. The – mostly white, – Southallians concluded, in the words of their guide, that 'this centre is not for us'. The local press carried further messages complaining of exclusion:

Old people are going to Hounslow and Greenford because they don't get what they want at the Dominion.   *(The Gazette, 19 February 1988, 11)*

Southall's Caribbean Focus and Beyond say management at the Dominion Centre, The Green, are holding purely Asian events that exclude both blacks and whites. [The organisation's] leader ... said: 'Black youths and also the white population are made to feel unwelcome at the Dominion, as though they were treading on Asian-only territory.'   *(The Gazette, 15 April 1988, 3)*

The political discourse and civic culture of Southallians is shown, in this case-study, as being highly susceptible to arguments on the basis of the *communities* of 'colour', rather than cross-cutting civic ideas and ideals. Public spaces and facilities are often judged first on whether they 'are *for*' one *community* or another. The few exceptions I have found among public institutions are the Labour Party, the churches, and the socialist or liberationist groups and initiatives. Yet these are not civic institutions so much as alternative communities of conviction. One example of such a rare exception should be given, though, both for the sake of its local tone and because it raises an important question which will be addressed later on, namely, how far Southallians of different *communities* might want to see themselves as forming one solidary 'Black' *community*. Reacting to the under-use of the Dominion Centre, the chief Afro-Caribbean proponents of better musical resourcing protested their claims by looking beyond *community* boundaries. They invoked three exemplars that anthropologists might call Southall's mythical 'hero martyrs'

(McCann 1985): the youth whose stabbing sparked off the formation of the Southall Youth Movement in 1976, the socialist demonstrator who was killed during the 'Southall riots' of 1979, and a prominent local businessman who was assassinated on the orders of Khalistan activists in 1985:

> Every empty room is
> a slander to the memory of Gurdip Singh Chaggar.
> Every unused piece of equipment is
> a travesty to the memory of Blair Peach.
> And every day the building is closed early,
> an abomination to the memory of Tarsem Singh Toor.
>
> *(Southall Musical Enterprises 1987, 12)*

Such cross-*community* appeals, even rhetorical ones, are so rare as to be precious in the local political culture. Southall has neither the municipal institutions of a town in its own right, nor the comprehensively civic institutions of a localized civil society that might integrate and amalgamate *community*-specific requirements and leaderships. In the political sphere, the notion of *community* has come to serve as shorthand for a category of people in need of civic resources and reliant upon the brokerage of *community leaders*, largely self-selected. In such a milieu, and faced with a scarcity of public resources, there is little chance for a political culture based upon individualist civil rights. Instead, rights and resources are claimed in the name of *communities* that must, in effect, compete with each other. What Southall culture the ethnographer can discover at first sight is a culture of people intent upon moving out and up and yet tied to the place by common economic problems, *community* bonds, and the recourse to *community* claims in the competitive public arena. To progress further in a study of Southallians, one must first study the dominant discourse as locals engage it. This is the task of the following chapter, which reviews each *community* one by one. So far as is useful, it will trace, for each *community*, the outlines of the dominant discourse, and will then explore the local migratory histories and local structural placings of each.

4

The dominant discourse applied: 'self-evident' *communities* of *culture*

On Sikhs: the 'majority *community*'
On Hindus: *cultural* cachet
On Muslims: marginalized as a *community*
On Afro-Caribbeans: *community* across island *cultures*
On whites: Irish without *community*, English without *culture*?
On youth: culture consciousness among children

If a group of strangers were to enter Southall with the task of delineating its *cultures*, it would quite obviously depend upon their interests which criteria they would choose. Cross-cutting as the town's social cleavages are, they could establish one classification by religion, another by class, a third by birth-place, another few by parents' or grandparents' region of origin. Just as plausibly, they could divide Southallians by nationality, their own or their parents', or rely on the criteria of ancestral language, mother-tongue, or the language preferred in one context or another. None of these would satisfy any researcher for long, since all these cleavages cut across each other as they must in a plural society.

Yet the descriptions of the town as a whole have already indicated that in most contexts and in much normative speech, Southallians tend to take for granted one near-consensual division: the commonest usage of *culture* in their everyday discourse equates one *culture* with each of five *communities*. Two are defined on 'racial' terms as Afro-Caribbean and white, and three are distinguished on religious criteria among the 'Asian' *community*. Most Southallians are aware, of course, that there are Muslims who are 'Black' and Christians who are 'Asian'; yet these are treated as classificatory anomalies, and most people are in most contexts content with a division into five *cultures*, each identified as a *community*: Sikh, Hindu, Muslim, Afro-Caribbean and white. This classification itself supports the prevailing tendency to think of a town as an assemblage of discrete *communities*: each defining its own *culture*, and each definable without reference to another. In most daily discourse, *cultures* can thus appear as self-evident, mutually exclusive, internally homogeneous groups. Thus, local classifications of the *cultures* and *communities* that surround one's own are able to translate the dominant discourse into a local one.

On Sikhs: the 'majority *community*'

The proportion of Southallians who identify themselves as Sikhs may amount to something like 40 per cent across the town as a whole and 60 per cent in the central wards. Prominent Sikhs are highly visible and influential in the business and political life of the town, and Southallians thus often describe 'the Sikhs' as 'the majority *community*'. This sounds plausible enough at first sight, but to appreciate what the usage implies, one needs to trace its presuppositions. I shall do so in the same order as with the other major *communities* that Southallians tend to identify: starting with a location of the dominant discourse, turning to the local history of migration, and ending on a general assessment of their local positions.

The formation of a dominant discourse about Sikhs as a unified, clearly bounded community of culture has involved British participation for well over a century. On the subcontinent, the British annexation (1849) of the Punjab set an end to 'the precolonial evolution of several Sikh identities, each embracing a selected set of cultural meanings' (Fox 1985, 12):

> These identities subsumed a range of quite different religious beliefs and social practices. Because the boundary between these several sorts of Sikh identities was indistinct, a self-denominated Sikh might follow an amalgam of religious and social practices drawn from different points along the range of identities. Quite against the actual diversity of belief and observance, the British usually treated one Sikh identity, the Singh or Lion one, as the only true Sikhism, and they often used the labels 'Sikh' and 'Singh' interchangeably.   *(Fox 1985, 7)*

The incorporation of a unified Sikh identity owed as much to the formalization of selected religious and customary practices in the numerous Sikh regiments, as it did later to the urban reform movement of the Akalis, and the widespread peasant unrest during the 1920s. Although Fox's detailed account is challenged by McLeod (1989, 78–9) who stresses the internal continuity of the 'Singh' or 'Khalsa' vision of Sikhism, McLeod too confirms the gradual and deliberate creation of 'a new consistency and a new clarity of definition' (1989, 80) during that period.

The view of Sikhs as a clearly bounded, internally homogeneous group was indeed enshrined in British law when the House of Lords recognized Sikhs as an 'ethnic group' in 1983. The case, known as *Mandla v. Dowell Lee (1983)*, had to determine whether the wearing of a turban infringed uniform regulations at an English school. The final ruling produced a translation of the dominant discourse into British law, determining that Sikhs constituted an ethnic group because two 'essential conditions' were fulfilled:

(1) a long shared history, of which the group is conscious as distinguishing it from other groups, and the memory of which keeps it alive;

(2) a cultural tradition of its own, including family and social customs and manners, often but not necessarily associated with religious observance.

> *(Lord Fraser,* Mandla v. Lee (1983), *quoted in Poulter 1986, 185–6)*

One should note in passing that other 'relevant characteristics', such as 'a common geographical origin, or descent from a small number of common ancestors' (ibid.) limit the application of 'ethnic group' status to many other contenders. Regarding the perception of Sikhs in Britain, however, the ruling confirmed the assumptions of the dominant discourse. How this dominant discourse is translated into a local one, however, will in part depend upon local historical factors. In the course of the past forty years, Sikh Southallians have been the first, and have become the largest and most influential, of Southall's post-migration *communities*.

With the 1947 partition of India, and the partition of the Punjab that it entailed, rural Sikhs faced renewed economic pressures in an economy long beset by land shortages and population pressure. Since the British economy was suffering from serious labour shortages, and British policies favoured labour immigration from the Commonwealth, rural Sikhs began to arrive in Britain during the mid-1950s. Most of them were the sons of farmers in the Doab region of the Punjab, with many coming from the district of Jullundur, the most densely populated of all India. That it was Southall that should prove such a magnet for Sikhs was a matter of chance, as I have mentioned already. A local manufacturing plant, specializing in motor accessories, was run by a managing director who had commanded a Sikh unit in the British Indian army. Now battling with a labour shortage, he resorted to active recruitment among his former servicemen's networks. There were further job opportunities in the surrounding food-processing plants of Middlesex and in the thousands of ancillary jobs growing up in nearby Heathrow Airport. The

migrants were by and large the sons of upwardly mobile farming families, and were sent out by them to spend a few years earning hard cash
for those back home to invest. Few, if any, thought of staying in Britain,
and the stories now told of groups of men each working two eight-hour
shifts in a row, and sharing the same bed in shifts as well, are wholly
credible. The priorities of these pioneers and 'new frontiersmen' (Aurora
1967) were still entirely directed at economic progress back home in the
Punjab, where the Green Revolution of the 1950s gathered momentum.
The region saw staggering advances in agricultural and infrastructural
development (Pettigrew 1975, 227). In such a climate of unprecedented
structural growth, regular remittances from Britain could yield enormous
benefits.

Quite apart from earning money to be invested by the family back
home, migrants were also useful to their home communities in that they
could officially sponsor other young men who wished to migrate under
an increasingly complicated British system of visas, permits, guarantees,
and certification. During these early years, the pioneers had little *community* life. Often living in all-male households, they were subject to open
hostility from neighbours, discrimination by foremen, and suspicion
from unionised fellow workers. What communal life there was between
the mid-1950s and mid-1960s revolved around some participation in the
culture of West London working men, be it at work or in a few 'mixed'
local pubs. Things were to change, however, as the second major phase
of Sikh migration gained pace. This was the movement of dependants
from the subcontinent, encouraged in part by the need to anticipate
British government plans to close the door to any further influx from
overseas. For Southall, this second influx, namely of overseas dependants, resulted in an unmistakable demographic shift.

Between the mid-1960s and the mid-1970s, the vast majority of
incoming Sikhs were the wives and children of the pioneers and of those
who had joined them in the process of chain migration. Within the space
of ten years, ever denser networks of kinship and friendship grew up in
a small local area. All-male households became a rarity, and family
households with complex local kinship networks the norm. The foundation of *community* organizations and networks, of gurdwaras and
women's prayer circles also resulted in a renewed stress on the Sikh religious heritage. This was all the more pronounced as there were now children to be brought up and enculturated, and often grandparents to watch
over the process. With the success of this second migratory movement,
the erstwhile Sikh pioneers had established themselves as the largest local

community of Commonwealth migrants. Their status as 'the majority *community*', however, was to be enhanced even further. Having been the first in the 1950s and become the largest in the 1960s, they also became the best resourced in the 1970s.

The third migration of Sikhs into Southall was on a far smaller scale numerically, but made up for this by its impact on the local economy. From the early 1970s, and especially after 1975, Southall attracted a steady influx of the East African Sikhs escaping from or expelled by policies of 'Africanization' in Kenya, Uganda, and Tanzania. These migrants, or rather expellees, from East Africa differed starkly from their fellow Sikhs already in town:

> Few of the generalizations which apply to South Asian migration and migrants apply to East African Asians ... Firstly, they are not primary migrants in that they have not moved directly from their ancestral homelands to Britain; secondly, they came from a different colonial structure from that which existed in India; and thirdly, they were refugees rather than voluntary migrants.
>
> *(Robinson 1986, 39)*

East African Asians shared a very different history and, by and large, superior economic resources. In East Africa, the British authorities had encouraged them to fill the skills shortages in the communications, commercial, and administrative sectors of the colonial economies. 'Before the Second World War', as Robinson excerpts the relevant statistics, 'Asians controlled over 90 per cent of the total trade in Uganda; in Tanganyika they were responsible for 80 per cent of the cotton trade, 50 per cent of imports, 60 per cent of exports and 80 per cent of transport services' (1986, 40). Through an emphasis on education and provision of their own schools, they had, 'by the early 1960s ... gained considerable access to both professions and civil service' (Robinson 1986, 40). They thus came to form a middle stratum between the British colonial rulers and settlers and the mass of Africans. Within a few years of their newly gained independence, however, the East African states had embarked on a policy of 'Africanization'. From 1967, the Kenyan government removed all non-citizens – and few Asians held Kenyan passports – from public employment, from employment in the transport system, and, by way of a new Trades Licensing Act, from the registers of entrepreneurs. Uganda followed suit. East African Asians had to think of their future security, material and even physical; many transferred their savings to Britain; and increasing numbers followed their savings to London, Birmingham, Leicester, and Coventry. In 1967, the number of Asians emigrating from Kenya doubled from 6,000 in the previous year to

12,000. A further 12,000 emigrated during the first two months of 1968 alone. From Uganda, some 4 per cent migrated to Britain during the 1960s; in 1972, when Idi Amin expelled all Asian non-nationals, the slow trickle turned into a forced mass exodus.

British authorities, worried about further concentrations of Asians, divided the country into green areas that, in their judgement could, and red ones that could not, 'absorb' further numbers. Southall, needless to say, was declared a red area; yet when the 1961 National Census had found a mere sixteen residents of East African birth, the 1981 Census counted 5,000, a number which excludes their children born after arrival.

The influx of East African Asians, especially those who were commercially experienced or skilled in crafts, transformed Southall's economy. The first local shop owned by a South Asian, and frequented then only by other South Asians, is said to have opened in 1954 in the very last house of a dead-end terrace facing the railway bridge. The same building now houses *Des Pardes* (*Home and Abroad*), the largest Punjabi-language newspaper in Britain; adjoining it is 'Sunrise Radio', the first Punjabi-language radio station in Britain and the first '*community* radio' to obtain a legal franchise. Next door, there is a bookmaker's office, then a night-club, then a restaurant, all in the hands of formerly East African Sikhs.

Other Sikh Southallians, not necessarily of East African origin, have come to prominence in the politics of the town. They shape the priorities and strategies of the Indian Workers' Association and co-shape those of the local Labour Party; they are highly visible on the Boards of Governors of the local comprehensive schools, and they serve on most other representative committees, be they concerned with local government or policing, trade unions or charitable organizations. This is, of course, as it should be. Yet their very interest in public affairs is seen, at times, as an imposition of sectional *community* interests, rather than a contribution of public-spirited service. In the atmosphere of *community* competition that I have outlined above in describing the political culture of the town, this can lead to misgivings, suspicion, and some apprehension.

The combined weight of numbers, and of economic and political potential, rendered the Sikh *community* the most powerful and influential factor in Southall's local affairs. Yet three things need to be borne in mind when saying this. Firstly and most generally, the description of the local Sikh *community* has followed the parameters of the dominant discourse. It has thus reflected the view of Sikhs as a unified group of 'them', despite the fact that this stylization is of relatively recent, and in part indeed colonial, provenance. That this dominant discourse cannot be taken at face value will become increasingly clear. Secondly, the Sikh *community* shows an internal cleavage between subcontinental and East African settlers that, in the course of time, has been accentuated, rather than bridged. Finally, the largest single category is always liable, of course, to inspire smaller ones to seek to ally themselves in response. The *community* most successful in counterbalancing Sikh influence in the politics of the town and the local economy is that of Hindu Southallians. In describing it briefly, I shall stick to the conventional 'ethnographic present' tense, since I cannot say how far the spectre of a 'Hindu fundamentalism' may have changed local perceptions between the end of my fieldwork and the time of publication. The perceptions I describe are those I found prevalent between 1986 and 1991.

On Hindus: *cultural* cachet

Just as Southallians often find it convenient to think of 'the' Sikhs as a unified *community* of *culture*, so they regard all local Hindus as members of an equally homogeneous and well-bounded group. Hinduism, in this dominant discourse, is associated with non-violence and religious toleration, and with the dignity of an ancient civilization. Such views are not surprising, of course, among Hindus; they are almost equally common, however, among white and Afro-Caribbean Southallians. Many of these also echo the claims that Hinduism gave rise to scientific achievements such as the invention of mathematics and the development of physics and astronomy, long before these advanced in the West.

The latter idea in particular will ring a bell with students of Hinduism: the claim to have invented science before its day formed part of Hindu thinkers' engagement with European ideas from the late nineteenth century on, and the fact that many Southallians, Hindu as well as Black and white, echo this idea must be contextualized within a consideration of the dominant discourse at large. I shall then, as before, turn to summarize the local history of migration and finally assess the *community*'s local position.

The very 'concept of Hinduism was established by outsiders', writes Burghart (1987, 226) who traces the term to the early nineteenth century, the 'sense of the term' to the mid-eighteenth. 'Implicit in these designations was the assumption that there was a religion ... which formed (or which at one time formed) a coherent system of beliefs and practices: Western scholars provided an intellectual space for [its] systematic description' (Burghart 1987, 226-7). This does not mean that Hinduism cannot or should not be described as 'a relatively coherent and distinctive religious system founded on common structures of relationships' (Fuller 1992, 10). But it is one thing to analyse 'the relative unity that exists despite the absence of an equivalent category' among Hindus of the past (Fuller 1992, 11); it is quite another to stylize Hindu beliefs into an '-ism' deemed to transcend all manner of regional, historical, and sociological cleavages. Yet it is precisely this latter, reificatory approach that has come to characterize the dominant discourse about, and sometimes among, Hindus in Britain. A good example of such essentialism is contained in a textbook used in some Southall schools:

The mass of religious achievement called Hinduism was not founded by any one teacher, like Jesus or Muhammad. Nor did it originate from any one book, such as the Bible or the Qur'an. Probably India has given birth to more great teachers and scriptures than any other country. But its teachers have lived in many ages, and the scriptures have taken greatly varying forms. Hinduism was not planned and built like a cathedral; rather is it a garden in which every kind of growth can flourish. The teachers have been gardeners, each turning over his own plot, planting this seed or that, crossing one result with another, and even welcoming shoots from intruders, in a ceaseless attempt to reproduce the root from which all fruits come.   (*Crompton 1971, 9*)

This view of Hinduism as a quintessentially tolerant, internally plural creed is shared by many non-Hindu Southallians, especially white and Black, and learnt by the youngest ones at school. It has become part of the dominant discourse. Yet this dominant discourse is concerned with ethnic minorities and ethnic groups, not with philosophies of all-encompassing truths. What it requires, thus, is ethnic closure, that is, a view of Hinduism as the religion of an ethnic group. The point has been made in the subtlest way by Burghart (1987) who enquired into the evidence for a specifically 'British Hinduism'. Starting from the observation that it was, in Britain, the laity rather than Brahmans or ascetics, that had taken on the role to represent what was Hindu, he found:

[M]any non-Hindus in Britain see Hinduism as the religion of an ethnic group. From the point of view of Hinduism's Brahman and ascetic spokesmen this is in certain respects inaccurate ... But the cultural awareness of Hindus has been sharpened in an alien cultural milieu, and they are ready to believe – as many non-Hindus do – that Hinduism is an ethnic religion ... Thus the redemptive Hinduism of Hindu religious traditions, with its ascetic spokesmen, sees itself as being neither ethnically Hindu nor British; and paradoxically it is a very British form of Hinduism, with its Hindu lay spokesmen, which claims with force to be ethnically Hindu.   (*Burghart 1987, 233–4*)

The dominant discourse about Hinduism in Britain can thus maintain two positions at once: on the one hand, Hinduism is seen as the cultural property of a purportedly ethnic group defined as 'the Hindus'; on the other hand, this 'ethnic' religion can assume the status of a meta-religion of such ancient sublimity that it can integrate what would otherwise contend or even conflict. In the specific circumstances of Southall, these considerations throw light on two mutually independent sets of observations: the remarkable absence of internal divisions within the Hindu *community* itself, and the cachet which the *culture* of the Hindu *community* enjoys in town.

The lack of internal divisions is remarkable in the light of Hindu Southallians' migratory history. The majority of Hindus in Southall are, like their Sikh neighbours, Punjabi by language and regional origin. There are, however, far greater numbers of urban Punjabis among them; and there are others who, although Punjabi by family history, have grown up in other cities of the Indian Union and may speak Hindi rather than Punjabi. The influx of East African Asians brought further Punjabi-speaking Hindus, as well as a sizeable proportion of Gujaratis who may also speak Hindi, but not Punjabi. Finally, the Sri Lankan civil war brought into Southall a growing number of Tamil refugees who, although distinct by their language and nationality, their calendar, and some of their religious festivals, join in worshipping in the Hindu mandirs.

There are two of these Hindu temples in Southall. The older one, founded and run by the Hindu Temple Trust, is located in Old Southall and dedicated to Shri Ram. The other, founded as the Vishwa Hindu Kendra in 1979 and dedicated to Vishnu, is located in New Southall. Both foundations can be traced to the same 'Hindu Cultural Society' which was formed in 1965, but in 1972 fissioned due to to personality clashes. Each group of trustees purchased vacant premises and turned them into a mandir. Yet no matter how many worshippers one asks, no difference can be established between these two temples. Although it is true that the management committee of one contains more East African Hindus than the other, numerous families attend them indiscriminately, and there is much cross-attendance whenever one of the two is visited by a *pandit* or *guru* from elsewhere in Britain or from India. That the two congregations have failed to differentiate into two sub-*communities* is remarkable. Sikh gurdwaras and Christian churches showed quite the opposite trend, as I shall show later on. There may well be supra-local reasons for this, such as the continuing importance of domestic worship.

Devotions in private may lessen the divisve impact of congregational forms, although these have certainly increased and diversified in recent years (Vertovec 1992). In addition, however, there may well be reasons that result from the local constellation in particular. The position of the Hindu *community* combines the weight of relative numbers with the weight of the dominant discourse.

By numbers, Hindu Southallians form but a minority: there are easily four times as many Sikhs in town as there are Hindus, and the Hindu *community* is no larger than the Muslim one. Yet the very threat of a Sikh hegemony is part and parcel of local Hindus' cachet. Hindu Southallians play an active part in the business life and the local politics of the town; yet even prominent businessmen, *community leaders* and local politicians are spared the, usually unproven, suspicions of rapaciousness, corruption, or dishonesty that circulate freely about some of their Sikh and white counterparts. Nor have I ever heard the Hindu *community* maligned with one of the scathing or dismissive commonplaces that Southallians may use in private conversations. Such commonplaces, for instance, as 'the Sikhs think they own this town', 'the Muslims don't mix', or 'the Caribbeans are rude', are not difficult to overhear. Yet there is no corresponding stereotype of the Hindu *community*, except perhaps that 'they keep to themselves', an observation that Southallians can apply to any and all *communities*. Even this is rare, however, and more than weighed up by the qualitative tone of the dominant discourse: the stylization of Hinduism into an 'ethnic' creed of tolerance and inclusiveness marks a stark contrast to the stereotypical view of Sikhism as 'a warrior religion'. Hindus thus appear as the 'natural' allies of anyone who fears 'Sikh' assertiveness and predominance.

The local cachet of Hindu *culture*, and of the local *community* that is taken to represent it, is thus a result both of the dominant discourse and of local relations. This combination appears in even starker outline when the position of Hindus is contrasted with that of 'the Muslims' in the town.

On Muslims: marginalized as a *community*

If Hindu Southallians can claim a remarkable cultural cachet among other Southallians, Muslims find themselves in a decidedly marginalized position. Their numbers approximate those of Hindu Southallians; yet very few Muslims indeed are visible in the public arena, and only three have gained even modest influence. To begin to account for this contrast, it may again be best to start with the dominant discourse itself. That

Muslims should form a cohesive community defined by a reified culture has for long been a commonplace in the Western search for an Other (Said 1978). One could say, in fact, that orientalism as directed at Muslims was the prototype of any dominant discourse which attempts to square putatively ethnic distinctions with stylizations of culture. Fox (1985) makes much the same point when he points to the 'organismic conception of culture' applied to Sikhs as a form of 'present-day orientalism' (1985: 211). Muslims are in some ways prevented by their own tenets of faith from countering such reifications. The doctrine of an *'umma*, a 'community' of all the faithful regardless of internal distinctions, forms part of 'the faith' (*ad-din*) itself. 'All Muslims', Halliday (1992) finds, 'do share certain tenets in common, and in this minimal sense there can be said to be a "Muslim community" in Britain. But, as with Christians, the unity ends there' (Halliday 1992, 137). None the less, Muslims face much greater discursive difficulties in negating or escaping the imposition of a reifying dominant discourse. It might be one thing for a Muslim to repudiate outsiders' views that all Muslims are the same; it is another to disown the doctrinal commitment to a unified *'umma* before fellow believers. The dominant discourse, which turns all Muslims into one community defined by its culture, is thus much harder to counter or relativize. Correspondingly, Muslim Southallians find themselves readily objectified as 'Muslims in Southall', with all the marginalizing effects that such thinking entails. These effects are exacerbated by a number of other factors, of which three seem to deserve particular stress. They concern, in turn, the recent history of the Indian subcontinent, the local history of migration, and the persistence of family links overseas.

On the subcontinent, tensions between Muslims on one hand, and Sikhs and Hindus on the other, have a long history. Most non-Muslim Southallians imagine the centuries of Muslim Moghul rule over Northern India as a time of oppression, and many Sikh and Hindu Punjabis blame 'the Muslims' for the Partition and war of 1947 and the horrific sufferings which these inflicted on all sides. After Partition, resentment against Muslims focused on the Muslim state of Pakistan, and while Pakistani citizens are far from the only nationality of Southall's Muslim *community*, they form its numerical majority and occupy most, though again not all, positions of internal influence. The resentment of Indian-born Sikhs and Hindus against Pakistanis is as intense in Southall as it is on the subcontinent. The Indo-Pakistani wars, the Indian-backed secession of Eastern Pakistan, the continuing territorial dispute over Kashmir, and various other political tensions have kept alive this heritage of distrust.

The mere fact of having Pakistani, Bangladeshi, or other countries' citizenships also has tangible organizational consequences in Southall's public sphere: Pakistani Southallians are only entitled to associate membership in the powerful Indian Workers' Association. Instead, local Muslims have set up their own separate *community* organizations and social or welfare associations, be they inclusively Muslim or specifically Pakistani or Bangladeshi.

A second reason for the marginalization of the Muslim *community* may be seen in its different migratory history. Contending with emigration policies very different from those of India, and often setting out from areas far poorer than the Indian Punjab, most Muslim Southallians arrived considerably later than their Sikh and Hindu neighbours. Many indeed arrived only after the post-war decade of labour shortage was over, and found it difficult to establish themselves as firmly as their neighbours had done. Even then, family reunions among Muslim Southallians tended to take far longer to complete. Often coupled with economic insecurity, but as often as a result of expectations 'back home', Pakistani Southallians are more likely than others to return to their families' homes for extended periods, sometimes interspersing a few years in Southall with as many spent on the subcontinent. The myth of return is far more widespread among them than it is among their neighbours, and extended visits to the subcontinent are also the result of distinctive cultural practices.

Among these, Ballard (1990, 219–49) has drawn attention to the funerary custom of interment in family burial grounds on the subcontinent, rather than cremation in Britain, and to different marriage patterns. While Sikhs and Hindus obey elaborate rules of 'clan' (*got*) exogamy, Muslim families continue to aspire to classificatory cousin marriages. The former produce fairly far-flung webs of kinship and affinity, while cousin marriage produces tightly knit families held together by multiple, and often overlapping, consanguinal and affinal bonds. A preference for cousin marriages necessitates lively contact with kin 'back home', and it helps define the highly cohesive, but strictly bounded familial networks which other Southallians sometimes interpret as a sign of Muslim 'clannishness'. 'The Muslims always stick together,' is a stereotype that I encountered time and again even among children and teenagers.

Such factors of history, migration, and custom would probably suffice to render the Muslim *community* the most marginalized of the three

South Asian *communities*; but distrust and resentments are fuelled further by the exposed position of Muslims in British society at large. Southallians, like other people in Britain, see television and newspaper reports on 'Muslim fundamentalists' who appear to 'stir up trouble' or 'make impossible demands'. During the few years of my fieldwork, Muslims certainly received a bad press: political news from Iran and Iraq, Libya and Egypt, Algeria and Afghanistan was mainly concerned with the 'threat' of radical Muslim leaders or fundamentalist Muslim agitators. Within Britain, the Rushdie Affair of 1989/90 seemed to pitch an entire community against the tenets of free speech and the rule of law. I shall return to this confrontation later. Even before it started, however, I noted in my fieldwork diary the British media's predilection for interviewing self-appointed '*community* leaders', whose 'radical' rhetoric was considered 'hot footage'. This lack of representative reporting may have contributed much to setting up Muslims as 'the bad *community*' for the late 1980s.

Even for those Southallians who can deal critically with media portrayals of Muslim 'radicalism', there remains a widespread weariness with what appear to be a plethora of impractical demands by Muslim campaigners. Examples can be seen most easily in demands aimed at schools, as in this case made by Wahhab (1989):

There are many changes to the educational process that Muslims would like to see undertaken. A model example that many Muslim campaigners follow is a paper produced by the South London Islamic Centre. Its demands include:

> withdrawal of Muslim pupils from religious education classes;
> prayer rooms to be provided in schools with substantial Muslim populations;
> Muslim children to be allowed to attend the Friday prayer at the nearest mosque;
> children to be allowed official holidays on the two main religious festivals;
> Halal provisions in school meals [...];
> segregated swimming and physical education lessons;
> music and dancing is judged unIslamic.   *(Wahhab 1989, 16)*

Southallians who encounter such demands very often fail to appreciate their plausibility for Muslim believers, and instead judge them to be exaggerated and immoderate forms of special pleading. It matters little, then, that most of these wishes are perfectly easy to accommodate, and have indeed been taken on board by Southall schools, as by many others in Britain and Europe. In phrases I often heard, such comprehensive schemata of requirements were taken as a refusal to 'fit in with the rest of society', and even an activism that 'gives Asians a bad name'. It is commonplace in such reactions to stress one's own *community*'s success in 'fitting in and making a contribution to society'. There are, of course, perfectly good reasons for these and other demands by Muslim campaigners, although to appreciate them requires a little more knowledge of the Muslim faith than most of their Southall neighbours have.

The tenets of Islam are by no means limited to the Five Pillars of religious observance. There is an extensive body of codified traditions of the Prophet's sayings, adjudications, and injunctions collectively named the *hadith* or 'tradition'. These customary injunctions, refined and specified over centuries of Islamic scholarship, and moreover highly varied across the Muslim world, are of a detail unparalleled among Sikhs, Hindus and Christians; their faithful application is difficult in any cultural environment that is not fully structured by the locally relevant Islamic norms, habits, and conventions.

Even if the devotional duties presented no practical problems in British workplaces and schools, the range and specificity of Muslim customary injunctions alone would suffice to necessitate active campaigning to make adherence possible at all. One need only think here of gender segregation and the protection of the honour of females, of dietary norms and laws, or of the problematic status of music and dance mentioned by Wahhab (1989). Most Muslims, in Southall as elsewhere, must thus hope for the success of campaigns which can sound immoderate and even 'fundamentalist' to their neighbours of other faiths.

Having lived among Muslims in the Sudan, I was impressed by the solidity of religious and customary observance among Muslim Southallians. Even among the young, alcohol and tobacco are widely shunned, Friday evening worship in the mosque is common, and observance of fasting during Ramadan is widespread and strict. I have seen children pleading with their parents to be allowed to join the physically demanding fast from which they are customarily exempt, and the survey data gathered among Muslim teenagers report a conformity to parental norms that is exceptional among their Sikh, Hindu, and Christian peers. Such conformity need not be construed, however, as religious fundamentalism. Anecdotally speaking, I have not once been challenged after joining numerous prayers in either mosque, although I was known not to be Muslim myself. Generally speaking, I have found very little evidence of any Islamic fundamentalism in Southall's Muslim *community*. Quite the contrary: Muslim Southallians tended to react with caution and even dismay whenever I asked them about their fellow religionists who burnt Rushdie's book in Bradford or their putative *community leaders* who assembled in the so-called Muslim Parliament. They were clearly aware that Southall was no place for Muslims to draw attention to themselves. Their marginal position among the town's *communities* made it seem inadvisable, and as one friend put it, it was 'best to keep quiet: live and let live'.

On Afro-Caribbeans: *community* across island *cultures*

While religious distinctions among South Asian Southallians are recognized as *community* cleavages, Christianity is not, in most contexts, validated as a *culture* capable of defining a *community*. Christian congregations include Afro-Caribbean, white, and indeed several hundred South Asian members, and these distinctions of 'colour' and 'race' are widely granted precedence when assigning them to one *community* or another.

Even among Christians, Afro-Caribbean Southallians are a small minority, counting some 3,000 according to the 1991 Census. Their numbers are so low because the migratory history of Afro-Caribbean Southallians differs from that of their South Asian neighbours in important ways. For one thing, it spanned little more than a decade, since the Commonwealth Immigration Act of 1962 severely restricted further labour migration, and Caribbeans tended not to send for their dependent relatives to the same extent as South Asians did. Further, while many Afro-Caribbeans arrived as early as the Sikh pioneers, they did not, by preference, settle in Southall. For the Sikh pioneers, it was privately owned factories that promised jobs in Southall; for many Afro-Caribbeans it was work for, and sometimes organized recruitment drives by, the National Health Service and London Transport that attracted them to the capital. Rather than gravitating to the suburbs, they settled in more central areas of West London, such as Paddington, Notting Hill, Ladbroke Grove and Shepherd's Bush from the mid-1950s. Some of these areas had been gradually vacated by a previous cohort of Irish and northern English migrants and provided inexpensive housing. As the market value of housing in these areas fell below the investment value of their desirable central location, and developers spearheaded the cyclical process of gentrification, Afro-Caribbean West Londoners underwent dispersal into the western suburbs from the 1960s onwards. One corridor led to the north-western suburbs of Harlesden and Willesden, the other along the Uxbridge Road, one of the capital's main westbound arteries. The housing estates along this road still shape the social geography of

West London's Afro-Caribbean *community*. Southall is located near its extreme western edge, and as a town without even an Underground station, it is thought far less desirable than, say, Shepherd's Bush, Acton, and Ealing, all of which were closer to central London. Many Afro-Caribbean Southallians can thus look back on residence in other, more metropolitan areas, and some retain close social links with friends and relations there.

That Afro-Caribbean Southallians should form, and be considered, one *community* is in itself remarkable. Most Caribbean islands had developed a heritage not of unity or even proximity, but of mutual estrangement and rivalry both as British Dominions and as independent states. The inhabitants of Jamaica, the largest of the British-dominated islands from which migrants arrived, dismissively spoke of people from 'the Smallies', such as Grenada, Dominica, Barbados, Trinidad, and St Kitts and often met reciprocal dislike. Among those from the smaller islands, in turn, mutual appreciation was rare. British authorities used island distinctions to facilitate the bureaucratic process of 'settling' these immigrants. Thus, Brixton in South London came to be an area in which some four out of five Afro-Caribbeans were of Jamaican birth; High Wycombe, a town some twenty miles west of Southall, was 'settled' almost exclusively with Vincentians; and the western parts of London were allocated to people from other 'Smallies'. Among Southall's Afro-Caribbean *community*, the largest regional contingents come from Grenada, Dominica, and Barbados.

The differences between islands were palpable and had been exacerbated by the communication structures characteristic of colonized peripheries: Hiro relates that it 'took ten weeks for a letter to travel directly from Jamaica to Trinidad, but only a month if routed via Britain' (Hiro 1971, 43). Further differentiation was established when each newly independent government proceeded to foster its own national culture, to 'write its own history and erect a pantheon of national heroes' (Hiro 1971, 105).

Yet this national differentiation of heritages came too late to influence most migrants. Their journey, again unlike that of most South Asians, was 'a journey to the mother country', as many migrants recall. 'The educational, religious and cultural centre of West Indian society lay not within itself, geographically or otherwise, but outside – in England. For the individual West Indian, coming to England was thus an inward movement, a journey into his cultural womb', comments Hiro (1971, 17). Yet the largely hostile reactions in the presumed mother country pushed into the background all inherited and constructed island differences. This decline of island boundaries was heralded by political activists who formed a 'West Indian Unity Association' as early as 1956 (Hiro 1971, 43), even before politicians in the Caribbean began to consider a Caribbean Federation for different reasons. The forging of cross-island links and the incipient fusion of a regional cultural heritage in the face of conflicts in Britain were accentuated politically by the first post-war 'race riots' that took place in 1958 in London's Notting Hill.

It is hard to say, and remains as hard in more recent years, how far this convergence upon a cross-island *community* was inspired by political activists, and how far by the day-by-day contacts across islands of origin. Perhaps the distinction is naive, for as a Southallian in his mid-twenties explained to Yabsley: 'The hate of injustice among West Indian people is common to all the islands. At the end of the day, it's a black man that's in trouble ... Island doesn't matter now. Most people have been born here. Blackness and being black means more. Islands have to unite. In England, through common experience and geography, people can unite' (Yabsley 1990, 96).

Birth in Britain or overseas apart, James phrases this coalescence most tangibly in pointing to the proximity forced upon different islanders by working in the same few service-intensive and low-paid public industries that had wooed them: 'Although island loyalties still remain, the people of the Caribbean have been brought together by London Transport, the National Health Service and, most of all, by the centripetal forces of British racism to recognize their common class position and common Caribbean identity' (James 1986, 264). But one should not overestimate the extent of this coalescence. James rightly equivocates on this 'common class position', and in Southall, too, one can observe processes of 'class differentiation and class formation taking place amongst people of their own colour and cultural background' (James 1986, 266).

Like class, so religious distinctions are easily overlooked, or at least hard to weigh. My own evidence differs from Yabsley's assessment that:

whilst there are differences between religions and faiths among African-Caribbeans, these did not constitute noticeable cleavages. People spoke of being Catholic, Church of England, methodist, baptist, or pentecostal within the Christian religion. Hiro (1971) describes some boundaries along these lines so perhaps in Southall – given the prevalence of other religions (rather than Christian denominations) such as Sikhism, Hinduism and Islam – Christianity transcends its internal denominations.   *(Yabsley 1990, 103)*

Yabsley may be right, especially when comparing these distinctions to the 'one religious boundary ... [that] was apparent, that between Rastafarian and non-Rastafarian' (1990, 103). Yet my own acquaintances among church-going Afro-Caribbeans, especially when they were of an evangelical faith, quite consistently delineated themselves from those of 'no faith', as well as from those professing a less evangelical Christianity.

Regardless of how far individuals may stress or discount these religious and denominational cleavages, they tend, organizationally, to have a centrifugal effect. While Sikhs, Hindus and Muslims can pursue *community* interests through temple and mosque congregations, Afro-Caribbean Southallians find themselves scattered over eight to ten congregations, most of which they share with white, and some South Asian, neighbours. It is important, therefore, briefly to describe the three most important non-religious associations that pursue Afro-Caribbean Southallians' *community* interests.

The oldest dates back to a West Indian Parents' Group founded in 1975 to campaign against the 'bussing' policies discussed above and against the misuse of the 'educationally subnormal' labelling applied to disproportionate numbers of Afro-Caribbean youth. By 1979, the group had widened its agenda to provide supplementary classes which continue to have two aims: on the one hand, they foster the creative development of youngsters through recitals of music and poetry, acting and some script writing; on the other, the content of many of these activities is designed to serve the transmission and deepening of the youths' cultural heritage. This heritage is by no means one of island cultures, nor indeed is it exclusively Afro-Caribbean in focus. Rather, it entails new elements which are orientated toward the African heritage that the 1970s liberationist movements validated behind the dispersal and oppression of all peoples of African descent. Thus, in 1982, the group performed a production about Marcus Garvey, the founder of the Back to Africa movement, entitled 'Africa: the Cradle of Civilization'. I shall discuss the pan-Africanist approach to Afro-Caribbean culture in the corresponding section of the next chapter.

Celebrations of Garvey's centennial year in 1987 were also held by the other two Afro-Caribbean *community* organizations, whence knowledge of this heritage had been disseminated from the 1970s. Both these associations go back, through personalities and values, to the group Peoples Unite which has been mentioned, in Chapter 3, in connection with the 'Southall riots' and the 'Stories of a Community Centre'. One is known as Unity of Afro-Caribbean People, the other began life as Caribbean

Focus and Beyond and is now called African-Caribbean Focus.

Unity of Afro-Caribbean People is, of course, an immediately plausible programmatic statement, given the island boundaries that Afro-Caribbeans in Britain had to overcome. There was more to its foundation, however, as an activist, now a Rastafarian and in his thirties, recalled to Yabsley:

> It was set up because there was a lot of money floating round the community, on behalf of the black community, but in the hands of the Asians who claimed to speak on behalf of the Caribbeans here as well. So a group was set up to cater for Caribbeans only. That's why we didn't use the word 'black' in the name, so that everyone would know who it was for.   *(Yabsley 1990, 111–12)*

Since then, Unity has become well-established and has been housed in offices in Southall's old Manor House, now in Borough ownership. Its full- and part-time workers organise activities for Afro-Caribbean youths which include supplementary summer schools and play-schemes, sports events, and occasional trips and outings to leisure and theme parks that include an 'African Village' located in Hertfordshire.

African-Caribbean Focus was founded in 1986, but again goes back, in personalities and values, to the Peoples Unite movement of the late 1970s. Some of the best-known members of Peoples Unite were the musicians of the Southall reggae group Misty in Roots which achieved international acclaim between the mid-1970s and mid-1980s. After the demolition of the Peoples Unite drop-in centre following the 'Southall riots' of 1979, the musicians and their manager formed a Peoples Unite Musicians Co-operative. This was an entrepreneurial as much as a *community* foundation, and it strove both to achieve professional success and security, and to campaign for better local provisions for musicians and Afro-Caribbean youth. The musicians and management of the Peoples Unite Musicians' Co-operative were invited, in 1986, to participate in events organized between the Commonwealth Institute and various Caribbean governments, in order to mark an official 'Caribbean Focus Year'. This collaboration, not always an easy one, gave rise to the foundation of the Southall-based Caribbean Focus 86 and Beyond, which, a year later, was renamed African-Caribbean Focus and, again, occupies premises in town owned by the borough.

Like Unity, it runs supplementary classes for youth and some evening classes; drawing on its musical connections, it organizes Reggae, Calypso, and Soca performances. Its political agenda inspired a large Marcus Garvey centennial celebration in 1987, and, two years later, a rally to commemorate Blair Peach, the demonstrator killed during the

'Southall riots' of 1979. Its political philosophy, inspired chiefly by Marcus Garvey, but also by personalities such as Maurice Bishop and Walter Rodney, will be examined in more detail in the corresponding section of the next chapter.

To conclude this introduction to the Afro-Caribbean *community*, it is useful to throw a last glance at its infrastructure. Unlike Sikhs and Hindus, but like Muslims, Afro-Caribbeans are not represented among the elected councillors and are few and far between in the other civic power structures. Unlike the Muslim *community*, however, there is no one place of worship around which *community* leadership, collective resources, and joint initiatives could crystallize. The settlement pattern in West London, spread widely and thus thinly, helps to render Southall marginal to many Afro-Caribbeans, and Afro-Caribbeans are often regarded as marginal to Southall. The peculiarities of West London's social map are mitigated only by communal associations, and by one other resource that figures prominently in many Afro-Caribbeans' heritage: regular musical venues, somewhat misleadingly called clubs or night clubs. These are of enormous importance for Afro-Caribbean Southallians because, to use Gilroy's words, 'they provide, among other things, important rituals which allow its affiliates to recognize each other and celebrate their coming together' (Gilroy 1987, 223).

'The biggest thing to happen for the black community in Southall recently', writes a youth worker in 1988, 'has been the opening of Tudor Rose nightclub, this has at least brought some of the focus back to Southall for night life' (Clayton 1988, 9). A year later, a further venue was opened nearby, and Afro-Caribbeans from across West London flocked to the regular Soul, Reggae, and Calypso nights. In Southall's dearth of night-time entertainment, these clubs stood out, and they assumed territorial significance, as Yabsley relates from an interview with a Jamaican youth worker:

He says that people are proud to have a nightclub in the middle of Southall, the Tudor Rose, and with enthusiasm: 'We are on the map, people identify Southall by the club.' I asked whether he felt it was strange for African-Caribbean people to come to Southall clubs, considering Southall's reputation as 'little India'. He pointed out that Southall night-life is different, the streets are so empty that outsiders do not know who lives in Southall. 'You don't see any Asians at eleven o'clock at night, [only] during the day people are flabbergasted.'

(Yabsley 1990, 79)

A far more competitive assessment, and a foreboding caution are sounded by one of the youth worker's colleagues who remembers:

There used to be three night clubs in Southall which black people from all over London came to. The Asians came and turned them into mosques and things. African-Caribbeans stopped coming to Southall from outside, and insiders went out of Southall for entertainment. Now with the 'Tudor Rose' and 'Mona Lisa' African-Caribbeans are coming back to Southall. It's been recreated. I don't know how long that will last for, before the Asians take them over, and they will: they've taken everything over in Southall.   *(Yabsley 1990, 86)*

Such sentiments are more often heard from Southall's white population, but then usually in the whispers of a private confidence that is aware of breaching the rules of pluralist co-existence.

On whites: Irish without *community*, English without *culture*?

To speak of a *white community* is commonplace among South Asian and Afro-Caribbean Southallians; yet it is rare among their white neighbours themselves. Their self-classification acknowledges only one internal distinction as clearly as this: that between Irish and English Southallians.

The 1991 Census counted some 2,000, or 3 per cent, of Southallians 'born in Ireland', a figure that excludes their offspring born in town. Teresa McGarry, whose fieldwork among them complemented mine, points to 'three distinct groupings of Irish people – an older network built up in the 1950s and 1960s [who are often] home owners; another stratum who arrived in the early 1980s ... [and are often] council tenants; and the newest arrivals who have appeared in the last two or three years [,are often not yet married and live as] council and private tenants' (McGarry 1990, 18). Irish Southallians are thus the only local category whose numbers continue to be replenished by younger compatriots; yet, like their Afro-Caribbean neighbours, they regard Southall as a periphery of their far denser settlements in inner West London.

The older cohort of Irish-born Southallians remember the 1950s and 1960s, when Irish dances, ceilidhs, and social functions were well attended in Southall; the 1960s and 1970s, when most white residents sold up their houses in Southall's three urban wards and moved to the surrounding suburbs; and the 1970s and 1980s, when the last public vestiges of an Irish presence were concentrated on some pubs and the Roman Catholic church. Perhaps half of Southall's pubs are run by Irish landlords or barstaff; they attract sizeable Irish clienteles and feature Irish songs on their jukeboxes and even Irish bands at live performances. Other Irish *cultural* events and activities are organized at the now multi-ethnic Roman Catholic Church. Yet while Irish *culture* is recognized as a heritage, an Irish local *community* can hardly be said to exist. Even the key organizer of Irish events admitted to McGarry:

Our social life here in Southall has gone dead, you see, because we haven't got – the community that's interested in the social life we do put on. – We put on dances, we've done everything we can, but it doesn't seem to take. – It's just you haven't got the community.   (*McGarry 1990, 28*)

Local people readily relate the absence of *community* to individuals competing instead of co-operating. Two women of the second cohort express this in stressing conventions of privacy and independence: 'The Irish keep to themselves' and 'The Irish don't like to help one another' (McGarry 1990, 83). A builder aged fifty-nine, one of the first cohort to arrive and in his 'very much a family man' himself, contrasts the economic individualism of Irish Southallians with the pooling system by which their South Asian neighbours have helped their kin to buy homes and shops:

the problem with the Irish is ... they are all for themselves, they won't spin nothing, but the Indian people stand together and if one buys a house, they all buy a house. If the Irish done that before my time ... [they] would have drummed this country no problem; but the Irish people were all for themselves when they came over first, which the Indians are different.   (*McGarry 1990, 77*)

Such individualism, as well as their small local numbers, seem to many Irish Southallians to seal the final demise of their former *community*. Yet to speak of a larger *white community* was as rare among McGarry's informants as among mine. Nor is this surprising, given the continued salience of the 'Irish/English' distinction throughout London, and local English Southallians, too, may spontaneously single out 'the Irish' as a category apart. Consider, for instance, these brief exchanges between a mother aged sixty and her daughter aged twenty-one, interviewed by Barbara Hawkes:

MOTHER: I know, up to a few years ago, there were no coloureds in the Working Men's Club in Southall. But I'm not sure about now. I'm going back five or six years.
DAUGHTER: They're mainly Irish, though. (Hawkes 1990 b, 41)
DAUGHTER: That's another thing which singles out people.
MOTHER: Religion?
DAUGHTER: Yeah, if it was just like everyone was the same colour, you'd still get prejudice. Against religion.
MOTHER: Like the Irish.   (*Hawkes 1990b, 44*)

Such a spontaneous singling out of 'the Irish' reflects their long history as a religious minority in Britain, and indeed as an ethnic minority before the term gained currency. Habituated as English people are to viewing Irish people as 'others', they, too, find a comprehensively *white commu-*

nity a far-fetched idea even in Southall. At the same time, to speak of an *English community* makes even less sense.

Before the word 'community' came to connote the idea of an ethnic minority, it was used as a matter of course to describe the character, perceived or merely normative, of long-standing local settlements with dense kinship bonds. As Young and Willmott (1957) put it so clearly in their classic study of East London communities:

> the interaction between length of residence and kinship is ... the crux of our interpretation. Neither is by itself a sufficient explanation ... Either length of residence or localized kinship does something to create a network of local attachment, but when they are combined, as they are in Bethnal Green, they constitute a much more powerful force than when one exists without the other.
>
> *(Young and Willmott 1957, 115–16)*

Although more recently settled than Bethnal Green, Southall streets likewise developed remarkably dense networks of kinship from the 1910s and 1920s onwards. Hawkes' (1990b) interlocutor Jill, born in 1929 as the third local generation of her family, remembers this as easily as her friend Rita, also born in Old Southall:

> Q.:   I was talking to Rita earlier, and she was saying that where they live, along that street, there used to be her Dad's brother and a couple of aunts, and a sister.
> A.:   Yes, that's right. In fact, most of *my* aunts and uncles used to live in Southall. But now they're either dead, or further out, or moved away. But when you come to think of it, you were more close-knit [then].   *(Hawkes 1990b, 17)*

Such close-knit community living was on the wane well before new Southallians arrived from overseas. Like Young and Willmott's (1957) East-enders, Southallians joined the post-war relocation schemes to ease overcrowded conditions, although some of them may well have felt what an East-ender described after his move to suburban Essex: 'We all come from the slums, ... but they don't mix ... You're English, but you feel like a foreigner here, I don't know why' (Young and Willmott 1957, 147). In Southall, of course, English residents did know why, and as the town attracted ever-growing numbers of overseas migrants, English Southallians moved out in large numbers. Those who remained usually blame those who left for the loss of *community* in the pre-war, pre-ethnic, sense. Thus, one of Hawkes' informants sometimes 'has a go' at old neighbours who have moved: 'If you and your friends had made an effort, and hadn't moved out so quick, you would still have your own community' (Hawkes 1990a, 60).

On closer inspection, though, there is more to English Southallians' reluctance to see themselves as forming a *community* than a mere loss of numbers. *Community* has become a word to describe ethnic populations, as opposed to 'English' ones, and culturally distinctive categories, rather than the perceived norm. This is made very clear in another exchange between the mother and daughter we have quoted already:

QUESTION: What do you think makes a community a community?
DAUGHTER: Community a community? It's people working together.
MOTHER: Living together,
DAUGHTER: Working together, as a – to make their lives better, having their lives moving together as one thing.
QUESTION: Which you see happening with the Indian people here?
BOTH: Hmm.
QUESTION: Do you see that with the West Indian, Caribbean people?
DAUGHTER: Yeah, they have got their own community. Though it's not as big as the Indian community ... Yeah, the Caribbeans do have a community. – Thinking about it now, what you were saying about the Catholics at St Anselm's, – they all go, Indians and English and – they're a community in themselves, and they mix quite freely, the Catholics. Their religion is so strong, they don't have to define against colour. They just treat each other through their religion. – I think if you were to say there was a mixed community in Southall, it would be the Catholics.
MOTHER: Yes, that's true.
DAUGHTER: That brings a lot of Irish into it as well.
MOTHER: Yes, that's true.
DAUGHTER: Yes, I know some Indian families who are Catholics; some English families are Catholic; some African Caribbeans are Catholics; and they all go to St Anselm's. It's all mixed. And they stick together as a group cos of their religion. Their religion holds them together.   *(Hawkes 1990b, 43)*

This exchange is remarkable in several ways. The two Englishwomen seem happy to grant the status of a *community* to a congregation that they know cuts across all other, that is, 'ethnic', *community* divides; they are happy to include in that religious *community* even those fellow-English who are Catholics. What appears to distinguish them is adherence to a 'religion' so 'strong' that adherents can 'treat each other through' it: a phrasing reminiscent of many anthropologists' understanding of culture. As a culture, Catholicism is thought so comprehensive that it crosses the distinctions of 'colour'. Whether these impressions gained from outside the congregation are shared by those within, is a question I shall discuss later, in the corresponding section of the next chapter. What matters here is the implicit doubt whether 'English', certainly not the name of a *community*, is the name even of a *culture*. To be 'English and C. of E.' appears almost as an existence in a cultural void. The daughter, now aged twenty-one, indeed recalls this sense of bewilderment when faced, at school, with the question: 'What are you?'

DAUGHTER: Thinking back to school, that's how everything was written, wasn't it. I can remember saying 'What are you?', and you wouldn't *think*: 'Oh I'm British, I'm Christian.'! If someone said 'what are you', then you'd hear them say 'oh, I'm a Sikh', 'I'm a Muslim' ...
QUESTION: And you would say?
DAUGHTER: [*laughs*] I was told to say by my Mum I'm C. of E. [*laughs*]
MOTHER: There's a history to that. It's only because you asked me, specifically on religion.
DAUGHTER: I remember coming here: 'I'm not Sikh, I'm – none of those, so what am I? [*laughs*] It's true, there's nothing left for people like me. Not that I don't believe in God or anything. It's just – I don't believe in religion. So I haven't got a label.   (*Hawkes 1990b, 44*)

English Southallians do not speak of an *English community* because the *cultures* that define *communities* are the distinctive possessions of others, not one's own. To be 'English and C. of E.' are not thought culturally distinctive attributes. Alternatively, one may point to the variety of conventions, life-styles and heritages in Britain that render the word 'English culture' an absurd simplification. An example is given by another of Hawkes' interlocutors, an Englishman in his late fifties who, on the one hand, is certain that all others are culturally different, yet, on the other hand, recognizes neither a British, nor even an English *culture*:

Any culture is different to us, doesn't matter what it is ... I mean, when you talk about cultures, it can apply to anywhere! Someone living in the South [compared] to the Midlands is different, or from the Midlands to Scotland is different, innit?
                    (*Hawkes 1990b, 3*)

Such refusals to recognize an English reified *culture* in the same way as one recognizes the reified *cultures* of ethnic minorities need not neces-sarily form part of a claim to superiority. Neither my fellow researchers nor I have found any English Southallians who credited their heritage with a supra-cultural neutrality towering over the contending diversity of the 'minority' *cultures* and *communities* surrounding them. Those who would claim superiority are likely to have long moved away, and would, in any case, not see the need to take recourse to such sophisticated ways of arguing their superiority. White English people tend to take it for granted that they form the native population or, in liberal parlance, the 'host society' that accommodates the *communities* of ethnic populations or immigrants. There may be more to the question, though, than this plausible difference in self-definition. Over the years of my fieldwork, I was repeatedly struck by established English ways of problem-solving and, as importantly, problem-evasion. I think of these as a pragmatist logic and a legal or legalistic formalism, respectively. For both of these, many English people claim the status of 'common sense', somewhat as if they entailed a supra-cultural validity. Two of my fellow fieldworkers remarked on compatible impressions of *English culture* being seen as something more than, and rather different from, an 'ethnic' *culture*:

They draw on two claims of universality as their cultural bedrock and out-of-group power: [the] Irish have [the] R.C. Church and a national heritage, [the] English have [their] G[reat] B[ritain] hegemony and TV, language, etc. which they think are 'universal'.   *(Hundleby, letter to the author, July 1992)*

Hazel Yabsley, like Hundleby an 'ethnically English' student opting for fieldwork among Afro-Caribbean Southallians, relates the point to ideas of nationhood:

Claiming an absence of community [as English Southallians do] is perhaps in itself a ... community process. Do they think they have nothing because they only feel the culture/community presence of others – they can't feel their own? ... Perhaps 'Whites' in Southall see themselves as National citizens in a town 'overrun' (from a probably racist perspective) by foreigners? ... If they look at themselves in comparison, they may see that they have pubs, churches, whites on TV, the spoken English language around them, but this is normal, this is everywhere in England. What whites in Southall feel more strongly could be notions of national citizenship, because they are surrounded by non-nationals?
           (Yabsley, letter to the author, 16 May 1992, 7)

This introduction of the *white community* started out with a seeming paradox: those outside it take it for granted, while its putative insiders deny it exists. To speak of a *white culture*, likewise, may make sense in an academic or, more likely, anti-racist discourse; yet it is exceedingly rare to hear a white Southallian use the term 'white' to designate a *culture*. Both observations beg serious questions of the dominant discourse, even when Southallians engage it themselves. Why should the idea that people fall into self-evident *communities* defined by a shared *culture* apply or even appeal to all Southallians when it does not apply or appeal to white ones, be they English or indeed Irish? Further, does it really apply to Afro-Caribbean Southallians who have forged one *community* out of a dozen contending island *cultures*? The dominant discourse equates *culture* with *community* and indeed ethnic identity. At its most subtle, it stretches to treat religious distinctions as if they were

ethnic ones, as is the case among South Asian Southallians. The dominant discourse is engaged, of course, by Southallians, too, at least when
they talk about their town in summary ways. But how useful is it in
observing, let alone understanding, the subtleties of Southallians' lives?
There is something deeply problematic, or superficially simplistic, about
the equation between 'ethnic' *cultures* and self-evident *communities* upon
which this dominant discourse is based. I shall argue in the next chapter
that this is true for all Southallians. When Southallians engage in the
discourse I have called demotic, as opposed to dominant, they effectively
disengage the equation of ethnos with *culture*, and of *culture* with
community. I shall argue that this is true for Sikhs, Hindus, Muslims,
Afro-Caribbeans, and whites in different ways; but that it is true for all
of them. Before I present the data to sustain this argument, I should,
however, point to some of the qualitative effects that this equation exerts
upon the thinking of very young Southallians.

On youth: culture consciousness among children

The previous sections have introduced each of the five *communities* that
the greatest number of Southallians identify as *cultures* in their normative speech. This delineation of five cultural groups reflects the reified
view of *culture* as an 'ethnic' heritage familiar from the dominant
discourse. It feeds, and is fed by, media, politicians, and many, though
not all, *community leaders*, and is reflected in many community studies.
At first sight, this understanding of *culture* may appear close to what
ethnologists once termed 'heritage'. Yet even in their appreciation of
culture as heritage, Southallians often appear remarkably neglectful of
the processual nature of keeping a cultural heritage alive. Even a purely
material heritage, after all, needs to be reinvested in order to be
preserved. Yet strikingly static conceptions of *culture* as heritage appear
not only among the oldest, but just as clearly among the youngest of
Southallians.

This is remarkable for two reasons. Firstly, it suggests that the adult
equation of five *cultures* with five *communities* is taken for granted and
already consciously expressed by children. Furthermore, it points to a
conscience collective among young Southallians that I have termed
'culture consciousness'. By this term, which I use to translate the German
Kulturbewusstsein, I mean a heightened awareness that one's own life, as
well as the lives of all others, are decisively shaped by *culture* as a reified
heritage.

The evidence for this contention will highlight three aspects of young

Table 5. *Criteria used to distinguish* cultures *by 312 Southall youth*

Criteria %	Used by: % of respondents
Religion (e.g. Sikh, Hindu, Christian)	75
Nationality (e.g. Indian, English, Jamaican)	31
Region or language (e.g. Punjabi, Gujarati)	11
A named ('sub'-)culture (e.g. Rasta)	9
A religious festival (e.g. Diwali, Christmas)	8

Southallians' thinking: their unusual fluency in the use of *culture* as a term of reification; an ability to recognize *culture* in one's own and others' lives; and a patterning of conceptions of one's 'own *culture*' that, before adolescence at least, equates each *culture* with 'its' *community*. In order to explore this culture consciousness among Southall youth, it is useful to start with some quantitative data gathered among youths at large, before then focusing on a case-study among the youngest cohort. Our survey among some 350 young Southallians aged twelve to eighteen contained a fair number of questions that were phrased according to youngsters' own usages as observed during fieldwork. One of these echoed a statement which I had heard innumerable times: 'Southall has many cultures.' I added the instruction: 'Please write down some cultures that you know are around.' The open phrasing was intended to allow for the widest possible variety of criteria that youngsters might choose to define what they themselves saw as *cultures*. Their lists would probably contain a plethora of polythetic classifications. Yet the results showed a remarkable uniformity. Table 5 shows the criteria that were used once or more by each of the 312 young Southallians.

Two things are remarkable about this result. Three-quarters of all respondents used religion to define at least one of the '*cultures* that are around'. The figure is increased even further by those young Southallians, probably the younger ones among the sample, who named a religious festival or ritual as the marker of *culture* or were unaware that 'Rasta' designates a religion no less than a life-style. The distinction between *cultures* on the basis of religion seems thus fundamental to growing up in Southall, and Larson (1989) has confirmed this impression in her qualitative research among Southall children from Muslim homes. The quantitative data are the more convincing since the sample, taken from all over the town, reflects the religious composition found at the largest of Southall's three secondary schools, and it is unlikely to hide

Table 6. *Religious composition of survey respondents and of pupils at a local secondary school*

Religion	Survey respondents (N = 355) %	School roll (N = 771) %
Sikh	51	56
Hindu	16	20
Muslim	15	14
Christian	8	10
Other	5	0
Parents of two religions	5	N/A
	100	100

Table 7. *Tripartite terms used to delineate* cultures *by 311 Southall youth*

Term %	Used by: % of respondents
'Caribbean'	15
'Black'	7
'Asian'	14
'Indian'	12
'British'	6
'White'	5

any distorting imbalance between young Southallians of different faiths. The figures are given in table 6. Southall youths thus focus on religion as the marker of *culture* to an extraordinary extent. Yet the table has also shown an awareness of other criteria that include the cleavages of nationality, region or language. It is instructive, therefore, briefly to examine their use of terms which relate to the purportedly racial division into three *communities*, familiar from much public discourse in Britain. Strikingly, none of the current terms is used by more than 15 per cent of the young Southallians, as table 7 shows.

In passing, one may note the marked preference for 'Caribbean' over 'Black', a pattern not reflected in the equivalent choices between 'Asian' and 'Indian' and between 'British' and 'white'. Young Southallians' delineations of *cultures* are thus overwhelmingly based on religious distinctions. This focus on religion is probably even stronger among the youngest cohort questioned, those aged twelve to fourteen. It is to some of these that I should now like to turn, in order to explore the culture consciousness among Southall children. The data were gathered among a small group of second-year High School students, all aged thirteen, whom I asked to write a mini-essay of three answers to three questions: 'What is Culture? What is tradition? What is my culture?' Pupils wrote their answers spontaneously and without consulting each other. They knew that their essays would not be marked, but were merely to help my research and our next classroom project. They were anonymous, although I later matched handwritings with names in order to analyse the patterns emerging.

Among thirteen-year-olds from Sikh and Hindu homes, the replies to the first question, 'What is Culture?', again show an astonishingly consistent focus on religion; in the few cases where this is lacking, it later appears in reply to the particular respondent's 'own' culture.

Culture mean in what type of world you live in your religion.

My culture is religion.

Way you live in the world. and religion.

Culture – the SURROUNDINGS the world you live in. + religion.

My culture is religion. follow the rules.

Culture = This means religion or some sort of [*deleted:* being. thing] club, cast, different from another. A [*deleted:* sort cast.]

My culture is true hinduism.

1. Culture. I think it is the way people live in their society, and also to do with their religion.

3. My culture is my religion. I go to the temples and pray to gods that we worship. I celebrate festivals in my religion, and I respect my religion.

Colour of skin may be added into this equation; but it does not figure prominently:

Culture: religious habits, colour of skin, religious celebration.

I think my culture is based upon the Hindu Gods. For instants culture can be a religious celebration.

Culture – religious habits, environment, religious celebrations, colour. [my culture:] Hindu Gods.

While the term *culture* is thus used with effortless fluency and consistency by all but one of these thirteen-year-old children of Sikh and Hindu families, their definitions of *tradition* present greater variability. Some simply equate *tradition* with *culture* and *religion*, as in these mini-essays:

> Culture   – Habbits
>
> T.[raditional] Culture – Religes Habbits.
>
> Tradition – celebrations, religious habbits.
>
> 2. Traditional Culture. I think it is something people do according to their religion like celebrate certain festivals in their religion.
>
> Traditional: celebration, religious habits, past time celebration

Yet others take account of the existence of cultural boundaries in explaining *tradition*:

> Traditional culture. a thing that happens often and is liked or disliked by other people.
>
> traditional culture – things that you do – different things – continues things that have been happen throughout the years
>
> Traditional = This means a thing that happens often, and is liked or disliked by people. Like Christan.

Among the replies from thirteen-year-olds of Sikh and Hindu families, only one appears to deviate from the shared norm in a significant way: it intimates a recognition that *culture* is not a possession acquired by birth, but entails individual choices of conformity:

> Culture = to do with religion, surroundings, to go along with something.

Most striking in this boy's continued mini-essay is the use of an active infinitive to describe his 'own culture' as a process:

> Traditional = normal things that you do, every day life. Your traditional custom.
> My culture is to follow my religion.

In summary, the young Sikh and Hindu Southallians saw *culture* as defined by religion, with sometimes a hint of 'colour' or 'custom' thrown in; *my culture* equals religion or religious ritual; and *tradition*, a less familiar concept, is construed as the same, or as that part of one's heritage that others might 'like or dislike'.

Granted the widespread identification of *culture* with religion, this last-mentioned point is worth pursuing. It is in relation to *tradition* only that the 'like or dislike' of other people is mentioned at all and, one might interpret, recognized as legitimate. To like or dislike another religion as such, makes no sense among the small peer group, and makes little sense to any South Asian Southallian of that age whom I know. That it does not, is connected with the attitude and value called *respect* which is so crucial that it deserves some brief explanation here.

The word *respect* is young Southallians' translation of the Punjabi, Hindi, and Urdu word *izzat*, which other ethnographies, certainly among adults, translate as 'honour', the opposite of 'shame' (*laj*). It has become a commonplace in the ethnography of South Asians that *izzat*, especially in the meaning of family honour, is an abiding social norm and personal motivation, and the Southall data do not contradict the widespread findings. Individuals will go to extreme lengths to safeguard and serve the *izzat* of their family, which can be tainted summarily by a single member incurring dishonour and thus shaming the entire family. Yet having done fieldwork among young Southallians as much as among adult ones, honour (*izzat*) appears less as the absence of shame than as the fruit of *respect* (*izzat*). To explore the *izzat* notion of respect, it is necessary to dispense with the implication of negative reciprocity that the English term evokes. Only then is it possible to appreciate that the *respect* that spells 'honour' is both the respect one pays and the respect one graciously receives. It represents not the opposite of self-respect, but its fulfilment.

In its simplest and most childlike meaning, *izzat* is the recognition of a subordinate position considered natural. Thus Sarbjit Lal, a fifteen-year-old Hindu girl participating in one of my Creative Writing classes, made this quite clear at the start of her essay, written spontaneously and without any instructions but the title:

'ON RESPECT'

There are jobs where you *give* respect: some jobs consist in giving respect, like the

POLICE: they must show respect to the society to set a good example.

WORKERS: These people show respect to show that they are capable of co-operating in their work.

BUTLERS: Butlers use both respect and loyalty to show other people that his master is superior.

WAITERS: Waiters have to show respect to customers in restaurants by seating them, to take orders and to bring meals to satisfy them.

Jobs where you *receive* respect: some jobs consist of receiving respect, like

MANAGERS: They receive respect by their workers in the fear of losing their jobs ...

What is it that this things does for us?
It makes givers and receivers of respect honour each other,
and have trust,
and both feel protected by respect.
There is no job where you receive respect without giving respect

At first sight, the essay seems to divide the world into two classes or even castes: the givers and the receivers of respect. Yet even within this hierarchical order, the police are seen as servants of the public, and the gentleman as dependent upon his butler's respect to convince others of his superiority. Even acknowledging the 'fear' that may motivate *respect*, the conclusion elegantly squares the circle between hierarchy and reciprocity, in that the giving and receiving of respect establish a relationship of mutual honour. This philosophy of *izzat* entails notions of hierarchy; yet its very conception of hierarchy appears to differ starkly from English-language notions of respect such as the denial of one's own honour or even self-respect. It is a matter of honour (*izzat*) to yield the appropriate respect (*izzat*), just as one's own honour (*izzat*) relies upon the appropriate reception of respect (*izzat*). To show and to expect *respect* is a value obvious to, and taken for granted by, probably all young South Asian Southallians, and it is intimately tied up not only with social rules, but also with their understanding of *culture* and religion.

The predication of *culture* on religion is also documented in Larson's work among Muslim children in Southall (Larson 1989) which includes a cohort much younger than the pupils quoted here. It is probably not limited to South Asians or, for that matter, to Sikhs, Muslims, and Hindus. Although detailed data are lacking, it seems highly probable that children of any strongly held Christian tradition equate their own *culture* with their parents' distinctive religious adherence to being Catholic, Baptist, Methodist, Pentecostal, or Spiritualist; though probably not often Church of England. I would further expect, again in the absence of sufficient data to show or disprove it, that this equation between *culture* and religion is made the more decisively the more the particular Church tradition relies on a further marker of distinctiveness, such as Irish Catholicism, Black Pentecostalism, or South Asian Christianity. Children of South Asian backgrounds are thus probably not alone in equating their *culture* with their religion; yet they appear to choose this equation more commonly than two other definitions of *culture* espoused by their peers.

Children who find themselves members of religious congregations that span the other important cultural divide, that of 'race', may well prefer to use either a political-sociological, or else an individualist, discourse to define their own *culture*. These two further idioms of culture consciousness among children appear to be used the more commonly the less their religion is associated with another useful, traditionally validated, or putatively ethnic cultural marker.

Examples of the political-sociological conception of *culture* abound among children of Afro-Caribbean backgrounds, although they did not form part of the present small sample. Their commonest descriptions of their own *culture* in the large-scale youth survey were: 'Afro-Caribbean culture' and 'Black culture'. Their marginal position, both in the British public culture dominated by whites, and the Southall local culture dominated by South Asians, makes this understandable enough. It also tallies well with the further observation, already alluded to, that many adult Afro-Caribbeans conceive of *culture* as a creative, dynamic, and aspirational process, rather than an inherited possession. I call this conception 'political-sociological' because it takes its cues not from 'colour' or region as such, but from an interpretation of 'black' as a marker of *culture* rather than skin colour. Yabsley (1990) clarifies the difference most concisely in two instances. In one context, she quotes a Rastafarian feminist speaking of 'not just black our colour, but our links with Africa'; in another context, and speaking of Afro-Caribbean Southallians who are not pan-Africanists, Yabsley takes up Taylor's term 'colour consciousness' which was originally coined to help understand South Asians. Among Afro-Caribbeans in Southall, she finds that 'there is an element of "consciousness"; this is not necessarily colour-based, it is more often political consciousness which has some grounding in colour' (Yabsley 1990, 83).

Examples of an individualist conception of *culture* are provided by two thirteen-year-old white English girls. Their replies to the same three questions, 'What is culture? What is tradition? What is my culture?' differ starkly from those of their peers:

> [Culture:] 1. I think it means the way you live.
> [Tradition:] 2. I think it means the way you do thinks.
> [My culture:] 3. Yes I have got a culture for playing games.

The plausibility, to an anthropologist, of the girl's first two definitions, enhanced by the paradoxically insightful spelling error, contrasts with her third statement. Yet it is in perfect keeping with her own definitions; and it seems to show 'my culture' not as membership in a pre-defined 'group' but as a markedly individual achievement. The other white English girl expresses the difference even more explicitly:

> Culture – means the background of people different colour from different countries – different religion – the way of life they live.
> Tradition – what they look like, where they come from [*deleted*: all that is with culture.]

> [My culture:] is means past time, new things, and job. New things made that
> there haven't been made.

Her initial sentences appear to imply that *culture*, and perhaps *tradition*
too, are the possessions of other people: those of different colours,
nationalities, and religions. Her description of her own culture replicates
her friend's individualist slant: it reads almost like a description of
gaining adulthood, and brings to *culture* a strong flavour of novelty,
development, and processual dynamic unparalleled in any other of the
mini-essays collected.

But individualist conceptions of *culture* are certainly not the sole
preserve of white youth, just as none of the three conceptions of *culture*
should be stereotypically associated with children of South Asian, Afro-
Caribbean, or white backgrounds. Nothing more should be read into
these small-scale qualitative data than two indications: firstly, almost all
these Southall children know, by the age of thirteen, how to use the word
culture; one could almost say that *having a culture* has become second
'nature' to them. To put it somewhat pointedly, pre-adolescent
Southallians are as used to *having a culture* as North Americans are to
being hyphenated, that is, ethno-culturally subdivided, Americans. I
suspect that in Britain this is still quite rare. Secondly, there are at least
three discourses of *culture* that can be distinguished, namely, the religious, the political-sociological, and the individualist.

That this culture consciousness should be predicated on a religious,
political-social, or pointedly individualist conception of *culture* makes
good sense not only ethnographically, but also theoretically. Each of the
three conceptions invokes an ultimate principle of classification that
promises quasi-objective certainties and values that are endorsed *a priori*.
The appeal to religion literally invokes the ultimate authority that stands
for what is right and just. The political and sociological point of reference, likewise, is widely thought to provide ultimate, objective truths, the
'undeniable facts of Social Science', however elusive. The individualist
approach, finally, is axiomatic to any young person who envisages social
life as the outcome of individuals striving for autonomy. All three
conceptions can rely on the semblance of self-evidence, and all three
value *culture* by reference to seemingly unassailable religious, political, or
individualist guiding lights or truths.

The detailed data I have discussed fit well with some general impressions gained over the five years of fieldwork. Regardless of *community*,
Southall children were used and ever-ready to explain, defend, or justify
what they had said or done with phrases such as: 'You see, in my culture,

we don't' and 'You know, in our culture, we always ...'. The legitimation
of one's behaviour by one's *culture* occurred with striking regularity: it
was rare only among white children who more often chose the phrasing:
'In England, we don't' or 'Here, we always ...'. These ready usages of
culture as an explanation for individual choices intimate a veritable
conscience collective shared among Southall children: an awareness that
whatever one, or anyone, does and thinks is intrinsically and distinctively
culture-bound, and defined both in relation to one's *own culture* and the
cultures of others.

This heightened consciousness of *culture* should be seen as an adap-
tive, rational, purposeful response. Despite its great reliance on reifications, it helps very young Southallians to assess and take into account
the multifarious distinctions among their peers, visible in parents'
language and places of worship, phenotypes and insignia, family conventions, parental expectations, and a host of other potentially confusing
differences. Their heightened awareness of *culture* allows children to
move with purpose and consciousness in their shared social world, and
culture consciousness provides a common *conscience collective* among the
young cohorts. It is not, in case this needs to be stressed, a situation of
some children belonging to ethnic minorities and developing such a
consciousness. Rather, it is a matter of all children growing up in a town
of palpable cultural diversity which is, at the same time, subject to the
reifications of the dominant discourse.

These reifications cannot be written off as irrelevant or even false: they
form part of Southallians' culture and need to be recognized as such. Yet
their descriptions throughout this chapter have placed a number of ques-
tion-marks over the adequacy of the dominant discourse on an analytical plane. In the case of the Sikh *community*, it shows traces of the
colonial construction of a homogenizing 'Singh' identity, in the case of
Hindus it relies on stylizations of Hinduism into a meta-religion of tolerance and non-violence. In the local arena, these reifications contribute to
a stereotypical view of Sikhs as a potentially threatening hegemonic force
and of Hindus as their counterweight. In the case of the Muslims, the
dominant discourse and its stress upon 'Muslim militancy' and 'fundamentalism' contributed to their marginalization as the purportedly
dangerous *community*. The supposedly self-evident *community* of Afro-
Caribbeans could be seen as a conscious and in part deliberate creation
which was to neutralize the distinctive and sometimes contending island
cultures. A local *white community* of *culture*, finally, was recognized by
outsiders far more often than by its putative insiders: the relationship

between *community* and *culture* was thought problematic by both Irish and English Southallians, for different reasons. All these qualifications have arisen from the description of each local *community* as the dominant discourse would have it: a self-evident grouping held together by a unified *culture*. To pursue these qualifications, the analysis must thus move beyond the dominant discourse.

5

The dominant discourse denied: *community* as creation, culture as process

> Sikhs and the creation of caste *communities*
> Hindus and the culture of encompassment
> Muslims and the multi-cultural *community* of Islam
> Afro-Caribbeans and four approaches to 'finding' *culture*
> Whites and three strategies in the absence of *community*

The dominant equation of each *community* with a reified *culture* forms part of all Southallians' discourse. Yet it cannot be taken at face value, and more importantly, it cannot guide either Southallians or their observers to an adequate understanding of local dynamics. If the dominant discourse were the only one that Southallians use, their social lives would be circumscribed by stereotypes, reifications, and insurmountable *culture* and *community* boundaries. In trying to understand how Southallians produce culture as a process of meaning-making, rather than 'have' *culture* as an ethnic heirloom, the dominant discourse needs now to be questioned. This chapter will review each *community* anew, and in doing so it will question the dominant discourse on its own premises. It will assume the saliency of the boundaries that the dominant discourse constructs for local *communities*, but will pursue a more questioning line of enquiry inside each of them. Its argument, in brief, is that the dominant equation between *culture* and *community* is thrown into doubt and disengaged within the confines of each *community*.

Sikhs and the creation of caste *communities*
To go beyond the *community* discourse and appreciate the complexities lived by Sikh Southallians, one may, surprisingly perhaps, go back as far as the origins of Sikhism itself. These harbour two general ambiguities that can also be recognized in the particular setting of Southall: the

importance or otherwise of caste; and the openness or closure of the boundary which determines who is a Sikh.

The founder of the Sikh faith, Guru Nanak (1469–1539), is widely believed to have advocated the overcoming of all caste boundaries and indeed to have attempted to bridge the enmity between Hindus and Muslims which at that time divided the Punjab. Preaching the Oneness of all divinities and the unity of humankind, his hymns comprise Hindu and Muslim texts as well as his own creations. Even today, all Sikh temples continue to follow the precept of the Third Guru, Amar Das (1479–1574), and offer meals every day to all comers regardless of caste and even religion. Around 1600, the Fifth Guru, Arjun Dev Ji (1563–1606) founded an exclusively Sikh place of pilgrimage, the Golden Temple (*Harmandir Sahib*) at Amritsar, and there began to compile the Sikhs' own Holy Scripture, the later *Guru Granth Sahib*. When the Fifth Guru was martyred in 1606, his successor, Sri Guru Har Gobind Ji (1595–1644), was the first to mobilize military might to defend the originally pacific movement. A century later, in 1699, the Tenth Guru, Gobind Singh (1666–1708) initiated the first Sikhs into the ranks of the *Khalsa*, literally 'The Pure', sworn to defend the integrity of the now autonomous Faith with the sword. This turn from pacifism to self-defence, however, also reaffirmed the original indifference of Sikh teachings to distinctions of caste. *Khalsa* initiates continued, like most other Sikhs, to adopt the caste-neutral names Singh ('Lion') and Kaur ('Princess'). Yet the integrity and completeness of Sikhism as an exclusive religion was sealed when the Tenth Guru ceded his authority (*Guru-Gaddi*) to the now completed Holy Book, rather than to a further dynastic follower.

Given the economic circumstances of the Punjab at the time, Sikh practice was largely shaped by the caste of land-owning 'tillers' (*Jat*); and it was to this caste, too, that the vast majority of Southall's Sikh pioneers belonged. The local Sikh *community* remained predominantly Jat until the arrival of the East African refugees. Since then, however, caste has returned to Southall Sikh *culture*.

'Caste doesn't matter in Sikhism – so long are you're a Jat', a friend once explained with a wry smile. He was of East African background and, like some 90 per cent of East African Sikhs (MacLeod 1974, 87), belonged to one of the Ramgarhia castes, in the main the Tharkan or carpenters, Lohar or blacksmiths, and Raj or bricklayers. In the Punjab, these castes had not normally owned land, and the colonial literature indeed describes them as 'village serfs' (Rose 1911–19). Needless to say, most Jat Sikh Southallians tended to regard them as inferior in the terms of caste. Nor did they look kindly upon the rapid economic progress and the superior aspirations shown by those whom they considered inferior by caste. They were, after all, the latest arrivals to Southall; had not shared the trials of the early years; were permitted to arrive in whole families at once; were saved bureaucratic humiliation by immigration officials querying marriages and, worse, the legitimacy of children; and often arrived with capital in a British bank, rather than the relentless pressure of sending off remittances. Moreover, some Jat Sikhs regarded them as impure, observing that a number of them followed precepts associated with Hinduism and indeed frequented Hindu, in addition to Sikh, temples in town.

Many Sikhs of the crafts castes, on the other hand, regard Jat farmers as little more than landless labourers, uneducated, crude, and rude, as well as unsuccessful in the British economy. The antagonism was palpable in many walks of life, but this is not the reason it is mentioned here. Rather, I draw attention to it because the caste antagonisms played out and, in the proper sense of the word, cultivated among Sikh Southallians have much to teach us about the *community* paradigm. There is no doubting that Southall's 'Sikh *community*' can act as one when it is expedient. Yet the local majority readily fissions according to the segmentary principle, and the history of Sikh *community* building has, since the 1970s, entailed several processes of differentiation by caste. One of these concerns the Ramgarhia Sikhs and articulates the ambiguity of caste with the distinctions of class; the other concerns low-caste followers of a further Guru, Ravidas, whom most Sikhs do not recognize as fellow Sikhs, and it articulates both the salience of caste and the ambiguity of who is, and who is not, regarded as a Sikh.

From the mid-1970s, East African or Ramgarhia Southallians were the first *community* to differentiate themselves from the Jat Sikh majority. The resulting distinctions have been described in detail by Bhachu (1985) who reflects her informants' sense of a distinct East African or Ramgarhia *culture* and even 'society' (Bhachu 1985, 56). Bhachu's data, collected within her own *community*, are of immediate empirical relevance to this book; even more, they are of theoretical interest since our two approaches to the same data differ in their analytic intent. Since Bhachu, understandably, wishes to counteract sociological generalizations about South Asian settlers in Britain, she documents their diversity through a portrayal of East African or Ramgarhia Southallians as a *community*. Since the analytic purpose here, however, is to question the community discourse itself, one needs to examine how informants construct *communities* in the first place.

In beginning to explore the creation of *communities* with reified *cultures*, it is useful to seek clarity about the boundaries of the community Bhachu describes. It comprises, most generally speaking, 'Twice Migrants', that is, South Asians who, having migrated from India to East Africa, had descendants who migrated from East Africa to Britain. It is clear that the Twice Migrants included Gujaratis as well as Punjabis; Muslims and Hindus as well as Sikhs; Sikhs of other castes than Ramgarhia; and, to labour the point, not only educated or professional people. The Twice Migrant or East African community thus comprises several cross-cutting cleavages of regional, religious, caste, and class categories. Even the smallest sub-set, Southall's 'Ramgarhia community', on the other hand, comprises Ramgarhia families who came directly from India. The bounding criteria 'East African' or 'Twice Migrant', 'Sikh', 'Ramgarhia', and 'middle-class' are thus mutually independent variables.

Bhachu knows this well and, despite seeming to translate her informants' *community* discourse into the dominant discourse of 'cultural communities', she gives just the sort of data that illuminate the process of forming *communities* out of cross-cutting cleavages. Here, a Ramgarhia Sikh directly from India constructs an astonishing contrast between Ramgarhia pioneers assimilating to Jat customs in the early days, and finding his way from the pub to the temple upon the arrival of his East African fellow-Ramgarhia:

When I first came to this country, there weren't any Ramgarhia families around. We used to live like the Jats because they were the only Sikhs we knew. We used to work with them, we went to the pubs with them, we drank heavily, we started to talk like they did, and we cut off our hair because they had done so. Also, because it was difficult for turbaned men to get jobs. Since the East Africans have arrived, we have associated with them and have started going to the temple.

(Bhachu 1985, 50)

The foundation of a Ramgarhia Sikh temple was indeed a milestone in Sikh Southallians' internal differentiation by caste and the establishment of a 'Ramgarhia *community*'. The East African Ramgarhia were especially well equipped for this by their dealings, over several generations, with the community discourse in its colonial form that Morris (1968) has analysed so well and to which chapter 2 has already drawn attention. Bhachu offers further trenchant detail on the process by which Ramgarhia Sikhs constructed a 'caste identity' in East Africa. To use 'Ramgarhia' as the name of a caste is a recent phenomenon, and even in

Southall, most Ramgarhia Sikhs I asked were able to specify which caste of Ramgarhia they belonged to, be it Tharkan, Lohar, Raj, Dhiman, or five or six others. The coalescence of these crafts into a Ramgarhia 'super-caste' identity appears to have been an East African development, as Bhachu explains: 'Caste categories grew large in Africa because members of one sub-caste, which in rural districts in India would never have associated with one another, since they often belonged to different regions, were [now] brought together' (Bhachu 1985, 26). Yet one should not reduce Ramgarhia *community* building to a mere continuation of colonial routines. Bhachu rightly emphasizes the point:

It is clear that ... *Indian* Ramgarhias were far more aware of their caste position in the U.K., especially in relation to the caste system in India, because they have actually lived there. For that reason, they are more conscious that their caste status is inferior to that of the Jats. *East Africans* [of Sikh faith and Ramgarhia denomination], on the other hand, are extremely aware of their 'East Africanness' but were not so aware of the traditional position of Ramgarhias in a caste hierarchy because they have been away from India for a long time.

(Bhachu 1985, 51, my italics)

The colonial amalgamation into a unified 'Ramgarhia caste' thus took on an entirely new significance in the changed surroundings of Southall. In the East African context, it had spelled the most comprehensive path of unification for most Sikhs; in the Southall context, it spelled a differentiation from the local majority and clearly negotiated not only caste status, but class aspirations, too.

Social and *community* differentiation along lines of caste is, of course, not limited to Southallian Sikhs alone. The most solid empirical study, rooted in a general discussion of caste boundaries among Sikhs, is Khalsi's (1992) ethnography based in Leeds and Bradford. In Southall, this differentiation has continued with the building of a new gurdwara to serve the Ravidasi *community*, whose patron, Guru Ravidas, is not one of the Ten Gurus recognized by orthodox Sikhs.

The building of this temple, which began during my fieldwork, was a challenge from the lowest echelons of the Sikh caste hierarchy. It began when Southallians of the Chuhra and Chamar castes collected money to build their own gurdwara. While they call themselves Sikh, they are denied recognition as such by many Sikh Southallians of other castes. During the 1980s, when the Ravidasi religious *community* built its new representative temple, families of these two castes began to gravitate toward Ravidasi worship, even when previously they had attended other congregations in which Guru Ravidas held no place of veneration. Some made their way from Sikh gurdwaras, some from Hindu mandirs, and some had mainly worshipped at home. By the end of my fieldwork, most South Asian Southallians tended toward the new consensus that there now was a 'Ravidasi *community*' that could be distinguished from, or perhaps within, the 'Sikh *community*'. The difference was ambiguous. There were Ravidasi Southallians who, despite attending the new Ravidasi temple, still considered themselves 'Hindu'. Their position was understandable despite the seeming contradiction between temple atten-dance and religious allegiance. Arguments about who is a Sikh and who is not carry much weight among South Asian Southallians. They are also reflected among a smaller heterodox congregation known as *Nam Dhari*; while these recognize the ten Gurus and the *Guru Granth Sahib*, they believe that the Sikh Scripture has been followed by further living Gurus. Many Sikh Southallians, again, are hesitant to recognize them as fellow Sikhs. Such arguments about exclusion or inclusion may appear to be doctrinal at first sight, yet they are by no means reducible to, let alone caused by, so abstract an interest.

Doctrinally speaking, all who recognize the *Sri Guru Granth Sahib* of Sikhism are also enjoined to endorse the ideal of a Sikh *panth*. The meaning of this ideal, postulated by Sri Guru Nanak himself, is, however, hard to interpret. Some Sikh friends translated it as a 'Commonwealth' which embraces all Sikhs and enjoins them to strive for the common good not only by religious commitment, but also by co-operating in economic, business, and political matters. Other Sikh Southallians, however, translate *panth* as meaning 'nation' and specifi-cally relate this ideal to aspirations for the Punjab to secede from India as an independent *Khalistan* or 'Land of the Pure'. The definition of the *panth* has been problematic throughout Sikh history, and McLeod (1989) has documented in dispassionate detail the contentions about exclusive *Khalsa* leadership that characterize successive temple reforms and the Sikh political party Akali Dal on the subcontinent. Khilnani (1990) rightly points out that the Punjab conflict is not 'a re-enactment of atavistic religious passions. It is a battle between competing descriptions of the Sikh community ... [in which] the moral and political stakes are high: to define, with authority, the identity of a community is to claim the right to represent and act for it, and to require of its members not just allegiance but obligations' (1990, 68).

Doctrinal differences thus reflect and serve social and political inter-ests rather than any disembodied orthodoxy. To clarify this does not mean levelling a charge of duplicity or cynicism at one party or another.

Deliberate lies and distortions assuredly happen; but even if everybody were always subjectively honest in their interpretation of doctrine, doctrinal argument would still, by necessity, rely on a process that squares *culture* understood as heritage with culture observed as a process that entails re-evaluation and rethinking. Much as intelligence has been defined as the ability to think anew in each new situation, culture here appears as the shared ability to reinterpret heritage in the light of changing circumstances and goals. Sikh Southallians have reinterpreted their heritages as circumstances demanded or allowed for. They have, in the process, created *communities* distinguished on lines of caste that artic- ulate with those of class and regional networks.

Yet this process is not one of simple segmentary fission, of a 'majority *community*' falling apart. Rather, it increases the institutional repertoire while leaving intact the multiplicity of cross-cutting cleavages. One may picture, for instance, an East African Punjabi Sikh of the Tharkan caste. He or she can speak to certain Muslim and Hindu Southallians as a fellow East African; they may do likewise with former East Africans who are Gujarati, rather than Punjabi; they may similarly speak to fellow Sikhs of the Raj or Lohar caste as fellow Ramgarhia, whether they hail from the subcontinent or from East Africa. Which of these mutually independent identifications they draw upon or stress will depend on the perceived context, the strategies of everyday life, and the classificatory choices deemed appropriate between the various parties. In saying this, I am indebted to the work of Wallman who was the first to go beyond the genre of community studies that merely adumbrate the reifications of the dominant discourse. In analysing 'ethnic origin' as part of a 'total system of resources necessary to the management of livelihood', she raised the question of 'how or when [people's] non-local identities become locally significant' (1982, 4). The plurality of identities that allows for strategic contextual choices is itself such an interactive resource.

The subsequent sections of this chapter follow the same analytical intent as has been anticipated here. They attempt to show how Southallians of all *communities* go well beyond the terms of the dominant discourse which sees ethnic minorities as communities defined by a reified culture. Competent though they are in invoking the dominant discourse, this second, demotic discourse disengages the equation between *culture* and *community* that the dominant one assumes *a priori*. The character- istic mechanisms to effect this creative disengagement can differ remark- ably between one *community* and another. In the case of Sikh

Southallians, new temple congregations such as the Ravidasis', or caste, or what has emerged in the new context as such, are articulated with factors of migratory history, class aspirations, and previous regional networks in order to establish new *communities*. The case among Hindu Southallians tends in the opposite direction. It shows a culture of encompassment that includes non-Hindu *communities* into the mould of Hindu *culture*. The distinction between *culture* and *community* is predicated on different premises and strategies, but it is negotiated just as visibly, pluralistically, and creatively.

Hindus and the culture of encompassment
There are several ways in which one may account for the remarkable cohesion of Southall's Hindu *community*. Local Hindus themselves often echo the idea of Hinduism as a tradition that values pluralism and toleration. In the dominant discourse about Hindus in Britain, this is certainly a well-established claim, and it found ready endorsement in Southall, and not only among Hindus. Up to the end of my fieldwork in 1990, most white as well as black Southallians continued to see the conflicts in the Punjab, and even the incipient rise of Hindu nationalism in India, as a case of 'the Hindus defending their [legitimate] interests'.

The *cultural* cachet that Hindus could command among many non-Hindu Southallians may have as much to do with their *community*'s structural placing. Under the guise of confidence, many Southallians readily echoed misgivings about 'the Sikhs running the place like they own it'. With both the Muslim and the Afro-Caribbean *communities* largely marginalized, Hindus and their essentialized tradition of tolerance could appear as a counterweight to Sikh hegemony.

The two explanations fit together well, since they combine to show the dominant discourse effective at two mutually reinforcing levels. The first recognizes its efficacy in essentializing an intrinsically tolerant Hindu '-ism', the second complements it with local considerations of a more or less widely desired balance of power between *communities*, the latter themselves a creation, in part, of the dominant discourse. Perhaps this is all there is to the question of Hindu Southallians' *cultural* cachet.

Yet the dominant discourse about an intrinsically Hindu tolerance must be credible to Hindu Southallians themselves if they are to fulfil the role assigned to them by outsiders. There may thus be good reason to give more specificity to this largely positional and relational explanation. Neat though it may appear, it reads like a rather mechanistic social physics, albeit in a relationistically up-dated form.

In Southall, the level at which one might seek this missing link of internal dynamics is most probably connected to the regional specificity of Hindu traditions. The largest single complement of Hindu Southallians are Punjabi by region and language, and according to Vertovec (1992), 'it has been especially in the Punjab that a rather broad (albeit Vaishnavite), less caste divisive, simple and easily adaptable set of Hindu beliefs and practices came into being' (Vertovec 1992, 259–60). Vertovec traces this development to the co-existence of the reformist Arya Samaj and the anti-reformist Sanatan Dharma, and Southall followers of the Arya Samaj on occasion credit their own movement in particular with the pluralist approach of Punjabi Hindus to religious diversity. They sometimes describe the movement as 'ecumenical', and stress that in some of its ritual practices it dispenses with the images of Gods that, given the diversity of Hindu beliefs, might hinder unified worship. They replace them, on occasion, with the symbolism of the sacred fire (*havan*) that may stand for cremation as well as for rebirth, for the cycle of beginnings and ends, and for the sameness of creation and destruction that all Hindus, regardless of their cultic orientations, strive to embrace. Followers of the Arya Samaj in Southall include not only subcontinental Punjabis, but also a large number of the East African-born Hindus.

The Arya Samaj in India undoubtedly contains elements of Hindu exclusivism (Fuller 1992, 60, 100); yet the integrative aspect stressed by some of my informants may help one to understand the internal dynamics of Southall's Hindu *community*. While among Sikhs, I have remarked on a pronounced process of internal differentiation, the dynamics of *community* building among Hindu Southallians might be said to correspond to the logic of encompassment. The term has been theorized in Dumont's (1980) influential account of the caste system and, in particular, in his design of a general theory of hierarchy appended to later editions. Hierarchy is, in Dumont's theory, 'a relation that can succinctly be called "the encompassing of the contrary"' (1980: 239), and encompassment is a holistic, yet intrinsically value-laden, operation which relates two contraries to one another. At a lower level of analysis, they are recognized as opposites, yet at a higher level, one of them is considered the whole which, as such, encompasses its opposite as now merely a part. The principle of encompassment of one opposite by another 'necessarily hierarchizes them with respect to one another' (Dumont 1980, 240–1). This logic of encompassment certainly makes sense in considering the ways in which Hindu Southallians redefine and expand the boundary of their *community*. The clearest example, the encompassment of 'low-caste Sikhs', has been mentioned already. A noticeable number of Sikh Southallians of the lower castes attend Hindu mandirs as well as Sikh gurdwaras. They are often not recognized as Sikh by other Sikhs, and mandir worship must in turn, of course, weaken their claim to be 'pure' Sikhs. Hindu Southallians, on the other hand, often like to adduce such cross-*community* attendance as evidence that Sikhs indeed 'are Hindus'.

'Sikhs are Hindus' is a phrase I have heard time and again from Hindu Southallians. On one occasion when I doubted the statement, a Hindu friend remonstrated quite angrily: 'Hindus back home used to bring up their youngest sons as Sikhs! Don't you know that? How can Sikhs not be Hindus?' This particular tradition is somewhat apocryphal, and while several scholars of Hinduism confirm that they have heard it, no one can remember where. In any case, the selection of a youngest son seems rather unpredictable. Yet an ethos of encompassment is certainly recognizable in this claim. How this ethos may work on a more observable scale can be illustrated by a short anecdote.

One day, I was visited by a Sikh friend who was traumatized by a suspicion of black magic (*jaddu duna*). He suspected his mother of pitching what he called 'witchcraft' against his intended marriage to a girl from a highly respected Hindu family. In a state of acute anxiety, he asked me to advise. Since I suspected him of feeling guilty toward his family about lapsing in his religious observance, I suggested he read the Sikh morning prayer *Sukhmani* every day. Baffled by a 'social scientist' making such an 'unscientific' proposal, he sought advice from a *pandit* often available in one of the town's Hindu temples. Seeing the turbaned supplicant, the *pandit* wisely reciprocated the crossing of an ambiguous boundary by recommending that he devote himself to daily recitation of the *Sukhmani*. This prayer forms part of the Sikh Scripture (*Sri Guru Granth Sahib*) and is credited to the Tenth Guru, ironically the leader who sealed the one-sided emancipation of Sikhism from the Hindu tradition. To the Hindu *pandit*, however, whom I would credit with a lesser dose of cultural relativism than a fieldworking anthropologist, it seemed an appropriate choice. The *Sukhmani*, he reassured my friend, was a Hindu prayer as much as a Sikh one.

Hindus can find further confirmation of their claim to encompassment in the fact that a number of lower-caste Sikh families perform the family rituals so fundamental to Hindu life. Thus, Sikhs who have accepted the cutting of hair sometimes perform the ritual *Mundan* to mark their sons' first haircut. In Southall, this happens only rarely, however. The most widely celebrated among the annual Hindu family rituals is the festival of *Rakhi* (lit. 'Protection') or *Raksha Bandhan*, which celebrates the reciprocal bond between sisters and brothers. Sisters tie a bracelet of interwoven threads, the protective *rakhi* or *rakhri*, on their brothers' right wrists and in return receive a small gift. Many Sikhs, not only of the lower castes, celebrate this ceremony at home, and there are even some cases of adolescent best friends sealing their platonic bond in this way. Such metaphoric extension occurs not only between Hindus, but between unrelated Sikhs, too. In the course of my fieldwork, I reliably heard of at least three such ceremonies performed between Hindu girls and Sikh boys. Gillespie (oral communication, August 1989) witnessed one between a Hindu girl and her Muslim best friend, performed in the presence of the entire family and alongside that between brothers and sisters. It may seem ironic that on this particular occasion the Muslim boy was not thought entirely acceptable to the Hindu host family; yet the claim to Hindu encompassment, and either personal indulgence or the obligation that the claim demanded, proved stronger than contingent social resentment.

Such practices of encompassment are used to support further claims, sometimes even seemingly self-contradictory ones. A father of two sons explained to me that he had allowed both his wife's brothers to 'marry into Sikh families'. This is an unusual way of expressing a marital alliance, for in normal usage it is wives or daughters who are said to 'marry into' the groom's family; nor of course was this double union one that needed his personal blessing or consent. The ensuing claim, however, was clear:

All Sikhs are Hindus.   A long time ago, when someone was wearing a turban, he was called a Sikh; that was all. Only later, some Sikhs said they were no longer Hindu – the way these things always happen. But of course they are Hindus. Guru Nanak wanted to protect Hindus from the Muslims that pressed them.

G.B.:   But the Tenth Guru, Gobinder Singh ...

[*interrupts*]:   The same purpose. The same thing. They are the same, and they are very close. Only these Khalistan people deny this. They are like the IRA. They say they're not Hindus. But no matter what they say. Whether they admit it or not: they are Hindus. It's in your blood!

It is worth noting how the idiom changes here from an encompassment predicated on religious ideas to one invoking the bonds of blood. Parry reports the same use of a quasi-genetic idiom in his informants' explanations of caste (Parry 1979, 85–7), and it provides the metaphoric key, in a sense, to his argument that the hierarchies inherent in caste, in agnation, and in marriage alliance are thought homologous by his informants. Yet encompassment, as the example of the *pandit* advising my Sikh friend has already shown, does not need to stake open claims of hierarchical superiority. Another example may be quoted from a Hindu friend, a former teenage migrant now aged thirty, who maintained:

Our religion always needs another one to make it full, to make it complete. Like Christianity or Buddhism or – the Jews' religion or, well, about half a dozen others. You see, if you tell me you worship that tree, or you worship that bottle there, I must respect it. Because it is your god.

The difference that the speaker implies between non-Hindus 'worshipping' and Hindus 'respecting' may, or may not, point to encompassment as a relationship that implicates hierarchy. Another passage from the same interview incorporates the myth of Adam and Eve into a Hindu's view of reincarnation:

But of course everything you do in this life that is wrong, you suffer for after your death. You get another life, for instance as an animal. – Or even as a tree, or even a rock. Yes, then you get kicked around, literally, you get kicked around for thousands of years. – Christians don't believe, of course, that animals have a soul. But Hindus, well, in our religion we do. It's all life.

Q.: What can an animal form have done that in a later life it takes a human form?

In the end, we're all children of Adam and Eve; I mean, that's the only human beings there was in the beginning.

Q.: But is that in your religion? Isn't that just the Bible?

Well, it's a mythology. They were the only humans, and well – they did wrong, didn't they? That's why you have to redeem yourself, and your soul goes back into a new life. Always into the life that will show you what you have most done wrong. Like if I treated you badly, I would probably come back into a life where I suffer from what I did most wrong to you.

The reference to Adam and Eve, and its defence as one 'mythology' among others, all equally true for a Hindu, represents an encompassment so embracing, of course, that believers speaking in the name of recognized doctrine could not possibly endorse it:

We get new bodies according to our previous actions. If I have committed a sin with my eyes, I may be born blind in the next life – and so on. But this process has many aspects, which would need to be explained in detail ... Every human being can fall or rise, but the sin of one person (Adam, for example) cannot have any effect on the whole race. Of course, the Hindu theory of creation is entirely different from the Semitic one held by Muslims, Christians, and Jews.

(Usharbudh and Crompton 1982, 4)

Yet no matter what is said by guardians of orthodoxy, Hindu believers such as the one quoted above seem almost intuitively to encompass what they understand of other religions. Where doctrinal spokesmen may guard and defend *culture* as a possession, the many anonymous believers perform their culture through acts of *bricolage* as much as through reproduction.

In this process, Hindu Southallians keep developing and validating new arguments that sustain the logic of encompassment, as well as professing an internal unity within the elusive boundaries of their *community*. Three factors are important in this continuing process of encompassment that Hindu Southallians pursue in the face of their local minority position, and possibly in response to it. The first is the prevalence of family worship; the second, the existence of cults that, in Southall at least, cut across the cleavages within the Hindu *community*; the third, what the guardians of orthodoxy, be they informed by Hindu Sanscritic or Western Orientalist approaches, would probably term 'ignorance'. One example of each may suffice.

Domestic worship is not, among most Hindus, considered inferior to worship in the temple, which even the most devoted believer is not obliged to attend regularly. Virtually all Hindu homes have a small shrine, called *mandir* like the temple, which may be a shelf or mantelpiece with a statue, postcard, or poster of a god and perhaps some flowers and incense. Here, the householder or family members perform daily acts of *puja*, worship involving an offering, or *arti*, worship involving the circling of a light. Some devotees hardly ever attend the temple, as a family following Sathya Sai Baba explained:

We pray in front of Sai Baba's picture every morning, and before lunch; and in the evenings we meditate here. The last time we went to the *Mandir*, oh, that's last year, or the year before even. We just pray to Sai Baba here.

Sathya Sai Baba, sometimes kown as 'the Guru that Gives Eyes', is a living saint whom his followers worship as an incarnation of Shiva-Shakti, as well as of his deceased predecessor Saint Shirdi Sai Baba. He is famed for having restored the sight of thousands of devotees in his *Ashram* in India and in the numerous 'eye camps' he and his devotees have set up. Among other cults in Southall, one might mention a Shree Prajapati Mandal with its own small premises, as well as the devotees of

Pujya Swamiji Krishnand Saraswati who has visited Southall on two occasions. These particular chosen devotions tend to cut across all sociological cleavages within the Hindu *community*, and they interlink believers who otherwise might have been divided by their caste or regional networks, their migratory history or class position.

A final contributory reason for the continued culture of encompassment is the widespread vagueness among the young about tenets of Hinduism of which an example was given above. The caste system in particular, such a distinguishing feature among Sikhs, is barely understood and is known only in fragments by many Hindu believers. Asked what caste (*jati*) they are, many claim to be of the Brahmin estate (*varna*), but need to consult with older relatives to specify their caste. An even more confused version is this one, given to me by a man in his thirties:

At the top, there are the Hindus. That's what our family are. Then there are the Brahmins, and then the Patels. The Patels are accountants. Then there are many, many others, I don't know them well. And then, below them, there are the Khans, and then the other Muslims.

Patel is a common surname in the *Patidar* caste of landowners-turned-traders in the Gujarat, and has become a byword for 'Indian businessman' in London (Tambs-Lyche 1980); Khan, similarly, is a family name associated with Muslims of various land-owning castes in the Western Punjab and has become a byword for 'Pakistani Muslim' among Londoners. With its unsystematic hierarchy from Hindus to Muslims, the above quotation may furnish an apt example of the third contributory reason to favour a culture of encompassment: a limited knowledge of doctrine.

Regarded as a *community*, Southall's Hindus stand out by their lack of internal divisions, remarkable in the face of such heterogeneity by region and language, caste and class, cultic adherence and devotional practice. Yet by their very readiness toward encompassing others and by their universalist claims, they have removed themselves all the further from boundedness as a *community* in the image of the dominant discourse. Where the Sikh *community* divides into caste-articulated congregational *communities*, the multi-caste Hindu *community* shades into an encompassing set of practices which defies hermetic *community* boundaries.

Muslims and the multi-cultural *community* of Islam

Among Muslim Southallians, the disengagement of the equation between *culture* and *community* proceeds in two ways. One of these results from the vast cultural variety within this local *community*, the other from the global spread of the multicultural *community* or *'umma* of Muslim believers.

To appreciate the cultural heterogeneity of the local Muslim *community*, it is again useful to take note of contending claims of membership. In Southall, there are a few dozen families professing Shi'ite, rather than Sunni Islam, and while outsiders may think of them as members of the local Muslim *community*, they do not attend either of the two local mosques. There are a further three dozen or so families that are members of the Ahmadiyya movement. Named after its late nineteenth-century founder, Ghulam Mirza Ahmad of the Indian city of Qadian, the Ahmadiyya began as a charismatic movement during British colonial rule. Its founder denied the legitimacy of a Holy War (*jihad*) against the colonial power, and the movement long retained a political stand of co-operation with the ruling authorities. Most Muslims do not regard followers of the Ahmadiyya as Muslims, and its Southall adherents maintain their own place of worship and instruction.

Internal cultural variety would be tangible, however, even if the Muslim *community* were defined as entailing only the Sunni majority. Its cultural heterogeneity is extraordinary on both linguistic criteria and those of national loyalties. The majority of Muslim Southallians originate from the Pakistani part of the Punjab, and thus speak Punjabi and write it in Urdu script. Other Pakistani Muslims, though, hail from provinces where Urdu, rather than Punjabi, is the common language. In the Pakistani part of Kashmir, migration has been intense, especially from the district of Mirpur, and these Southallians speak Mirpuri, rather than Punjabi or Urdu. Smaller numbers of Muslim families hail from Pakistan's northwest, and speak Pashto. While most of these share a common national loyalty to the state of Pakistan, the cultural differences between the regions are palpable, and there are sometimes bitter mutual rivalries and regional resentments.

Other Muslim Southallians have migrated from Bangladesh and thus speak and write Bengali. Their national loyalties are to their own homeland which seceded from Pakistan after decades of discontent and the Indian-backed war of independence in 1971. Yet other Muslim Southallians have migrated from India, especially from Gujarat, and their languages are Gujarati and, among the educated, Hindi. They are joined in the mosque by Muslim families who originate from various cities of India and who, at the time of my fieldwork at least, shared in the Indian national loyalties of their fellow countrymen across all religious divides.

In the mid-1970s, Southall's Muslim *community*, hitherto mainly of rural backgrounds, was joined by a number of often successful business and crafts families from East Africa. Dispersed among this proliferation of South Asian backgrounds, Southall's Muslim *community* counts a few families from Mauritius and the Seychelles, from Fiji and Trinidad, Indonesia, Malaysia, West Africa, and Somalia. It stands to reason that their shared adherence to Islam can hardly ever suffice to overcome their great cultural differences. 'Of course I go to the mosque, and I think I'm a good Muslim as things go', a friend once remarked on our way back from Friday prayers, 'but there's a lot of people there I've got nothing in common with. I mean, Islam is *all* cultures, innit, just like *your* church where they've got all sorts.'

Such perceived ethnic differences aside, there are also cross-cutting distinctions by religious practices and conceptions. Some of these are associated with the existence of two local mosques. Southall's central mosque is located in Old Southall and its affairs are run primarily by believers from the Pakistani Punjab. It follows a strict interpretation of Muslim doctrine which leads it, for instance, to desist from celebrating the Prophet's Birthday, lest believers might be confused into worshipping Muhammad, rather than the One God. The smaller second mosque, located in New Southall, does observe this Day, and some of its members suspect that 'the people in the main mosque don't respect the Prophet'. Regular worshippers at the smaller mosque sometimes say that their own congregation 'is for all kinds', associating the main mosque with an exclusive claim to orthodoxy, and its management committee with a political endorsement of 'traditionalist' Pakistani leaders.

These differences should not be overestimated, and are in no way comparable to the distinctions between Sikh temples, for instance. Yet Muslim Southallians are aware, of course, of the disjunctions that characterize even the interpretation of Islamic observance, custom, and Law. This awareness was tangible during the months of the Rushdie Affair when the British media reverberated with endorsements by radical Muslims of the, notably Shi'ite rather than Sunni, Ayatollah Khomeini's death verdict for the author of *The Satanic Verses*. Public disquiet over the radical Muslim position was such that far more students and friends asked me about Muslim Southallians' reactions than ever asked me about any other local matter in five years of fieldwork.

Most Muslim Southallians were, in fact, extremely reluctant to discuss the dilemma, let alone to join public demonstrations. The prevailing attitude seemed to be one of lying low till the storm might pass, rather than exposing an already marginalized *community* even further. In Ignatieff's (1992) words, quoted earlier, 'at the height of the affair, Muslims in Britain could be forgiven for wishing no one had ever thought them a community at all'. When a Muslim friend of mine endorsed the death threat to Rushdie in a conversation with a Muslim neighbour, the neighbour took a spontaneously philosophical attitude. Showing his right hand, he explained: 'Look, Islam is the hand, and every finger is a part of that hand. But every finger is different. It wouldn't be a hand if it didn't have five fingers, all different.' Such resignation in the face of contending judgements within or about the Muslim *community* shows how used many Muslims are to both internal dissent and the reified stylizations that the dominant discourse imposes upon their culture or cultures.

Locally even more important are the obvious cultural differences between the varied Muslim populations, be they Punjabi from Pakistan or Mirpuri from Kashmir, Pashtun from the Afghan border regions, Muslims from Bangladesh or India, or other, smaller minorities from across the globe. What they have in common is a religion, rather than a culture, and within the Muslim *community*, however defined, a marriage between, say, a Pashtun and a Punjabi, or a Bangladeshi and a Gujarati, would certainly be judged highly problematic, and considered a crossing of ethnic and *culture* boundaries that responsible parents should prevent at all costs.

The cultural heterogeneity of the Southall Muslim *community* is, in ethnological terms, just a reflection of the fact that Islam, unlike Sikhism and Hinduism, has expanded to the most diverse parts of the globe. Its spread has established a global *community* of believers that is held by no common bond save its internally all but uniform religious observances. A Southallian who goes to worship in the Central Mosque in London's Regent's Park is surrounded by Arabs and Africans, Indonesians and Malaysians as much as by people from the subcontinent. All of them worship the same God in the same sacred language; yet even a good knowledge of Koranic Arabic, which takes years to acquire, does not enable them to communicate with each other. This is done in English or Punjabi, Urdu or Mirpuri, Malaysian, Pashto or Somali. Nor would Muslims expect, any more than Christians do, that the bond of a shared faith should render their multiplicity of *cultures* mutually intelligible or even compatible, let alone 'the same'.

Muslim Southallians are thus members of a global *community*, but that *community* is one of faith, and its bounds far exceed the horizons of any one *culture* or any one person's cross-cultural competence. By the same token, they are members of a local Muslim *community*, which again is not co-extensive with their own ethnic or reified *culture*. It is only to be expected, then, that Muslim Southallians of East African backgrounds, or of Punjabi or Gujarati backgrounds, see cultural affinities to others of the same background, even if they are not of the Muslim faith. In regional cases such as these, it is easy to see that Muslims, even more clearly than Hindus and Sikhs, are members of religiously defined *communities*, yet that much of the social life by which they perform and re-create their culture relies upon the mutually independent cleavages of language, regional background, national loyalties, class, and other factors that cut across the boundaries of all *communities* as the dominant discourse would have them defined.

Afro-Caribbeans and four approaches to 'finding' *culture*
The divisions between different islands of origin have been bridged to a large extent; yet many Afro-Caribbean Southallians do not recognize the commonality thus established as a complete, integral, and sufficiently defined *culture*. In the processual making and remaking of culture that all Southallians perform, the greatest awareness of culture as process is perhaps shown by Afro-Caribbeans of post-migration birth. A campaigner for musical provisions who figured in the 'Stories of a Community Centre' above, put this very clearly in replying to a question by Hundleby:

Q.:   Could you explain your position as someone who can call Asian musicians 'comrade' and at the same time want a separate Afro-Caribbean facility?
A.:   In the perfect world, I don't want a separate facility. But I think that, just as it's important for them to keep their culture alive and their music alive, so it's important for us to do the same. Even more important 'cos we've had our culture taken from us through slavery and the likes for hundreds of years. It's not a process of just keeping a culture alive for the Afro-Caribbeans; it's a process of finding that culture as well. We need somewhere for young Afro-Caribbean people where they can find their own culture.
(Hundleby 1987, Appendix IV, 3)

This perceived need to 'find' a *culture* that is not yet 'known' is reflected in a view that Afro-Caribbeans do not even 'have' a *culture*. Yabsley reports of our survey among Southall youth that it 'contained the question: 'What is your culture?' One Afro-Caribbean man (thirties, works for a market research company) ... came across the question and remarked: "How would West Indians answer that? – We *have* no culture!"' (Yabsley 1990, 119).

The perception that Afro-Caribbeans have been robbed of their culture through deportation from Africa and plantation slavery is sometimes also reflected in the academic literature. Thus, Pryce opens his Bristol ethnography *Endless Pressure* by recalling that 'the cultural losses of the African slave were substantial. He lost not only his language, but the essence of his religion as well, and his entire family system' (Pryce 1979, 3). Though I shall want to return to the loss of African family systems below, most Afro-Caribbean Southallians would probably agree with Pryce. A Rastafarian Southallian endorsed the view of a lack of culture and gave her own solution to Yabsley: 'West Indians have got not much culture. Jamaica belonged to the Arawak Indians ... I like to see myself as an African' (Yabsley 1990, 118).

In this search for an Afro-Caribbean culture, four approaches can be distinguished. They may be summarized as the religious, the political, the historical, and the musical. I shall discuss each of these in turn, exemplifying the religious approach by Rastafarianism, the political by pan-Africanism, the historical as a growing interest in African 'Roots', and the musical with regard to Reggae and a local Southall group. I shall turn to the religious approach first.

When plantation slavery had destroyed both individual liberty and the cultural autonomy of the African heritage, the religion of Rastafarianism promised to restore both at once. The Black Church movements of North America, knowledge of the Black Christian Empire of Ethiopia, and specifically Jamaican readings of Old Testament references were combined to form a consistent Black Redemptionist doctrine.

In the post-migration context, Rastafarianism stresses the unity of all African peoples, including the overcoming of Afro-Caribbeans' own island boundaries. In Southall, Yabsley interviewed:

a Rastafarian woman (Jamaican parents, born in Aylesbury, thirties) [who] argued that 'people realised that we are all one people, especially in the Rastafarian movement. People want to create bonding – unity – people realise that they are from the same country' [meaning Africa].   *(Yabsley 1990, 94)*

'As a black person in England I don't know if I'd ever consider England as my home. I feel I've never been accepted – I have a dual nationality – I can conform to the British way of life [but there is also] – the blackness: I like to see myself as an African. I think that's where my true culture lies – me going to Jamaica is like the tip of the iceberg.'   *(Yabsley 1990, 94–5 and 118)*

But this 'true' *culture* is not yet a possession; it needs to be acquired, and, as the same speaker concedes immediately, 'the obstacle is that Africans see us as West Indian' (Yabsley 1990, 118). There are further obstacles preventing most Afro-Caribbeans from exploring their African heritage. Leaving aside the superiority which the older cohort of migrants some-times feel over migrants from the African continent, and its mirror image among African migrants in London, strict adherence to Rastafari injunc-tions requires a strong conviction in the face of recent events in Ethiopia. There is an almost apologetic note in the following statement:

I'm a Rastafarian, but not dedicated ... I eat meat; dedicated Rastafarians are vegetarian. I see Haile Selassie as a great man, not a god ... he can be traced in the line of David, he's the twenty-fifth descendant in the line of David. Because it's a religious line, people see him as a god.   *(Yabsley 1990, 127)*

I was confronted with a more outspoken disavowal of the Rastafarian life by a Southall Afro-Caribbean friend who started to wave a red sheet almost before he was past my front door: 'Look what *I* got in the post!' The sheet, adorned by an icon of Emperor Haile Selassie, read:

The Ethiopian World Federation Incorporated
Research and Repatriation Committee
Cordially Invites all
Come Celebrate
The 58th Coronation of
His Imperial Majesty
Emperor
Haile Selassie I.
on Saturday 5th Nov. '88

Before I could kindle hopes that he might take me along, Winston poured scorn on the idea of repatriation: 'They want to repatriate us? Where to? – Effin' Ethiopia!? – If anybody wants to repatriate me, they can give me ten grand, and I'll go to the West Indies and open a business!'

Given such obstacles even in appreciating Rastafarian ideas, the African heritage can be claimed in another way, namely through a polit-ical pan-Africanism. This approach in its most comprehensive form was explained by a Southall *community leader*:

Through slavery, Africans were scattered all over the globe. Their culture was destroyed, they had no link with Africa. The aim of unity is to join African-Caribbean people – people of African descent and African people. They were forbidden to know about the mother-land, Africa. Coming to England united those who had been separated for 300, 400 years. They can go to France and meet Africans from Senegal, to Holland and meet Africans from Surinam. They go to Africa and are accepted (he claims in objection to my statement otherwise). ... Blacks in the American situation identify with Africa ... there are African traditions in Brazil, etc.   *(Yabsley 1990, 113–14)*

This pan-Africanist approach has tangible consequences for assessing the position of Black culture in the Caribbean, in the United States, and in Britain. In the Caribbean, it can spell African cultural hegemony.

Older African-Caribbeans don't identify with Africa, only those born in the sixties began to, it developed through Rastafarianism ... The Caribbean has got a culture, it is partly African, Asian and European. It is dominated by African culture but people don't realise it. *(ibid. 114)*

The Chinese, English and Indians in the Caribbean haven't had the same history in the Caribbean ... The islands must identify with Africa before there is a real Caribbean culture. *(ibid. 114–15)*

My generation is the link between what was and what is. We keep the link with the Caribbean. The Caribbean now belongs to Africa, we inherited it. *(ibid. 114)*

It is worth noting here that this version of pan-Africanism not only disinherits 'non-African' inhabitants of the islands, but is also reluctant to take its leads from Black North American culture. These latter, however, are probably the most widely accessible and plausible to most younger Afro-Caribbean Southallians. Yet convinced pan-Africanists tend to discount them unless they explicitly endorse the globally Africanist philosophy. Yabsley points to this in an instance of the good ethnographer noting not only what is, but also what is not the case:

I find it surprising that there is little mention of Martin Luther King or Malcolm X in Southall. It may be because they are contradictory in their proposals for the means to racial justice ... Their absence in Southall may be due to the fact [that] the African-Caribbean 'community' leaders in Southall are Rastafarian or Pan-Africanists; it may be that a debate over violence is thought inappropriate in Southall. *(Yabsley 1990, 127–8)*

Jesse Jackson, likewise, figures in the pan-Africanist exposition above, only as a new convert: 'The [new] link-up with trade must be with Africa. Not only in the Caribbean but also those in America. Jesse Jackson is realising that. Now he calls himself an African American. It is better to link with Africa than compete with Europe' (Yabsley 1990, 115). Such a link faces difficulties on the African continent, of course, which stem from the colonial heritage: 'French countries have a harder time. The French never let go, they annex the colonies to France. They see it as part of France, they participate in French elections. They are sent to prison in France' (Yabsley 1990, 117). Yet these colonial differences are known from the Caribbean islands already: 'People from the French Caribbean are more French-thinking, but they still do some African things' (Yabsley 1990, 113–14). Thus, as the Caribbean islands have come to co-operate, so a united Africa can be expected, on a larger scale, to emerge as a fourth great power in the world, sustained in its autonomy by a socialism of its own moulding:

The West doesn't want anyone to talk about unifying Africa, African determinism and destiny, Africans deciding who they want to trade with. The West wants to exploit Africa ... Nkrumah began the philosophy of Africanism. It will be socialist because it's been exploited. It is socialism in [an] African context, not an inherited philosophy. Africa is opposed to China and Russia. It doesn't want to fall under another domination, [when] it comes to an armed struggle, we don't need their help ... Young leaders are coming up in Africa, in Ghana, in Ethiopia. They are Pan-Africanists.   *(ibid. 116)*

For the position of African-Caribbeans in Britain, the consequences are equally stark:

There is a need to keep Africa alive. You need to identify with your nation, then you become stronger within yourself. You are a nomad if you can't identify with anyone. For example, black youth are not British but African.   *(ibid. 114)*

Such political pan-Africanism, however, requires considerable rhetorical competence unless it can be expressed symbolically through celebrations of great personalities such as Garvey, Rodney, Bishop, or, theoretically at least, Nkrumah. I do not know many Southallians of Afro-Caribbean backgrounds that would underwrite their classification as Africans, even if this were not meant to exclude their being British, too. A rediscovery and reinvention of an African cultural heritage, however, is undoubtedly taking place. This renewed historical interest is a far more accessible approach to Afro-Caribbean culture and its 'roots' for most Southallians.

The most popular inspiration of this new historical orientation reached Southall from the United States in the television series *Roots*. Its popularity is well remembered: 'When *Roots* was on, there was a hype over that! – Everyone! Everyone watched it!' Despite the broadcasts predating my fieldwork, I shall briefly consider *Roots* because it achieved one thing that previously would have been thought impossible: it rendered imaginable the society and culture of plantation slaves.

Plantation slavery is a fraught subject and the nearest to a taboo that there is in discussing Western, Afro-Caribbean, or indeed African history. As with all taboos, its status as the unspeakable prevents the spread of factual knowledge. Such factual knowledge is in any case most sparse where it would be of most use, namely in revising the image of plantation slaves as subjects without culture. Historians have tended to study the written sources of the slave trade and the regimes and economics of plantations; anthropology, which might have recorded the slaves' own social and cultural adaptations and group-internal processes, developed too late, as even in the United States it post-dates legal Emancipation. What little knowledge we have of the social and cultural dynamics in the slaves' own quarters is based on the scant oral history that survives, and on a body of testimonies that survives in music, rather than analytic words: the traditions of Gospel song, Spirituals, and, indirectly, the Blues.

Given these obstacles, *Roots* was thus remarkable in two ways. It made plantation slavery imaginable, and by force of its 'family saga' conventions, it could show that there was social and cultural creativeness among slaves themselves. The epic thus allowed a historical imagination of life in slave quarters that was not predicated on the two models that for decades misled many people's understanding: Beecher-Stowe's *Uncle Tom's Cabin* and the equally inappropriate parallel of Nazi concentration camps. While the heroic narrative conventions of the one tended to block, rather than open, the view of plantation slaves as the makers of culture, the popular imagination of the other tended to disregard the constant remaking of culture and sub-cultures even under conditions of total terror (Kogon [1946] 1974). The complex cultural processes developed among plantation slaves themselves had been documented for readers in Genovese's portrayal of *The World the Slaves Made* (1974); but it was only with the drama of *Roots* that they were made widely accessible for the first time. In rendering slave society imaginable, *Roots* effectively questioned the widespread assumption that slavery was a time without *culture*.

Roots could help little, however, in reclaiming the pre-slavery African heritage, as increasing numbers of young Afro-Caribbeans wish to do. Much current literature portrays this African heritage as having been entirely lost through slavery, and some Southallians quoted have reflected this view. Yet there may be genuinely African roots even to the matrifocal family arrangements which are so often blamed, in Britain, as a 'cause' of diverse 'social problems' among Afro-Caribbeans. Matrifocal domestic arrangements are widely traced to the disruptive impact of plantation slavery, and even Pryce (1979, 16) accepts that they 'stem directly from the institution of slavery'. Yet there is a case to be made which validates these patterns as a part of Afro-Caribbeans' original African heritage (Herskovits 1947, Henriques 1949, Matthews 1953). The ethnological literature on the question is hard of access, of course, and the cultural orientations of Rastafarians and many pan-Africanists veer toward Ethiopia as a spiritual homeland, rather than West African societies as the historical one. Yet the debate might assume a new interest amidst the processes of cultural rediscovery and reinvention that have led many young Afro-Caribbeans to enquire into their African heritage.

This search for an African heritage takes its most articulate form perhaps in music and dance. Thus, at the Marcus Garvey Centennial celebrations, Southallians hosted two groups of Afro-Caribbean Londoners performing African-derived music and a 'Zulu War Dance'. The dissemination of contemporary African music through the 1980s' marketing of 'World Music' found some delighted listeners in Southall. Some attention to this musical mode of 'finding' and re-creating an African-Caribbean *culture* should complete this review. Unlike the religious, the political, and the historical approach, the musical mode is, after all, far more widely accessible, is performative in its character, and affective in its appeal.

Studies of Afro-Caribbean musics have been unique in their validation of much that this section has argued or implied. They were the first to take seriously the African heritage that slaves kept alive and re-created; they are clearest also in acknowledging that plantation slaves were not cultural nobodies, but creators of culture, albeit under appalling constraints. Thirdly, they see culture as a process, rather than a possession, much as this entire chapter suggests. Among the most lucid examples of this scholarly tradition is Jones (1988) who may be quoted to exemplify all three of these insights that music, valued as a way of knowing, can reveal to the scholar. Jones is aware that slave quarters were not a culture-less vacuum:

For the slave owners, these apparently 'non-material' aspects of African culture proved almost impossible to eradicate. For while plantation slave cultures developed within the parameters of the slave system, they did so at a relative distance from white institutions.   *(Jones 1988, 4)*

Jones' assessment that music came to be one of the most effective ways of articulating a collective response to racial domination, (1988, 9) is especially useful in that it goes hand in hand with a validation that much of the Southall data, too, make clear:

The domination of slavery was experienced collectively ... It only followed, then, that their specifically cultural responses to such repression should become the raw material out of which their resistances were manufactured. This is not to suggest that all ... cultural expressions ... were ... reducible to conditions of political and economic struggle. Rather, it is to acknowledge *the specificity of black ideological struggles over the signification of 'culture'* – struggles at the heart of which lay a complex negation of European cultural dominance.   *(Jones 1988, 6, my italics)*

This negation of European cultural dominance is also visible in Southall, and the development of Afro-Caribbean musics is interpreted, by this Southallian, as a process of growing cultural self-awareness:

Blues came with African slaves. Calypso happened when carnival happened; it's fun music and quite political. Calypso came from the West Indies, followed the migration of West Indians to America and then England. Reggae was Jamaican and emerged with the 'rude boys'; reggae is the politics of the island, they identify the music as their own. Ska was West Indians trying to be Americans. Lovers Rock was English, the input of commerce was put into it, female voices. Dub came out of England; rap came out of America ... Black people were beginning to get an identity. They were no longer West Indian immigrants but Black British.   *(Yabsley 1990, 130)*

While 'Black British' as a term is not widely used in Southall, and is anathema to pan-Africanists, such parallels between musical styles and an increasingly secure 'cultural identity' are very widespread indeed. The reggae group Misty in Roots is a particular local focus of such a symbolization of self- and cultural awareness through musical fusions, and it brought eight Afro-Caribbean Southallians international stature.

Misty in Roots has for long occupied a pivotal place in young Afro-Caribbean Southallians' peer culture. Formed in the early 1970s, the group came to prominence in the 'Rock Against Racism' campaign of 1976, an alliance of musicians that mobilized vast popular support against racist and skinhead violence. In keeping with the radical political message of their 'Roots Reggae' music, the group formed a core part of Peoples Unite, the liberationist youth group which, in 1979, occupied the derelict Dominion Cinema and later developed into the *community* organization African-Caribbean Focus. These links between reggae music and political action are well known among the local fans of Misty in Roots. The group founded an independent record label, Peoples Unite Musicians' Co-operative. Its combination of politically radical and pan-Africanist philosophies is evidenced in the titles of Misty in Roots songs such as 'How Long Jah' (1981) and 'Own Them Control Them' (album 'Earth', 1986), as well as the names of other groups released on their label, such as Abbacush and Pauline African Woman. The ethos of the group is best outlined in this local appreciation:

Their music has developed from the spiritual vibes of Africa coupled with the Jamaican Reggae sound and other Caribbean traditional sounds, but inspired by their experiences of living and growing up in England. The band emerged from a group of young musicians living in Southall. Southall was the meeting place, London the inspiration, [Southall] the Ghetto of the city, from which these young musicians could come together to create their musical vision and spiritual aware-

ness ... West London has long been a home for black music, in fact it is said that
the first black Afro-Caribbean band in Britain started in Southall. Bands like the
Crescendoes, The Hipstars, Dave and the Nightingale and Calabash played
calypso, R[hythm] & B[lues], RockSteady, or whatever happened to be the music
of the day. This was the first generation of black immigrants from the West
Indies. It is from the second generation, their children, that MISTY IN ROOTS
was born, yet it was from their parents that the young musicians were to gain
much of their inspiration and training.   *(Anon. 1986)*

The passage bears testimony to a long local continuity of Afro-
Caribbean culture in Southall. It connects the process of reclaiming an
African heritage with a recognition of 'roots' in West London. These
may assume all the more importance for Southallians who have forged
an ethnic *community* as the dominant discourse demands, but so consistently disengage the dominant equation between *communities* and their
reified cultures.

Whites and three strategies in the absence of *community*
The position of white Southallians amidst the local *communities* is
ambiguous and often equivocal. While Irish *culture* is recognized as a
distinct heritage, an Irish *community* is seldom acknowledged either from
the inside or the outside. An English *culture*, by contrast, is hard to define
not only for locals, but for the ethnographer, too; and while there were
local communities of English people until they dispersed, an English
cultural *community* is not seen to exist. To call the entire white population one *community*, again, is far more plausible from the outside than
from the inside. The word that most white Southallians most readily use
of themselves is that they are a 'minority'. Demographically, this is clear,
of course, in the three urban wards of town, although the white population of the surrounding suburban wards is larger. But even here, white
young people tend to move 'out and up' when they can. Wendy, an
English woman of twenty-one, makes a case in point: 'My old friends
that I sort of grew up with and when I was young, all moved away.
They're all gone from Southall' (Hawkes 1990b, 39). The Irish population is rejuvenated to some extent by young and unmarried people
seeking work and inexpensive lodgings; they, too, however, tend to move
when they can afford it.
    To deal with this 'minority' position among *communities*, three strate-
gies can be discerned. A political option open to Irish Southallians is to
seek recognition as an ethnic minority or ethnic community in accordance with the dominant discourse of ethno-cultural communities. A

second option, open to all white Southallians, is a cognitive strategy. It consists in cultivating a shared minority consciousness, and it is achieved most easily by stressing white Southallians' exclusion from public services distributed by ethnic targeting. A third option consists in a pragmatic strategy, and is the one that best avoids subjective alienation: it involves the creative forging of affinities and alliances across *community* boundaries.

Recognition as an ethnic minority, and thus a distinct community, status, have been demanded by Irish '*community* activists' in several boroughs of London. During my fieldwork, the Labour politicians who controlled the Borough of Ealing and its resources were genuinely responsive to this corporatist approach. They fully endorsed the principle of ethnic targeting of public resources, since they saw each community as having 'special needs' that were to be satisfied separately. Thus, in 1988, a grant of £200,000 was given to an Irish housing association to establish a short-stay hostel specifically for Irish homeless people (*The Leader*, 6 January 1989, 5). Such ethnic targeting of the Irish community, however, owed more to the corridor dynamics of Ealing Town Hall than to the cultural dynamics prevalent among Irish Southallians, as the following anecdote will show.

A year or so earlier, the press spokesman of a social-democratic opposition party had vociferously blamed the ruling party for 'deliberately discriminating against Irish people'. He had objected:

to Ealing [borough]'s racial equality committee describing Irish people as those 'born in Eire or Northern Ireland'. ... [The politician] had objected because the gaelic word 'Eire' includes the six counties of Northern Ireland, so in his opinion gave 'offence to Irishmen who long for the reunification of Ireland'. ... In addition, [the politician] objected to a council advertisement for a director of education which said that Asian and Afro-Caribbean candidates would be particularly welcomed, but it gave no visual welcome to Irish or Polish applicants.

(Ealing Informer, 25 March 1988, 3)

The Council Department so accused abstained from questioning the logic of either of the spokespersons' contentions and merely denied an intent to discriminate:

'The use of the word Eire was never intended to give offence. It was used as the term used by the Irish government, on Irish passports' ... the council had funded a one-year research project devoted to establishing the needs of the Irish community in Ealing. 'In addition to this [...], various council departments have set up their own projects aimed at the Irish community.' These include the establishment of an Irish women's network and a working group on services to Irish women. The community services department recently hosted an Irish social evening in Acton and are planning more similar events, while the police [monitoring] unit have undertaken projects examining crime and community safety issues and the effect of legislation in relation to Ealing's Irish community. 'The very fact that our ethnic monitoring survey of service users included Irish as a category is evidence that Ealing Council does acknowledge the discrimination faced by the Irish community, and is taking steps to identify ways to redress this.'

(Ealing Informer, 25 March 1988, 3)

I do not wish to quote verbatim the language used by some twenty Southall Irish acquaintances with whom, on a few occasions, I discussed the article and who, one and all, pointed to the rates bills that then provided the mainstay of local government taxation. Most Irish Southallians see little benefit for themselves or their friends in demanding ethnic minority status. McGarry (1990) quotes the only example I can find that endorses the corporatist community approach as an antidote to the perceived economic individualism that was mentioned in the previous chapter. It comes from a recently settled young man with firm political commitments:

Everyone is cutting each other's throats and all this sort of thing. – They like to be together, and they drink together and everything else, but as for getting organized and saying, right we want to get bloody houses for the Irish here – they don't do that – they don't get involved in local politics – to get fair play in Southall.   *(McGarry 1990, 83)*

Such a corporatist approach is more widespread among committed Irish activists in North London pressure groups and policy committees, than among Southallians. McGarry points to an interesting reason to account for the absence of '*community* action':

Thus, while an Activist might from the outside unproblematically claim that an 'Irish' group does exist in Southall and equate this with notions of 'community', this is to ignore the fact that notions of 'community', like 'ethnicity', are socially constructed. To achieve this 'sense of community', Cohen (1985) presupposes the existence of a definite power by 'the people' – a power to change and construct the environment in which they live in a way which is meaningful to them [...], whereby the street, the pub, the corner shop, etc. become articulations of *communal* space.   *(McGarry 1990, 82, my italics)*

Precisely this loss of control over the environment is what most Irish, like most English, Southallians protest, when they journey to other suburbs to shop or to visit the friends that have moved out. It is one of the local perceptions that white residents most readily share with each other. While McGarry (1990, 100) lists some twenty Irish projects and pressure groups in London, she finds that, only three of my informants appreciate the work of the Activists. The feelings of the majority were summed up by Mrs. S., when she said: 'Well I think some of them [the Activists] are talking out of line really. They are stirring up more trouble really, because a lot of people want to live in peace with their neighbours and with one another, but they are bringing in these things. – I think sometimes they are only doing it for their own benefit.'   *(McGarry 1990, 45)*

The reasons for such distrust are not hard to find. When earlier Irish immigrants were previously considered an ethnic minority, they were subjected to open discrimination. Prejudice continues in British theatrical images of the Irish as 'drunken' or 'thick', as well as in anger misdirected at Irish people because of the actions of the Provisional IRA, as happened to this Southallian:

I've had a lot of problems when all The Troubles have been going on. – It's been dreadful – even the recent Troubles here with the soldiers being killed at the funeral in Northern Ireland – that was very bad. They forget that you are human and that you feel it as well. You see, [at work] one of the drivers of the ambulances came in – he just blasted in the door and he said: 'those barbarian Irish!'
          (McGarry 1990, 43)

To the politically committed, such occurrences prove all the more conclusively that ethnic minority status is required to ensure equal opportunities and rights, freedom from discrimination and abuse, and 'the right to play a full part in the social and political life of this country without fear of harassment and imprisonment by the security forces' (IBRG 1989, 12). British state forces can indeed use the Prevention of Terrorism Act, constitutionally so exceptional that it requires annual parliamentary renewal, to detain on suspicion citizens of Ireland and Northern Ireland. Correspondingly, 'some activists' interviewed by McGarry 'proclaimed that this hesitancy [in wishing for 'ethnic minority' status] is due mainly to the Prevention of Terrorism Act and the fear that it generates. Possibly. Or maybe it could just be that most ordinary people don't want to be mobilised politically' (McGarry 1990, 83-4).

While most Irish Southallians see little benefit in demanding ethnic community status, the option is not available, of course, to English Southallians. Even to point this out may seem banal, and few readers would expect to find an officially labelled 'English ethnic community' in England: they, after all, form the nation hegemonically identified with the state. Yet the point is of interest. It shows how recognition as the nation excludes recognition as an ethnic community and how, conversely, designation as an ethnic community may entail a tacit exclusion from the nation. I need not say more of it here, but later shall argue that there is indeed a nexus between the postulation of ethnic communities and the postulate of a state-forming ethno-cultural nation.

During the 1950s and 1960s, many English Southallians did indeed engage in the rhetoric of a nation 'swamped' by immigrants from ethnic communities. The vast majority among them moved out of the three central wards of town, sometimes because they held racist attitudes, other times because, like so many other Southallians, they equated moving out with moving up. Those English people who did not join the white exodus, remain in Southall largely by choice, and they have redefined their place in town. Neither Hawkes (1990) nor McGarry (1990) nor I have encountered much rhetorical emphasis on a white status as 'nationals' when others are members of ethnic communities. Rather, white Southallians rely almost entirely on the second and third options of minority consciousness and selective alliance, respectively.

Minority consciousness builds on two processes of generalization. One generalizes the shared marginal position of white Southallians and often blames public policies for favouring the ethnic minorities; the other generalizes about the surrounding *communities* by stereotyping their *cultures*.

A resentment that white Southallians are 'left out', and indeed disadvantaged by public policies thought to practise positive discrimination, is a common theme among Irish and English Southallians. During the time of my fieldwork, it was often directed at the Borough Council's ethnic targeting of its resources. This young white woman does not blame the council explicitly, although her examples may derive from some of its job advertisements:

[...] you know, this racism thing works both ways. Because you get jobs advertised for purely for Black people or Indian people, and if that isn't racist, you see, the white people don't like that. A job is a job, and the best person who can do that should get it. Not if you're a Lesbian – unless you're a Lesbian and an Indian. If you're Lesbian and Indian and go for a job – and you've got the same qualifications as a white person, you're more likely to get the job.

Q.: Is that general for most firms around here? Or are you thinking of anyone in particular?

A.: No, I'm not thinking of anyone in particular. It's what being – Ealing has a big black community. I don't know if it's a good or a bad thing. But the thing about advertising for Indians only – I'm not sure if that's a good thing. Cos that is racism working the other way; but the white people can't say anything because they would be classed as racist, if you see what I mean. But I think the person best qualified for that job should get the job.   (*Hawkes 1990b, 76*)

The fear of being branded racist keeps many white Southallians from spelling out in public that, in a widely used phrase, 'things have gone too far the other way': 'I'm not a racist,' explains a middle-aged, locally born Englishwoman, 'but there are things that I want to complain about. Except I can't. Because I would be labelled a racist, and I'm not.' An English employee of the council itself expressed most blatantly what probably most white Southallians would have endorsed at the time: 'According to Ealing Council, if you're white, you're a racist' (Hawkes 1990a, 64). This resentment was further incensed by the council's declaration of 1988 as 'Anti-Racism Year'. The idea arose because the Borough had been under a Conservative administration when the first 'Anti-Racism Year' was launched by the then Greater London Council in 1984. Of the dozen or so conferences and workshops targeted at ethnic minorities, political activists, and council employees, white Southallians heard little. The campaign to raise public awareness, however, was broadly aimed, and reached many households, as well as voluntary organizations dependent on the Borough Council's grants. Forms were sent out that asked citizens to endorse the campaign without qualification:

I pledge my support to the Ealing Anti-Racism Year campaign.

1. I recognize that racism runs through all aspects of life in the borough; I cannot ignore it, condone it, or gloss over it.

2. I agree with the fundamental right of all Ealing's Residents to enjoy a level of real equality, justice, freedom and security that currently does not exist.

3. I shall strive to create conditions, at home, at work and in the community that make it impossible for racism to operate; join with all ordinary people in Ealing to fight the disadvantages common to them all, and examine, challenge, criticise and change the structures that perpetuate racism in organisations.

Signed _____

To 'join with all ordinary people ... [and] to fight the disadvantages common to them all', is one thing; to join with politicians avowing that 'racism runs through all aspects of life in the borough' is another, even to those who do not wish to ignore or condone it. It was felt to be an insult by many white Southallians I questioned on the subject. It is not hard to see why, since it makes no allowance for people who, after all, had not moved out; and it blatantly stereotypes the white, or perhaps only the English, cultural heritage as a consistently racist form of life. Such labelling can engender a sense of fatigue, especially when it ignores

the class inequalities among whites themselves. Thus in a local pub, I
overheard a white dustman and an Afro-Caribbean acquaintance sharing
a lunchtime pint and chat, talking about British and West Indian history.
'But it wasn't the slave trade that kept the Brits in the West Indies', the
Afro-Caribbean companion insisted: 'it was the minerals and the trade
profits'. 'Oh come off it, mate, honest, I can't hear it any more. You
know, *we* had boys going up the chimneys and boys going down the coal-
mines!'

Given the history of Southall, an area of economic decline from the
1930s, it is not hard to understand a strand in white Southallians'
thinking that a social worker of twenty years' local standing paraphrased
to me in these words:

They're not racist. The racists have moved out, first the semi-racists; and then the
hardliners. No they're not racist. But they're – you know – ruffled. They say:
'These people complain too much. Look at the community centres. They never
built *us* any community centres?! But all you hear is complaining. I mean, most
of them just get on with it. But some of them, really, they're swinging the lead a
bit!' That's what they say.

That so many of the white Southallians we interviewed confided that
'things have gone too far the other way' may be due, in part, to the
timing of my students' and my own fieldwork: it followed the said 'Anti-
Racism Year', a campaign which among white Southallians was singularly successful in accentuating resentment and even provoking
professions of minority consciousness.

Minority consciousness is seldom, however, the only strategy that
white Southallians choose in the absence of *community*. To rely on it too
much would, after all, only heighten the sense of alienation and isolation
that white Southallians wish to alleviate. In daily life, most white
Southallians in the central wards, and many in the surrounding suburbs,
depend upon recognizing affinities across *community* boundaries, and on
validating these by forging selective alliances.

These affinities and alliances are forged in creative individual acts.
Wendy, aged twenty-one and quoted above, has 'got one friend, and
she's like family ... We started off as friends and got to know her whole
family. And they're like family now' (Hawkes 1990b, 11), so much so
indeed that Wendy accompanied her best friend's mother on a journey
to the family's home in the Punjab. She indeed sees herself as being 'more
in the Asian community' than in the, hardly existing, white one, as 'all'
her friends are Asian (Hawkes 1990a, 66). Another of Hawkes' English
informants, aged fifteen, answered the youth survey question to name his

own culture by writing: 'English/Black. (I hang around more with black people', explaining that 'only about 30 per cent of my friends are white' (Hawkes 1990a, 42). Such peer friendships should not be discounted or marginalized as a youthful phenomenon only. Adults forge similar individual bonds through their aspirations toward good neighbourhood. They can indeed do so to a point where differences of colour are not merely ignored, but expressly confronted. An unusually explicit example should be quoted from Hawkes' interview with a white Southallian woman who, in the presence of her husband, recounted her interactions with a South Asian family next door. Her husband, it should be noted, has forged an alliance with Afro-Caribbean, rather than South Asian neighbours:

Q.:   It must have been a real trauma next door when she married a white bloke?
HUSBAND: Well, – they just disowned her.
WIFE: She hasn't got another [unmarried] daughter. Weeks, wasn't it, Mum kept crying. She kept calling me in there every evening: 'What shall I do? Where have I gone wrong?' – 'You haven't gone wrong, it's just a fact of life that Parmjit fancied the white fella, and not an Indian.'
Q.:   Did it occur to her that it might sound strange to you that she was really upset because her daughter wants to marry a white man, – and you're white?
WIFE: Oh no. In fact, I was in there all one evening, trying to get her to eat something. [...]
Q.:   So were they really upset because she had married someone of her choice, or because she had married a white man?
WIFE: Of her choice, I think.
Q.:   So it was irrelevant that he was white?
WIFE: Yeah! Oh yeah. I mean, [her] Dad turned round in front of me and said: 'If you marry a white, he'll do nothing but hit you!' And I said to him: 'Hang on a bit!', I said, 'what about the youngster you used to have upstairs [as a tenant]?', I said, 'she was Indian enough, and so was her husband, and no one hit any-one more than he hit her!'   *(Hawkes 1990b, 6–7)*

Such bonds forged between peers and neighbours are important and make all the difference to those who do not wish to move out and up. Dozens more examples could be given; yet their individual character limits what they can tell the anthropologist about the cultural dynamics within the white population at large.

To observe such affinities and alliances on a collective scale, one must turn to the public domain. I have mentioned already that politically, Southall was represented by a locally born white Member of Parliament, and have drawn attention to his perceived non-partisan stand amidst the concert of contending *communities*. Similar cases of voters electing a representative of 'unrepresentative colour' have continued to occur on a local level. Such ethnically unrepresentative elections happened not only in the suburban wards, where English and Irish Southallians are large minorities, but also in one of the central wards where they are virtually absent. The councillor who represented the ward with the highest proportion of South Asian voters, had been re-elected for twenty years. Speaking of the confrontation and the white dispersal of the 1960s, he recalls: 'I got a lot of abuse in the early years from some whites. They called me "Indian-lover", traitor, and all sorts' (Hawkes 1990a, 74). After twenty years of a genuine and new alliance, he concludes that his South Asian electors:

have never seen me as a white Englishman ... Whenever there was any trouble, I was always over at the Gurdwara ... The local council was always trying to resist their aspirations. I campaigned with them on bussing, on trying to get community languages taught in the schools ... I've got 11,000 friends around here, since I've got well-known and become part of the new community here, they look upon me as a Punjabi, just like them.   *(Hawkes 1990a, 66)*

Another 'new *community*', which he served as church warden and organist, may exemplify a further collectively forged cross-*community* affinity and alliance: the fusion of white, South Asian and Afro-Caribbean Christians in joint religious congregations. It is worth casting a brief glance at these congregational developments, since white Southallians continue to form the majority in both Roman Catholic and Anglican parishes and see them, understandably, as among the few remnants of a once-white Southall.

   To speak of ethnic fusions in Christian congregations is by no means a foregone conclusion. There are 'churches that mix', and others that do not. Reference has already been made to some Anglican Southallians' perception of the Roman Catholic congregation as a cultural *community* whose members 'just treat each other through their religion'. The perception may be more convincing to outsiders than insiders, if McGarry's data are taken into account: '[An informant] ... suggests that: "they [the Irish] dominate the church to the exclusion of groups like the Afro-Caribbeans [because] ... the only outlet that the Irish have for their Irishness at the moment is through the domination of that little aspect of power which they have got, which is the church"' (McGarry 1990, 61). Her ethnography indeed details a case in which:

Mr. G. did attempt to 'undermine' this authority when he suggested that the Church and Church Hall should be places where Asians and Afro-Caribbeans could express 'their own culture'. As a result, he was voted off the committee, and the older Irish/English network became ever more vigilant as to whom they would appoint in positions of leadership.   *(McGarry 1990, 84)*

Such an exclusive strategy for some of the white local minority to retain a niche of control seems, none the less, to be highly exceptional in my experience. In other congregations, difficulties in forging new religious *communities* are of an opposite nature. Those of the Church of England may serve as an example.

The Anglican Communion in general has become almost a by-word for doctrinal and liturgical pluralism. In Southall, internal differences of emphasis in worship and faith are widely associated, and indeed roughly aligned, with different *community* heritages. Many South Asian Anglicans received their religious education from missionaries on the subcontinent; the religious heritage of many Afro-Caribbeans is predicated on an Evangelical understanding of Scripture; English Anglicans in Southall are divided, as everywhere, by their preferences for Anglo-Catholic, High Church, or Low Church liturgical conventions. Where vicars or parish consultative committees take a strongly partisan line on these, they risk losing part of their congregations, possibly indeed on ethnic lines. Where they refrain from mediating, some of their congregations feel themselves outnumbered by the liturgical or doctrinal consensus of the majority. The processes of mediation can be intricate and laborious, but in some parishes they succeed in forging 'new *communities*' that reach across, but do not deny, the inevitable contestations along perceived ethnic and doctrinal cleavages.

White Southallians, who did not see themselves as forming a white *community*, have made choices among three strategies. The first, open to Irish Southallians, was to seek recognition as an ethnic minority in accordance with the dominant discourse. In Southall, this strategy had few supporters and even fewer protagonists. The second strategy, that of cultivating a minority consciousness by stressing white exclusion from ethnic targeting was far more widespread. The third option, and the one which best avoided subjective alienation, was the forging of, usually selective, allegiances and affinities across *community* boundaries. In these processes, as in many others described in this chapter, one can see how Southallians are able to set aside the strictures of the dominant discourse, depending upon their judgements of context.

The dominant equation between culture and community is thus questioned and disengaged in various ways within each of the local *communities*. Among Sikhs, one could observe strong dynamics of forging new *communities* on a basis that combined differences of caste, migratory history, and perceptions of class. Among Hindu Southallians, Hindu *culture* could carry a claim to encompassing ideas and people of other *communities*. Muslim Southallians were clearly aware that the local *community* of believers entailed a contending variety of *cultures* divided on criteria of language and migratory path, as well as national and ethnic loyalties. Among the *community* of Afro-Caribbeans, one could identify several approaches aimed at 'finding', and thus consciously creating, a *culture*. White Southallians, finally, have developed three fairly distinct strategies in response to their own equivocation about the *communities* or *cultures* ascribed to them. All of these data make it clear that Southallians are able to disengage the dominant equation whenever the context appears to be suitable. This does not mean, of course, that the dominant discourse is thereby revoked altogether. Southallians continue to engage it, depending on their judgements of context and purpose. What the data thus show is a dual discursive competence.

6

Culture and *community* as terms of cultural contestation

On youth: assessing and discovering an *Asian culture*
Questioning *Asian culture*: socialist and feminist networks
Contesting political *community*: 'Are Asians Black?'
Questioning religious *community*: interfaith networks
Contesting religious *community*: convergence, encompassment, and
'multi-cultural' equality

In certain contexts, Southallians engage the dominant discourse; in others, they deny its essential equation. This dual discursive competence turns *culture* and *community* themselves into terms of contestation. Their definitions and boundaries become the object of questioning and reinterpretation, and spark off argument and even controversy. This is what the present chapter intends to show. It no longer assumes that Southall *communities* can be understood one by one, for it is clear by now that Southallians do far more than acting out the dominant discourse. In asserting their personal agency and pursuing their various commitments, they question what the terms *'culture'* and *'community'* may signify in the first place. The terms themselves become pivotal points in the making of a Southall culture. To show the two concepts as matters of debate, I shall begin with data gathered among Southall youths. Pages 98–108 have drawn attention to the culture consciousness of Southall children, and the next section will show how their ideas of *culture* and *community* change during their adolescent years. To start out with young people, however, should not be construed as pitching a dynamic 'second generation' against a purportedly conservative first. New debates about *culture*, *community*, and their interrelations proceed among adults no less than their offspring. Here, however, they spring not so much from daily exposure to ethnically plural networks such as one finds in schools and youth clubs; rather, they tend to react to challenges first voiced by cross-

Table 8. *Statements about relative isolation endorsed by 179 Southall youths*

Statement	Agree %	Disagree %
Southall is too isolated, it's like an island.	35	65
My community is like an island in Southall.	17	83
Every community in Southall is like an island.	15	85

community interest groups. I shall focus on two of these and then show, in both cases, how Southallians at large have reacted to such challenges. First, local socialist and feminist networks have come to question the legitimacy of *Asian culture* and to postulate a comprehensive *Black community* that unites Asians with Afro-Caribbeans. The ensuing controversy, known as the 'Black or Asian?' debate, will show how Southallians at large contend with the idea of a *Black community*. At the same time, local Interfaith networks have come to question the exclusivist truth claims of religious orthodoxies, and an ensuing controversy about religious assemblies at schools will show how Southallians contend with the claims of religious *communities* in a consciously 'multi-cultural' setting.

On youth: assessing and discovering an *Asian culture*
Southall children acquire consciousness of *culture* as a possession before they have acquired functional literacy or a sense of 'who they are in the world'. As they grow into their teens, their cultural and cross-cultural capabilities develop side by side with their curiosity about themselves and 'the others'. Juveniles often discover that in a variety of contexts they perform a *youth culture* of peers, as distinct from the *cultures* of their elders. This can result in an increasingly relativist and dynamic view of their elders' *culture*, conscious of generational as well as contextual differences. In the fieldwork diary of my second year in Southall, I had once written: 'This place is like an island. And all the communities in it are islands again.' Vague and subjective as the impression was, it seemed to me to describe something of the attitude of adult Southallians when they engaged in the dominant discourse of 'five *communities* of *culture*'. We later decided, despite its vagueness, to treat it like many of the statements gathered among young Southallians themselves and to submit it to their assessment on a larger scale. The survey respondents did not endorse it to any great extent, as table 8 shows. Strikingly, only half of those who endorsed the island metaphor for Southall at large applied it

Table 9. *Sources of learning about the best-known 'other' religion endorsed by 264 South Asian Southall youths*

Sources of learning	Endorsed by: % of respondents
Religious education at school	51
Other school subjects	35
School assembly	28
A friend at the same school	37
A friend of another school	20
Family	33
Other relatives	18
Television	30
Other visual media (cinema, VCR)	10
Printed media (books, magazines)	11

to their own, or others', *communities.* These *communities* tended to be defined with a remarkable emphasis on religious *cultures,* as table 5 has shown. It would be good to know, therefore, how they manage to go beyond religious boundaries in their social life and in their acquisition of cross-*community* knowledge.

To explore how young Southallians learn about religions other than their own, 264 of them were asked to name the religion other than their own that they knew best, and to endorse a variety of sources of learning. The results are contained in table 9.

The largest single source of learning about a religion other than one's own was located in school activities. Yet no respondent validated these as the only source. School-friends and friends from other schools; family and other relatives; and television and other media had each been drawn on by more than half of the young people. Qualitative research by Gillespie (1995) has explored in detail how television viewing accentuates young Southallians' awareness of religious differences and commonalities.

Friendships across religious boundaries appeared to be common among the respondents. A separate question asked them to 'think of the five people you spend most time with outside school. Does any of them have a different religion from you?' Almost half, just over 47 per cent of the 324 young people asked, answered this with 'Yes'. This may seem unsurprising in a town of such wide religious variety; yet even among young Sikhs, who by their weight of numbers could easily confine their circle of best friends to fellow-Sikhs, 42 per cent of boys and 47 per cent of girls sustained the general pattern. It comes as far less of a surprise,

Table 10. *Social divisions thought important among adults and among youths, endorsed by 185 Southall youths*

Factors thought divisive among adults	Endorsed by youths %	Factors thought divisive among youths	Endorsed by youths %
Religion	65		
Culture	54	Culture	55
		Religion	55
		Racism	47
Class	38	Class	39
Race	38	Race	37
		School	36
		Competition	36
		Parents	35
Money	34	Money	33
Racism	30		
Fear	23	Fear	29
Politics	20	Politics	16
Competition	20		
Media	14	Media	11
School	11		

therefore, that respondents seemed unanimous in rejecting single-faith schools. The question, put to 185 of them, was phrased: 'In your opinion, should there be separate schools for different religions?' While fifteen youths were undecided, only seven endorsed the suggestion, and 163, or 88 per cent of the sample, answered 'No' to the idea. The vote in this case shows the largest consensus recorded for any of the ninety survey questions. I should expect that it will surprise large numbers of local parents, though I do not expect that it will deter the more single-minded campaigners for single-faith schools. These need not, after all, seek their mandate from the wishes of young people themselves so long as public debate on the matter is conducted in the reified terms of the dominant discourse alone.

Yet in understanding young Southallians' crossings of *community* boundaries, it is insufficient to concentrate on religion as the only criterion. Prominently though religious differences figure in their delineations of *culture*, they are also aware of other cleavages, both among their parents and their peers. In order, therefore, to explore their own assessment of 'what divides adults' and 'what divides young people in Southall', they were asked to endorse two lists of divisive influences for each. Again, these were collected in qualitative fieldwork before being submitted to quantitative research. The results, contained in table 10, may most easily be read by regarding 'class' and 'race' as the centre-line of perceived agreement across the generations. The top of the list shows that 'religion' is thought to be a divide more important than 'culture' among adults, but not among youth. It indicates that ten per cent of the sample at least have dissociated the two terms, and the figure may be far higher since the question allowed for multiple endorsements. 'Class' and 'race', by contrast, are viewed as equally divisive among adults as among youth. Above and below that centre-line, there appear telling differences. 'Racism' is thought to divide youth more than adults. Unlike 'race', 'racism' is of course a term of blame, and the many youths who recognize it in their peers even more than their parents can be presumed to resent it intensely.

Remarkably, the young respondents attested to more divisions for youth than they did for adults. It is possible that they underestimated the divisive effects upon adults of social class, money, and competition. At the same time, they may have confirmed very liberally those divisions among themselves that could be blamed on their elders, such as school, competition, and parents themselves. Yet there is certainly evidence of a critical attitude to one's peers, as the mention of racism has already indicated: money as a divisive factor is acknowledged for youth as much as for adults, and fear considerably more. I certainly have never interviewed even one young Southallian who thought his or her own generation more divided than that of their parents. The interpretation I am drawn to by qualitative fieldwork is twofold: youth are more aware of their own divisions than of their parents', and thus endorse them more completely; and youth resent their own divisions more intensely, partly by blaming them on adults, partly even by blaming mere fear – an emotion that teenagers will neither admit to lightly nor respect in their peers. So far, the data suggest that teenage Southallians begin not only to disengage their childhood equation between religion, *culture* and *community*, but are able also to distinguish between adult divisions and their own.

It is in keeping with this growing self-awareness that young South Asian Southallians begin to differentiate between their parents' views and their own, especially when they concern matters of *Asian culture* seen as a normative heritage. Two of these in particular, the customs of 'arranged marriages' and the divisions of caste, are associated with a 'traditional' *Asian culture*, and are subjected to questioning and local debate.

In reviewing these assessments, I need not spend time here to deconstruct stereotypes about 'arranged marriages' as 'the social problem' by which ill-informed protagonists of the dominant discourse identify their own version of 'Asian culture'. Roger Ballard (1972, 13–15) has elucidated the economic and legal conventions that governed marital contracts in the rural Punjab; Catherine Ballard (1979) demolished stereotypical views of marriage arrangements more than fifteen years ago, and found even then that:

In Britain, as well as in the sub-continent, young Asians are now asking for, and often getting, the chance to meet one another properly ... before the engagement takes place. Most of them are now able to veto a proposed match, but many would like to be able to choose from a number of prospective spouses ... Sometimes an already established relationship can be presented as if it were a conventionally arranged marriage, so saving face for the family.

(Ballard 1979, 125)

The ambiguity of 'arranged marriage' as a sociological category is so apparent, indeed, that it takes little or no sociological knowledge to discern it. Dervla Murphy (1987), a travel writer rather than an academic, observed much the same among Mirpuri families in Bradford and Leeds:

there are 'arranged' marriages, 'approved' marriages, and 'forced' marriages. It is not always easy for the families concerned – never mind outsiders – to be sure into which category a particular marriage fits. Dutiful offspring may go through the required matrimonial hoops without complaint while feeling so inwardly rebellious that their marriage really belongs to the 'forced' category. But blatantly forced marriages are rare and their victims usually come of very rich or very poor families ... The majority, even now in Britain, do not envy their white contemporaries who are left to cope unaided with the awesome responsibility of selecting a congenial partner for a life-long relationship.   *(Murphy 1987, 17)*

The latter assertion may, at first sight, seem a rather daring, as well as apologetic, act of interpretation. Yet it accords well with Catherine Ballard's impression, formed among Leeds Punjabis a decade before, that 'many of the second generation would maintain that ["arranged" marriages] are based on sounder foundations than "love marriages" and that they are probably less likely to fail' (Ballard 1979, 125). Having known some young Southallians who happily sailed into an arranged or approved marriage and found intimate bliss, and some others who desperately struggled to evade one or elope from it, I do not know. It is hard to assess people's marital happiness and more useful, in the present context, to try and assess how young Southallians might think about marriage decisions. Following our usual method of collecting informants' statements first, we put a number of them to a larger sample of Southall

Table 11. *Statements about arranged marriages endorsed by 172 South Asian Southall youths*

	Total N = 172–4 %	Boys 76–7 %	Girls 96–7 %
People who marry should be of the same culture.	36	26	44
People should be free to marry whom they like.	78	83	73
People should marry in their own caste.	19	17	21
I personally would prefer a marriage within my own culture.	51	55	48
I would only enter a mixed marriage if my family agree with it.	47	43	51
If I wanted a mixed marriage, I would do it against my family.	25	25	25

Note: The discrepancy of one in the number of boys and girls is due to an error in the manual keying-in of the data which we have not been able to correct. Percentages are calculated from the lower N throughout.

youngsters. The question as put to the survey respondents read: 'Here are some statements that people have made to us. Please tick the ones you agree with.' Again, the statements that guided the quantitative exercise were based on qualitative fieldwork, and in formulating the options we followed the vocabulary and set phrases we had often heard. In using this method, one cannot, of course, escape the subjects' own views of 'the problem': they may, on the one hand, underestimate how much leeway there is in negotiating the acceptability of a partner with parents who might not, at first, agree with the choice. They tend, on the other hand, to import their own imprecisions. Thus, a 'mixed marriage', in Southall parlance, may mean one that crosses a boundary of *culture*, however defined by the people concerned, or one that crosses the boundary of caste. This fluidity is part of the ethnographic reality itself; yet even taking it into account, one can see patterns emerging from table 11. Three-quarters of the respondents endorsed the normative statement that 'people should be free to marry whom they like', while less than a quarter affirmed the rule of caste endogamy so vital to 'arranged marriages'. Yet the matter is more subtle, as the fluid boundary between *culture*, *caste*, and *mixed marriage* has intimated already. Most importantly, the figures show a telling difference between normative statements and statements of personal intent. They reflect the distinction drawn by almost a quarter of the young Southallians who affirm that 'people should be free to marry whom they like' yet add in the same breath that, 'personally, I would only enter a mixed marriage if my family agreed with it'.

A similar ambiguity can also be discerned in young people's attitude to caste in general. By school age, most children are aware of their own caste and of some version, at least, of its relative purity and status. Many indeed feel curious about the caste of peers at school.

You see, I met this boy called Tethi in Second Year [aged twelve], and I thought I'd get on with him. So I asked him was his dad a Carpenter [i.e. of the Tharkan caste]? – And he was, so I said: 'That's good. We're both the same then!'

It's funny that, you really want to know somehow what caste someone is. Once you know, it's no longer important. It doesn't matter for anything. But you want to know. Everybody at school susses each other out that way.

I used to go and ask my dad whether a boy called So-and-So was a Sikh, and if he was a Tharkan.

All three statements happen to come from Sikh boys of the Tharkan caste and thus from the Ramgarhia congregation that has profiled itself *vis-a-vis* the Jat temples. Yet the same growing awareness of caste can be observed among young Sikhs of the Jat caste, as well as among Hindus and Muslims. Deprecation on the basis of caste can go from the supposedly lower to the higher as easily as vice versa, as is demonstrated in these extracts from essays written by three seventeen-year-olds:

The notion of one caste feeling superior to another can be seen in the attitudes of several youngsters. For example, many Jat boys believe that they are 'hard' because of their caste, and are more pure than Ramgarhi groups.

Sometimes I am sweared at because I am a Ramgarhia. Because I have a surname of a Ramgarhia, people can tell who I am.

Everybody says the Jat boys are bad. Everybody, just ask around!

'He's a Singh', is a phrase I heard dozens of times when Sikhs of other castes wanted to disparage a Sikh of the Jat caste. 'Singhs' are thought crude, unsophisticated, and yet proud to the point of arrogance. Caste knowledge turns into prejudice as readily with regard to the lowest castes, the Chamar or leatherworkers and Chuhra or sweepers. Yet with these, the lack of fit between the systems of caste and of class is recognized most readily, as is illustrated in two further school compositions by girls aged seventeen. Both contain a nice twist, in that one excuses her description as an exaggeration, and the other describes the effects of class inferiority on those used to caste superiority.

Occupation has confused everything in the traditional caste system. There are for e.g. Chamaars who are electricians and Jats [who] are cleaners, to slightly exaggerate!

A person's whole life is based upon what cast[e] he/she is, so the notion of purity is taken to a far extent [*in the margin:* – with some, or perhaps I could go as far as saying the majority of people in Southall.] However, I've experienced and known people in Southall who are traditionally 'considered' to be at the bottom of the system, at the bottom [inserted: apparently] meaning that their [they are] slaves, non-pure, untouchables, etc. and only work for the higher castes and yet go round driving exprensive cars, wear enough gold to open up a shop!, and have huge house[s] etc. They have all the luxuries and I know people who consider themselves to be 'pure jats' and they look up to these people.

The lack of fit between class position and caste status is probably far harder to take for adults raised in India, than for youth raised in a class system and sent to school to succeed in it. One youth who protested to a friend's father that he knew a Chamar who was a doctor, received an instantaneous answer: 'My son could be a road sweeper, but he'd still be a Tharkan.' The differences between generations in their understanding of the caste system is nicely pointed to in this incident reported by a Sikh friend then aged nineteen:

When my grandad came to visit from India, we were out in the garden, he and my dad and me. And two doors down the neighbour was pottering around in his garden. So my grandad asked: 'Is that the Chamar?' – My dad nearly pissed himself: 'Shuush, shuush, not so loud!' – But my grandad didn't understand that at all: 'Why,' he said, 'what's wrong with that? It takes all sorts, sure?' – 'No, but here they're more touchy,' I told him. But he didn't understand, you see. To him, a Jat is a farmer, and a Tharkan is a carpenter, and a Chamar is a shoemaker, and it takes all sorts – obviously.

It is impossible to say how far adult Southallians' ideas of caste and its relationship to class might reflect expectations that would be considered outdated on the subcontinent. It is, after all, not uncommon for a migrant cohort to perpetuate traditions which back home have long been revised. Yet be that as it may, the 'traditional' *Asian culture* which young Southallians have to assess is that which their parents construct for them, and the ambivalence with which youngsters assess it is part of their *conscience collective* as 'young Asians'.

It is remarkable how many young Southallians see 'arranged marriages' and the strictures of caste as a part of *Asian culture*, rather than a specifically Hindu, Muslim or Sikh *culture*. It is widely considered an 'Asian custom' or 'rule' that 'Asians' should marry within their religious *community* and their caste. This way of speaking enables South

Asian Southaliians to discuss their views as 'young Asians' together, and
it thus contributes to their discovery of a shared 'Asian identity'. This
commitment to a comprehensively *Asian culture* marks a point of convergence that noticeably removes juveniles from the culture consciousness
observed among children. While their younger siblings largely predicated
their *culture* on their religion, South Asian Southallian adolescents come
to see their own identity as 'young Asians'. Their discourse of *culture* and
community can be seen to widen, with time, to include this new, secular,
cross-religious, cross-caste, and sometimes political, discourse of an
'Asian' identification.

To speak of an *Asian culture* in the sense of a unified *community*
heritage is highly implausible, as all Southall children know. It would
demand blindness to the enormous diversity and the momentous
contention that have long characterized the subcontinent. In Britain, at
any rate, Asian as a term to designate a shared *culture* signifies a new
departure, rather than a tradition or heritage. The departure is
consciously innovative, and in some ways recalls Fischer's description,
formed from reading recent works of 'ethnic' American fiction, of:

the paradoxical sense that ethnicity is something reinvented and reinterpreted in
each generation by each individual [...]; it is something dynamic ... that institutionalized teaching easily makes chauvinist, sterile, and superficial ...

Secondly, what is discovered and reinvented is, perhaps increasingly, something
new: to be Chinese-American is not the same thing as being Chinese in America.
In this sense there is no role model for becoming Chinese-American. It is a matter
of finding a voice or style that does not violate one's *several* components of identity. In part, such a process of assuming an ethnic identity is an insistence on a
pluralist, multidimensional, or multi-faceted concept of self: one can be many
different things, and this personal sense can be a crucible for a wider social ethos
of pluralism.   *(Fischer 1986, 195–6)*

In passing, one should be wary here of playing a sociological generation
game, as if the forging of an *Asian* post-immigration *culture* were the
preserve of youngsters alone. Mannheim (1982) has shown up the spuri-
ousness of using generation as a sociological category. There is, however,
an articulate awareness, among young South Asian Southallians, that
being 'young and born here' involves them in, and qualifies them for, the
conscious creation of a comprehensively *Asian culture*.

A first sign that young South Asian Southallians are developing a
shared post-immigration culture may be seen in their use of Urdu,
Punjabi, and Hindi. Their shared idiom shows all the levelling that a
linguist would expect in such proximity, and I have never failed to get an

assenting laugh when remarking that young Southallians spoke 'Southalli', rather than Punjabi, Urdu, or Hindi. 'When you go back [to] India,' I was told by a friend who had done so, 'everyone knows you're a *bilati*' [here: a South Asian living in Britain; based on the word from which English 'Blighty' is derived]. 'In fact,' another young informant elaborated, 'they sometimes know you're from Southall as soon as you open your mouth. Even at the Customs in Delhi, they asked me if I was from Southall. You can hear it; it's easy.' Amar, a 32-year-old Punjabi educated in a Hindi-speaking military school, likewise explained that:

a Southall accent you can tell a mile away. Partly, it's a mixture of Punjabi and Urdu, and some bits of Hindi maybe. Partly it's the vocabulary. Partly it's also the softer pronunciation; it's lost all the contours, it's no longer as hard as the real village Punjabi.

Some young Southallians are complimented, and some are laughed at, because of the 'pure' Punjabi they speak: its 'pureness' can be admired as authenticity, or ridiculed as reminiscent of a 'peasant' or *pindhu*; but its difference from the new standard '*Southalli*' is readily recognized either way.

To characterize this evolving *Asian culture*, three elements spring to teenagers' minds. They concern classification as Asians by others, be they white or Afro-Caribbean; an aspiration, like Afro-Caribbeans to achieve a unity within that imposed classification; and a wish, like the 'other two *cultures*' symbolically to express this unity, often through music. A few words should be said about each of these dimensions of an *Asian culture* which is increasingly recognized as a unifying factor by the young.

The avowal of an *Asian community* of *culture* can be seen as a response to classification by others. The young Southallians who, in their teens, begin to apply the term to themselves are far less likely to have heard it from their parents than from Afro-Caribbean and white peers at school, from teachers, and notably from television. Sometimes this inclusive self-categorization as Asians can begin to take on a political significance. In this sense, they explain that 'Asians should unite' in the face of discrimination and racism, as Afro-Caribbeans are seen to have done. Reference is sometimes made to the 'Southall Riots' of 1979 and 1981, when 'Asian youth united and took the lead' in protesting their common grievances. But this is rare, and an explicitly political approach tends only to develop later in adolescence. For the vast majority of young Southallians, though, politics is far less interesting than having fun with peers. And, as among so many youths whom anthropologists have studied, it is music that plays an eminent part in their expressive and symbolic peer culture.

Probably the greatest boost to a comprehensively Asian cultural consciousness that occurred during my fieldwork was the 're-invention' (Baumann 1990) of Bhangra, a traditional Punjabi folk dance, music, and song form which was turned, from the late 1970s, into a genre of amplified, modernized pop music to listen to on records or dance to at discos and parties. One can hardly overestimate the popularity of Bhangra among young South Asian Southallians during the 1980s. The adaptation of Bhangra that complements traditional lyrics and drum rhythms with electric keyboards and guitars, synthesizers and new sampling and scratching techniques of recording, is indeed largely a local invention. It was known originally as 'The Southall Beat', championed by the local groups Alaap, Heera, and Holle Holle, and popularized further by some sixty West London groups. What is of greatest interest here is its expressive and symbolic contribution to young Southallians' conceptions of a new *Asian culture*. This was explained most clearly by three musicians interviewed in Southall's *Ghazal and Beat* music monthly. The first, lead singer of the East London group 'Cobra' refers to the impetus for *cultural* unity and autonomy that many South Asian youth received from, and then defined in contradistinction to, young Afro-Caribbeans:

I can remember going to college discos a long time ago, when all you heard was Reggae, Reggae, Reggae. Asians were lost, they weren't accepted by whites, so they drifted into the black culture, dressing like blacks, talking like them, and listening to reggae. But now *Bhangra* has given them 'their' music and made them feel that they do have an identity. No matter if they are Gujaratis, Punjabis or whatever, – *Bhangra* is Asian music for Asians.   *(Dewan 1988, 8)*

This acknowledgement of internal divisions is widened to include a critique of 'racism' identified within the Asian *community* itself by Kuljit Bhamra, probably the most thoughtful producer of Bhangra records during the 1980s; his analysis again refers to Afro-Caribbeans in validating 'their' word 'roots':

I think people maybe felt the need to identify themselves, and in order to do that a medium was needed, and that medium was *Bhangra*. There is always this roots feeling, and people will always want to know where they came from: we are a different colour, we are from a different country originally, so where do we fit in? The Southall Riots made me aware of this, as they did others. – Racism exists between societies, within societies, and within cultures, but the whole of the Asian society is taking part in *Bhangra* because there is always this need for a roots feeling ... There really is a need to stay together and be amongst your own birds of a feather owing to racism, and *Bhangra* music has provided [for] that need.

(Ghazal and Beat 1988a, 14)

Bhamra makes several points about *Asian culture* that are worth noting. It is defined in contradistinction both to Afro-Caribbean and white cultures, and it is called not only a *culture*, but a society. As both *culture* and society, it must overcome racism within and racism outwith by unity. This unity is distinctive from that of the other *cultures* or societies and shared between elders and youth by force of their common roots. Bhamra's condensed comment throws into relief the most tricky of questions. If Asian *culture* and society are, as yet, also divided within, then how far should youth go in validating the roots they share with their parents, and how far should they turn against the internal divisions rooted in their parents' pre-emigration cultural heritages? Mac, lead vocalist of the group Dhamaka, echoes the contradistinction of *Asian culture* to both Afro-Caribbean and white *cultures* in the context of defending 'Daytimers', that is, Bhangra discos that youths attend while pretending to their parents that they are at school:

Daytimers reinforce our culture and values, girls dress in sulwaars [*salwaar-kamiiz*, the traditional dress of Punjabi women], boys can come in with their turbans and get no hassle. The music is our music, and it's their show, not a goray [*gore*, lit. 'whites'] gig or a kale [*kale*, lit. 'blacks'] show. Do parents want for kids to go out to *gora* shows? Would they rather have Asian kids disowning and abandoning their culture, to become the Sharons and Garys of tomorrow?

(Ghazal and Beat 1988b, 13–14)

Most South Asian Southallians do not want their children to neglect school any more than they want them to lose their *cultural* distinctiveness. Yet this *cultural* distinctiveness is defined, by most parents, not with regard to a shared 'Asian identity' or even the reassuring sight of Punjabi clothes, but with regard to their own, pre-emigration, traditions. These have no use for a category of *Asian culture*, as if Sikhs, Hindus, and Muslims, Punjabis, Gujaratis, and Bengalis were 'the same'. Yet this is precisely what growing numbers of teenage Southallians wish to see emerge among themselves. They tend, by an overwhelming majority, to marry within their own *communities* of religion, as well as caste; those who do not, tend to leave Southall. Yet the discovery of an *Asian culture* and *community* among the young presents a first example of the processes by which *culture* and *community* become objects of debate and terms of contestation.

Questioning *Asian culture*: socialist and feminist networks

South Asian Southallian parents may well have enough on their hands in dealing with youths who describe their *culture* as *Asian*. Yet this is far from the only case in which *culture* and *community* become the verbal sites of cultural contestation. The very term *Asian culture* can be used to disown traditions and customs that many Sikhs, Hindus, and Muslims consider as sacrosanct. The socialist and feminist networks which will be described below are local minorities; yet there are several reasons why they deserve ethnographic attention. To start with, it is decidedly strange to read so many community studies in which no one local seems capable of fundamental dissent and everyone seems engaged in reproducing the same, indiscriminately shared, ethnic culture. The lacuna is a direct result of the assumption of cultural uniformity which underlies the dominant discourse. Secondly, I take it as read that socialist or feminist convictions can establish alternative cultures, that is, comprehensive systems of meaning-making with and about 'others'. Finally, even relatively small networks of dissenters can influence ideas of *culture* and *community* prevalent around them, as is shown, for instance, in Pryce's (1979) exceptionally pluralist community study of Afro-Caribbeans in Bristol. As the data will indicate, the counter-cultures of Southall socialists and feminists contribute to the agenda that Southallians at large have to face. In the present case, these agenda are concerned with a critique of *Asian culture* from what the dominant discourse would call within, and I shall review the responses by Southallians in the section after this.

The Southall Monitoring Group is an initiative which provides support and case work for victims of racially motivated violence, runs workshops and public campaigns, and monitors the activities of police as they affect minorities. Funded by local-government grants, its two or three salaried workers and their voluntary helpers are widely known for their effective public-relations work. Their network of supporters includes Southallians of all ethnic and religious *communities*, and the political orientations they share are broadly left and sometimes Marxist. This orientation necessitates a reassessment of 'traditional' *cultures* and their heritage. Thus, the group's full-time coordinator takes issue with the idea of 'preserving Asian culture': does this project, he asks, 'also include the preservation of practices such as dowry deaths, sati (bride burning), killing of "untouchables", retention of the caste system?' (*The Gazette*, 5 August 1988, 10.)

Such criticism of 'traditions' is seen by many South Asian Southallians as discrediting their *culture* in an already hostile environment, and the political dilemma it poses is obvious enough. It appears even more clearcut when Asians are not only the victims of racist attacks, but are themselves among the perpetrators of other violent acts, some directed against women.

A partly overlapping network of Southallian socialists and feminists supports a group named Southall Black Sisters which is pledged to confront these issues. Organizationally, it resembles the Monitoring Group, in that it relies on local-government grants to pay three salaries and the cost of running classes and pursuing case work for women victims of domestic violence. Unlike the Monitoring Group, Southall Black Sisters face the problems of reassessing their *community*'s cultural heritage in two sharply defined ways. One is related to the commitment openly to confront traditional cultural tenets, the other to their self-appellation as 'Black'.

The problem of critiquing *Asian culture* would be easier, of course, if South Asian Southallian feminists could limit their criticism to a populist chastising of individual violators; yet a feminist analysis obliges them to challenge institutions seen as fundamental to many Southallians' *culture*, such as arranged marriages and the dowry system:

within the Asian community our priorities remain to challenge head-on practices such as domestic violence, arranged marriages, the dowry system and sexual abuse in the family. If we do not confront these patriarchal structures and forces we will be guilty of colluding with them.   *(Southall Black Sisters 1986, 2)*

Such open criticism of 'traditional' *culture* is apt to incur the wrath of established *community leaders* intent upon the good reputation of 'their' *communities*. Thus, Southall's most powerful South Asian *community* organization, the Indian Workers' Association, addressed a letter to the Borough Council responsible for funding both the Black Sisters and the Monitoring Group. I quote from a leaked copy which I consider authentic, and have taken the liberty of italicizing passages that carica-ture the dominant discourse:

We *on behalf of the community* would like to inform you that both these groups play a negative role through their activities in Southall ... their *whole life style*, activity, and involvement is totally *alien* to the *customs, language, tradition* and *culture* of *the* black community.   *(my italics)*

The dilemma of the two sides here facing each other is rooted in the dominant discourse itself. *Community leaders* working on the premise of having to represent whole ethnic-cum-cultural *communities* must underpin their efforts by demanding and gaining respect for the *culture* concerned. This *culture* must be represented as a monolithic body of life-styles and convictions hallowed by custom and shared among all their constituents. Those, however, whose culture entails a re-assessment of the status quo, and implies an appreciation of culture as continually remade, must then be disowned. They are, in effect, declared 'aliens' in relation to the reified *culture* that *community leaders* are supposed to represent. The dilemma of the other side is equally poignant. Those whose chosen culture of conviction does not allow them to endorse some of their ascribed *culture's* traditions and values, must say so even in the face of a general public that may well be ignorant, lacking in respect, and ill-intentioned. The tensions documented in a letter such as this are far more than the result of personal animosities or local-level politicking. They are an index of a dialectic that applies more widely between *culture* as reified in the dominant discourse, and culture performed, in this case consciously, as a lived process. 'Our lives', as one of the Black Sisters writes, 'will not be defined by community leaders. We will take up our rights to determine our own destinies, not limited by religion, culture, or nationality' (Sahgal 1990, 24). It is not my intention here to play one lot of Southallians against another. I have sympathy for both sides, not merely because I am liberal and white, but because both sides struggle against odds determined by others. Just as the Southall Black Sisters face being cast out of the certified ethnic fold, the established *community leaders* face a dominant discourse that obliges them to deliver culturally homogeneous *communities*.

The very delineation of such communities, however, forms part of the Southall Black Sisters' political agenda. Like many other groups allied with the anti-racist movement of the 1980s, Southall's feminists and socialists regard themselves, for the most part, as members of a comprehensive 'Black *community*'. The term 'Southall Black Sisters' in fact dates back to an informal network of both Afro-Caribbean and South Asian Southallians who, from 1983, received local government grants to run a 'Black Women's Centre' and refuge. Three years later, however, a group led by three South Asian women seceded from the larger group on account of personal, strategic, and ideological differences. Which of the two groups held the right to call itself 'Black Sisters' continued to be a point of bitter contention for several years. Over the course of my fieldwork, the secessionist group succeeded in securing the name, managed to find independent premises, and induced local government to split its grant evenly between the two rival associations. Resentments, however, remain bitter between the two groups, and the traumatic split continues to demonstrate the ideological and cultural difficulties involved in reassessing one's *community* and *culture* in the light of what might be called a new culture of conviction. These reassessments, however, also have tangible consequences for Southallians at large. *Culture* and

community have, in the discourse of Southallians themselves, become the
verbal sites on which one fights battles of meaning. That these battles
matter is shown by the variety and ardour of Southallians' responses.

Contesting political *community*: 'Are Asians Black?'

When Southallians who maintain cultures of conviction question the
value of *Asian culture*, they incur the wrath of *community leaders* intent
upon protecting 'the good name' of the *communities* they are to represent. Very often, the matter ends there, thanks to the imbalance of
resources between the protagonists of the dominant discourse and the
pioneers of an altogether different one. It so happened, however, that my
fieldwork coincided with a burst of public debate about the very question that Southall's socialists and feminists had so far deliberated only
among themselves. The ensuing controversy made it conspicuous that
communities and their relationship to *culture* are objects of negotiation
and argument, and it shows how both self-identification and recognition
as *communities* are matters of conscious, and sometimes fierce, contestation.

On the face of it, the controversy presented a conflict over words,
concerned with the question whether Asian settlers in Britain should be
called, and call themselves, Black, the term most commonly associated
with settlers from the Caribbean and Africa. The identities at stake,
however, were not merely ethnic, but political in a peculiar and cultural
in the most comprehensive sense. The use of 'Black' as a term to subsume
both the Asian and the African-Caribbean *community* emerged from an
alternative variant of the dominant discourse.

The idea that all citizens disadvantaged on the basis of their dominant
ethnic-cum-cultural classification form a single community united under
the term 'Black' as its 'political colour' had emerged among political
activists of radically anti-racist convictions. The wider political background is summarized most lucidly by Modood (1988) who recalls:

Over the last few years a consensus has developed amongst race equality professionals and activists that the term "black" should be used to describe people who
are unfavourably treated in British society because of their colour. While this
idea originated with the Left, particularly with the Black Section movement in
the Labour Party, it has now acquired commonplace public usage. The argument
behind this use of 'black' is that it provides the means of effecting a unity between
very diverse, powerless minorities that is necessary for an effective anti-racist
movement. The argument is thought so decisive that it is rare, at least in print,
to see it critically considered.   *(Modood 1988, 4)*

This rare breach of taboo occurred when a major West London weekly newspaper published an article written by a Community Relations Officer working in Hounslow, the London Borough adjoining Southall to the south and a place where many South Asian Southallians aspire to move. The article called for a determined campaign to ensure that South Asians be classified by their culture as 'Asians', rather than subsumed under the term 'Black':

Time for the silent majority to speak out:
BLACKS – THE NAME THAT BETRAYS OUR PEOPLE'S CULTURE

Asians ... contribute a great deal to the life of this country. However, there still is a lack of security. Asians are not quite sure they are accepted for what they are ... But now a threat is coming from those who Asians would expect to be their friends and allies ... They have been exploited by politicians and race relations professionals who want to imply that all Asians should march behind them under a single banner as 'blacks'. A silent majority of Asians are deeply offended by this, but until now they have not spoken.

In opposing this use of the word 'black' I am not in any way attacking or claiming superiority over Afro-Caribbeans or any other of the groups who want to be known by this name ...

For example, they [the Hounslow Borough Council] set up a meeting for 'black' women and were surprised when very few Asians turned up ... Asians are proud of their background, culture and way of life and would therefore like to be referred to as Asians ...

Often the term black is used to mean Afro-Caribbean only, and then in the same breath to include Asians – even Chinese. This creates the impression that Afro-Caribbeans are the real blacks, while Asians are somehow second-class blacks ...

Asians will not feel fully accepted if they are called by a strange name ... A community under the wrong name is like a book under the wrong title, a source of much confusion and little knowledge.   (The Gazette, *22 July 1988, 10)*

This comprehensive use of the term 'Black' was the language policy of the Ealing Borough Labour Party and the Council administration controlled by it, just as it had previously been the policy of the Greater London Council. Within a fortnight of local publication, the author was asked by West London's 'Senior Community Relations Officers' Forum' to face a vote of no confidence or tender his resignation from the professional group. A press statement released by the caucus argued that his views 'perpetuate stereotypes of African, Afro-Caribbean and Asian people. The discussion on whether Asian people and others could come under the umbrella term "black" was argued more than a decade ago. We find it disturbing, dangerous and divisive that it is raised now, at a time when anti-racist work is under attack' (*The Gazette*, 5 August 1988, 10).

The article, however, galvanized the Readers' pages of the local weekly for some time to come, and encouraged Southallians to give vent to their assessments of the relations between Afro-Caribbeans and South Asians. The language issue had first confronted a large number of Southallians when an Ealing Borough survey of schools had asked students to identify themselves as 'Black/Caribbean', 'Black/Asian' or 'Black/other'. Many 'Asian' students, as well as most parents, had been confused and at times tangibly alienated by the language policy imposed on them. There was thus considerable public interest in the controversy, and contributors were not limited to *community leaders* alone.

In reviewing the range of published contributions, I shall be guided not only by sorting positions into pro and con, but also by recognizing the enormous variety of considerations brought to bear on the question of a Black *community*. Many Southallians were plainly unfamiliar with the logic of using 'Black' as a 'political colour', and some saw the word itself as having negative connotations for several reasons. Given this gulf between local usages and anti-racist political intentions, a number of Southallians took to pointedly pragmatic approaches in order to resolve this apparent incommensurability. These, however, had to be seen within the context of *communities* competing for civic resources, and this context itself provided arguments, not only for, but also against the anti-racist language convention.

The lack of familiarity with the rationales for using 'black' as a 'political colour' is exemplified in this response from a Muslim Southallian who assumes that 'black' is merely a blanket colour term to subsume all populations who are not white:

They are called black because they are grouped together with the Africans and West Indians on the basis of the pigment of their skin which is different from the native Europeans, [even] though some Asians have fair complexions.

(The Gazette, 26August 1988, 11)

This lack of familiarity with the political logic proposed by the anti-racist strand of opinion was common in my experience. It is entirely understandable. As an accepted technical term even for people of African extraction alone, it reached Britain late and from the United States. Until well into the 1960s, American sociologists described African-Americans as 'negroes' and would have found the demotic 'Black' an offensive term. Only the Black Power and Black Consciousness movements decided to adopt as a self-appellation what hitherto had been a term of deprecation. South Asians in Britain can hardly be expected to be aware of this

American-inspired use of 'Black' as the 'proper' term even for people of African extraction.

On the contrary, the term 'Black', just like its Punjabi equivalent *kala*, is perceived by many South Asian Southallians as rude when used as a personal label or face to face. Many of my acquaintances in Southall preferred the term 'coloured' when they meant Africans or Afro-Caribbeans: children may have done so because of its phonetic similarity to *kala*, the term that parents might have used in private. Many adolescents, and at least six of my friends with a tertiary education, used the term 'coloured' as a matter of course to refer to Afro-Caribbeans and Africans, but not to South Asians.

There is thus an obvious incongruence between 'Black' in the post-1968 North American sense, 'Black' in the anti-racist sense, and 'Black' in the sense given to the term by many South Asian Southallians. The latter, indeed, can still be subject to the South Asian association of dark skin with low caste. This, too, helps to understand the reluctance of many South Asian Southallians to use the term to designate themselves, and, with the best of intentions, to shy away from using it about others. That this argument carries emic force is shown by a writer of low caste who embraces the term 'Black' precisely in order to protest against the caste system:

I am a Hindu, a harijan (untouchable) and black. I am leaving Southall but would like to comment on Inder Singh Uppal's 'Asian' article. He writes of 'our people' yet insists on calling them 'Asians'.

An Asian can be an Inyuk from the north, a Mongol from the east, a Yemeni Jew from the west or a Maori from the south –, what common culture have they?

Not the culture of the majority of the peoples of the Indian sub-continent. Their culture is varna, the designation of people by colour and the basis of the caste system.

When the Aryan racists invaded the sub-continent they repressed the brown-skinned Dravidians (also incomers) and the indigenous black proto-Australoids. The Aryans developed the caste system with four classifications, and krsna-varna (black) was the colour of all the people in the lowest caste.

For one of our people to call himself black is to admit to being a sudra (the lowest caste). Indians identify each other by caste – Brahmin, Ksatriya, Vaisya or Sudra – never Asian.

Inder Singh Uppal is right with his headline 'Blacks: the name that betrays our culture'. I am one of the betrayed indigenous blacks – my shadow can defile the food of a higher caste Hindu and my consolation is [that] the shadow of those other untouchables, Europeans, does the same.

This is written, using the words of Inder Singh Uppal, 'in pursuit of fairness and enlightenment'. The Gazette should run some articles on caste in Southall and what specifically is the culture of 'our people'.

K K Chamar
Villiers Road
Southall.
(The Gazette, 5 August 1988, 11)

The writer gives as his family name the designation of an 'untouchable' caste; I am not entirely convinced that the letter is authentic, and sometimes suspect that it may have been planted by a protagonist of 'black as a political colour'. Be that as it may, its critique of 'Asian' as the name of a 'culture', as well as its criticism of certain South Asian heritages, accords well with the anti-racist discourse as evidenced in the following contribution:

Black is a political colour. It arose from the struggles against colonialism and then developed through the struggles against racism in British society ... In Britain, from the Fifties onwards, Asian and Afro-Caribbean people have had to unite in their fight against injustice and violence, wherever it arose, in housing, at workplaces, in schools or on the streets. The struggles were organised ones and took the form of community organisations, defence committees and self help projects. The whole history of Southall is a testament to this.

(The Gazette, 5 August 1988, 10)

Later in his letter, the writer outlines the present-day threat to this united struggle, and hints at the political paradigm within which his political analysis makes sense: one of citizens divided by a class society and manipulated by the state:

By the Seventies the organisations of self-reliance were being eroded by the state. Black struggle was 'ethnicised' – reduced to its individual components: West Indians, Indians, Pakistanis, Irish etc. Simultaneously, the black middle classes began to move up in the system, occupying positions of power and authority in the race relations industry and local government. Another category of 'representatives' was created, that of community leaders. Their position was legitimised by their role as mediators between the black community and the state.

(The Gazette, 5 August 1988, 10)

This political analysis is linked with cultural concerns in two ways. Firstly, it is attributed to a unitary 'Black' solidarity that migrants in Britain preserved their cultural heritage:

The usage of the term Black empowered the different black communities. It meant unity and strength. *It* gave us the confidence to retain our own identity and culture – language, religion, art, music and customs.

Secondly, there is an explicit disavowal of what might be called 'traditional' culture, for it is thought both divisive and unjust:

What does Asian mean? ... Tamils? Hindu Punjabi or Muslim Punjabi? We share the same continent but we do not have a common culture. In fact, Mr Uppal is referring to ... Punjabi culture. He talks of the necessity of preserving it. Does he then also include the preservation of practices such as dowry deaths, sati (bride burning), killing of 'untouchables', retention of the caste system?

(The Gazette, *5 August 1988, 10)*

The cultural frame of reference for this text is clearly not an Asian or a Punjabi *culture*. Rather, it is a political culture shared by socialists in the widest sense: internationalist in outlook, supra-ethnic in aspirations, and class-orientated to a greater or lesser degree. The status and indeed aspiration of this framework as a culture in its own right is also expressed in this short excerpt from a speech at a conference sponsored by Southall's Indian Workers' Association:

We define Black as a political colour. It is an education, an experience, and above all it locates us structurally. We as black people are offering a new definition of culture; commonality of experience.   *(Yabsley 1990, 59)*

Socialism is not a cultural framework, of course, which most Southallians operate in their daily lives or in their explicit value systems and beliefs. South Asian, Afro-Caribbean, or white, most are even less likely to be convinced by exalted rhetorical exertions such as these:

I am writing with great concern about the recent regrettable trend amongst some fellow Asian citizens towards identifying ourselves as a group politically separate from our Afro-Caribbean brothers and sisters.

The history of Southall has proved the point that without unity, our community will remain powerless to challenge the racism black people continue to face in this country. The term "black" has less to do with colour than it has to do with a common experience of oppression and injustice.

To drop that term, therefore, is effectively to give ammunition to those racially hostile elements in society who still uphold the belief in divide and rule.

To be addressed as a black person is, for me, neither an error of judgement nor a term of insult, but a re-affirmation of my identity as a citizen of the UK.

(The Gazette, *5 August 1988, 11)*

What is clear from both advocacies of the term is the enormous gulf that separates them from the cultural heritages, as well as the down-to-earth West London culture, of those they wish to speak for. It appears that 'Black' as a 'political colour' and 'black' as a colour of skin form part of two incommensurate discourses.

To bridge the gulf between them requires a mixture of equivocation and pragmatism as evidenced in the following contribution by an established moderate *community leader*. In this view, a comprehensive use of the term 'Black' does not require a critique of *Asian culture* as such or the formulation of an alternative, embracing, post-immigration socialist culture. Although it advocates more than mere political alliance and it does embrace the comprehensive use of 'Black', it none the less speaks of 'categorization', rather than identity:

The word black used for Asians, West Indians and Africans in this country is not our creation but comes from the racial attitude of the host community. The words wogs and niggers were used for those coming to this country. In my experience of 31 years of community service, we are categorised as blacks not only on the basis of the colour of the skin, but on the basis of our status in the society. We are disadvantaged, discriminated against and an under-privileged community. As long as we do not enjoy equal status and equal opportunities, our common interest lies in our unity and common struggle.

(The Gazette, *5 August 1988, 11)*

Even this stance, however pragmatic it might appear, is unlikely to be endorsed by most Southallians. The following letter, written by the President of a Sikh temple in Hounslow, may be unusually robust in tone, but reflects what the large majority of my Punjabi neighbours made of the controversy:

It is only us who can decide what we should call ourselves and not a handful of activists who have no respect for our culture and way of life. We have nothing against blacks. We claim no superiority or inferiority over them. We are keen to put our best into society, but can only do so if we are allowed to maintain our self respect and our cultural dignity. Surely that is not by calling us blacks, a word quite alien to us and one we will not acknowledge ... We are Asians, we will stay Asians, and integrate with the rest of society as Asians and not as blacks.   (The Gazette, *9 September 1988, 5)*

It is not possible to say how far this statement might be endorsed by the majority of Southallians. Given what I heard over the years, however, I was surprised at the result of a telephone 'vote' on the question, phrased clearly as: 'Should Asians be called Black?' Viewers of 'Network East', a weekly 'programme for Asians' then broadcast by BBC 1, were asked, on 12 March 1989, to phone in their opinions. The result announced a week later read:

> Total phone calls received: 3,132
> Callers endorsing the term: 1,182
> Callers rejecting the term: 1,950

The fact that as many as 40 per cent of callers endorsed the term 'Black' for 'Asians' seemed most unexpected to me, given prevalent opinions in Southall and assuming that all callers were of South Asian backgrounds. It is impossible to gauge whether the television audience was more representative of South Asian opinion in Britain than Southallians might be. Modood, in the article referred to earlier, intuits that:

Of course some Asians, including prominent figures, do accept the term black of themselves. But others don't. The largest group is, perhaps, that which knows that society now refers to them as black, and tolerates this while studiously avoiding referring to themselves as black. Then there is the group that feels polit-ically obliged to talk of themselves as black. They see that their political cham-pions, sponsors and other sympathisers, talk of them in this way and expect them to do so too. Finally, there is the group of Asians to whom it simply has not occurred that when local authorities, politicians, or media speak of blacks, (as in job advertisements which say 'applications from black people are welcome'), that they are being referred to. They can still be found in large numbers in areas such as Brent [the London borough adjoining Ealing]. Their own understanding of themselves and of other groups is so different from the assumptions of the local public vocabulary, that those assumptions do not even register as possibilities within their framework of understanding. *(Modood 1988, 5)*

I suspect, although there are no data to prove or disprove it, that a very similar situation pertains in Southall. The linguistic conventions and indeed prescriptions of race-relations professionals and activists emanate from a culture that is not widely shared, understood, or even known among most Southallians.

Interestingly, the only time that I heard a spontaneous self-identifica-tion as 'Black' outside of the context of a political debate occurred during the first meeting, in my house, of Farouque, a man in his late twenties who was born in Mauritius, grew up in Leeds, and identified himself as a devoted Muslim and an 'Asian', with Narinder, a young Sikh Southallian. Describing his new job as a hospital porter in West London, Farouque explained:

At first the job was great, a really cushy number ... Then they gave me this ... bleeper, and now they're constantly bleeping me all over the place, for all sorts of stuff. I'm the only – sort of – black guy there, you see, and all these white cunts are sitting there and watching TV!

In this context of discrimination, the term 'Black' offers itself as the word for 'their', the whites', perception of 'us'. To be identified as 'Black' helps not only to describe, but also to explain the fact of discrimination. Farouque does not trace this to being the only 'Asian guy' in the work-place, which was also the case. Others thought of him as 'sort of – Black', and this is why they took to discrimination. By the same token, to be abused on the grounds of being Asian or a Muslim, identities that Farouque, like many others, is proud of, would be far more threatening and insulting than to be ill-treated because one is, or is thought to be,

'Black'. That aspect of one's social identity that is subject to discrimination, is 'black'. This perception is a long way from thinking that one 'is' black in any simple sense, or indeed that one is anything like an Afro-Caribbean, a Hindu, or a Jew. The same person who calls himself 'black' in one context, may in another blame the hostility of whites on the misbehaviour of 'blacks'.

The local controversy has shown evidence of unfamiliarity with the logic of 'Black as a political colour', unease among South Asians with the term 'Black', and the complication of both factors by an association of dark skin and low caste. Further, it has highlighted the incommensurability of anti-racist and local discourses, and the pragmatic solution advanced by some, and dismissed by other *community leaders*.

That the controversy is not a disinterested debate about words, but part of a tangible, and far from symbolic, battle over scarce resources claimed for *communities*, is clear from contributions from both South Asian and Afro-Caribbean Southallians. Thus, the Vice-Chair of a Southall Asian Parents' and Governors' Association writes:

As we had always feared, we find that the Asian people are discriminated against at every place and level. When Ealing Labour Party talks about Black people, it only means Afro-Caribbean people. The same can be said of the Race Equality Committee, who gear most of their work and public functions to the Afro-caribbean community ... What is most worrying is that the majority of the newly created [Council] jobs in the last two years have gone to the Afro-Caribbean candidates, although they are a very small minority compared to the Asian population in the borough.
(The Gazette, *5 August 1988, 11*)

A similar note of rivalry is sounded also by a Sikh writing from one of the town's temples, known at the time for the political support that some of its leaders gave to the movement for an independent Sikh state in the Punjab:

Asian people feel that their strength is being used by bracketing them with black people, but when it comes to the allocation of resources and jobs, most of it goes to the Afro-Caribbean community. This is why they feel that they must assert their own identity as Asian people and demand a fair share of resources and jobs ... We are not against Afro-Caribbeans but we feel the Labour Party is giving everything to them and actively discriminating against Asian people.
(The Gazette, *5 August 1988 11*)

The Labour Party and the Borough Council are not distinguished in these protests at second-class treatment meted out to South Asians; nor indeed could they have been. For the Labour Party had, at the time, unchallengeable control of the Council, and the leading councillors were well known for their radical stand on anti-racist policies.

Significantly, such misgivings about the Council engaging in preferential treatment were mirrored among Afro-Caribbeans. Among political activists, the fact that the Race Equality Unit established by the newly elected Labour Council comprised only South Asian employees was often quoted as proof positive of this discriminatory treatment. The Preface to the brochure of the Marcus Garvey Centenary celebrations in Southall contained similar misgivings:

The present labour administration came into office with a manifesto of equal opportunities for women, black people and other minorities in our community. It is now one full year since the election of that administration and although things have improved on certain fronts for the Afro-Caribbean community ... The fact remains that our communities still receive less assistance than any other ...

The creation of the race equality unit should have set the tone for positive changes in the unfair employment practices not only in the council but in the community as a whole, however from the offset the Caribbean community was not invited to play any constructive role in the setting up of this unit and one year later the Race Equality Unit have not taken steps to employ Afro-Caribbean people in any key positions. This is most disappointing and could be seen as willfull neglect ... The employment of Asian people in key posts is most welcome but should this be at the expense of the Caribbean community once again. This could only lead to greater division in our community, therefore we challenge the council to take steps towards real equal opportunity in our Borough.   *(Jabal 1987)*

It can thus be Afro-Caribbeans themselves who deny the legitimacy of South Asians claiming a 'Black' identity; the claim can be viewed, not as a sign of solidarity, but as an opportunist ploy in the pursuit of public resources. The point is made most clearly by a Rastafarian feminist activist:

Asians call themselves 'black' or 'coloured' when it suits them ... I don't mind them calling themselves 'coloured', but they do it for political reasons.

(Yabsley 1990, 66)

These reasons are judged here to be political in the lowest, rather than the acceptable, sense of the word. South Asians using the term are suspected of jumping on the band-wagon of emancipation that Afro-Caribbeans built and got rolling.

Underlying this suspicion is the notion that Afro-Caribbeans are politically more experienced, seasoned, and determined. When evidence is cited for this view, it often refers to the counter culture of Reggae and Dub music, to the less compromising attitude and styles of Afro-Caribbean youth, to the old tradition of the anti-colonial Black movement, to the culture hero Marcus Garvey whose centenary in 1987 was celebrated in Southall, and, most commonly, to the longer and earlier experience of racial discrimination in Britain. The latter point is connected to the 'Black or Asian' controversy by an Afro-Caribbean part-time youth worker in his late twenties:

Asians don't want to be 'black' because white people have always put down West Indian people ... They are the next lot coming in, and they don't want the same ... Asians haven't lived here for as long as West Indians; few Asians have been here for twenty-five years, most West Indians have.   *(Yabsley 1990, 67)*

Both the scepticism about South Asian politicians' and activists' motives in using the term 'Black', and the claim to a more advanced culture of resistance are endorsed in the acutely dialectical assessment by the Afro-Caribbean musician and music campaigner introduced already in connection with the Dominion Centre story. In an interview with Hundleby, he, too, suspects opportunism in South Asian activists' use of the comprehensive term; yet he also shows how locally the comprehensive term has weakened, rather than strengthened, his hand in negotiating for the interests of the Afro-Caribbean minority:

Five years ago, if you said 'Black', everyone would know that you were talking about Afro-Caribbean people. Nowadays, you have to state: 'Afro-Caribbean', you have to be quite specific when you're talking about them. This makes things harder, it helps no-one. It means you have to be divisive, you have to stay 'Afro-Caribbean', you can't speak for a community any more.

Q.:   Because of the use that's been made by Asians of the term 'Black'?
A.:   Yeah – [*chuckles*] – when it suits them.
Q.:   For example?
A.:   They command such authority cos of the Southall Riots and the repercussions of that. It was never expected that a predominantly Asian community would riot. It was always something that was reserved for the Afro-Caribbeans. It meant that politicians on all levels of politics had to look, and look seriously, at their policies. And that gave organizations like SYM [Southall Youth Movement] which is basically a boys' club, so much clout and power. And [gave] IWA [the Indian Workers' Association] – which should be just a union! – [chuckles] immense powers.   *(Hundleby 1987, Appendix iv, 5)*

The description of the semantic shift and the loss, rather than gain of influence that it is judged to have brought Afro-Caribbeans appear paradoxical, especially when one considers the local circumstances. The speaker implicitly credits the clout of Southall's South Asian politicians and actvists to the 'Southall riots' of 1979, in which Afro-Caribbeans, such as the activists of Peoples Unite, played a prominent part. In statements like this, it is clear that to speak of any simple competition or rivalry between Afro-Caribbean and South Asian Southallians would be to miss the point. 'We're tied to each other, back to back, and struggling for fuck's sake to get freedom', is how a close friend once put it to me. It matters little, given his simile, whether he was of one perceived ethnic group or the other.

To assess the public controversy, and some of the private voices overheard in its course, two things seem worth recalling. Firstly, the question was phrased, on both sides, as a binary choice. Some Southallians noted this, as Yabsley (1990) points out:

> The debate appears in Southall as an either/or debate; but as an African-Caribbean sociology graduate working in the Dominion Centre in Southall pointed out: 'People are members of several groups ... it depends on the issue as to which loyalty is made at a particular time; it is difficult [even] to predict.'
>
> *(Yabsley 1990, 57–8)*

One of the public contributors, the first of those cited above, made a similar point despite his lack of familiarity with the logic of 'black' as a 'political colour':

> The terms blacks and Asians are valid in different contexts and one fails to understand how their use could affect the political and community unity and racial harmony.   (The Gazette, *26 August 1988, 11)*

Yet most Southallians faced the question: 'Black or Asian?' as it was put to them: as a decontextualized choice. This observation relates to the second point in assessing the controversy: its terms themselves were set and defined for Southallians, rather than by them. Yet Southallians clearly took it seriously and recognized *community* boundaries as matters of argument and contestation. In questioning how *communities* might relate to 'ethnic' identities and the notion of *culture*, moreover, the lines of local debate did not follow any simple ethnic cleavage. There were South Asian Southallians who considered themselves as part of a unified Black *community* and others, very likely the majority, who did not; similarly, there were Afro-Caribbean Southallians who endorsed the new joint *community* and others who distrusted it. The lines of the argument did not follow the cleavages of ethnic differences or reified cultures. The multiplicity of criteria that participants drew upon in their intense debate shows all the more clearly how far the idea of *community* defines part of the problem, rather than offering a descriptive solution, in the negotiation of collective interrelations.

Questioning religious *community*: interfaith networks

If the postulate of a unified black *community* challenges certain assumptions about ethnic and political identifications, the postulate of a *community* that reaches across established religious boundaries challenges the idea of religious *communities* as self-evident and discrete entities. In Southall, this challenge assumes a particular poignancy for two sets of reasons. Given the local constellations, *community* boundaries based on religious allegiance carry enormous weight. One need only recall that the three *Asian communities* in the town divide upon religious lines, and that the culture consciousness of many children fixes upon their religious heritage in order to define *culture* itself. At the same time, Southall is one of the centres, in Britain, of the movement known as 'Interfaith', which propagates a 'community' aimed at uniting all 'people of faith'.

Interfaith can be called a tendency, a movement, or even a religious philosophy, depending upon the intensity of rethinking among its adherents. To approve of Interfaith as a tendency requires little more than an interest in the tenets and experiences of those who believe in other religious creeds. In this minimal way, which is usually called 'Multi-faith' rather than Interfaith, it relies upon cross-cultural curiosity and the liberal desire to develop one's tolerance and understanding of doctrinal differences. Followers with a deeper commitment may go further and value Interfaith worship to widen their experience of faith. They may even acknowledge shortcomings in their own religious heritage. The commonest of these acknowledgements concerns devotional practices. Thus, Christianity may be enriched by stressing the meditational aspect of devotion familiar, for example, from Hindu and Buddhist forms of piety. Beyond these matters of method, Interfaith activities may encourage a culturally relativist appreciation of doctrinal differences. Those, finally, who embrace Interfaith as a philosophy may profess a faith in the Divine that transcends the boundaries of any established religious heritage. Interfaith is thus a renegotiation, more or less daring, of one's own religious heritage in the light of that of other believers. The more committed the adherent's approach, the more clearly it establishes a new spiritual culture and a new cross-religious *community*.

In Southall, the local Interfaith networks combine to produce an unusually well-resourced initiative which, among Christians, can draw upon the support of both the major churches. The Anglican Bishop of Willesden has continued to foster various local groups devoted to interfaith dialogue under the programmatic title 'Christians Aware', and the Roman Catholic 'Westminster Interfaith Programme' provides diocesan funding for a full-time organizer, helpers, and premises in town. Their regular activities range from the educational to the devotional. Mutual knowledge is gained in seminars and lectures about other faiths; shared devotional experiences are fostered through joint sessions of meditation, weekend retreats, and pilgrimages to other places of worship. Within the limits of Christian doctrine, to which I shall return, Interfaith activists devise joint acts of worship that incorporate the symbolic repertoires of several traditions.

The most active non-Christian partners in these initiatives are, notably, the smaller religious congregations, such as the Sikhs of Ramgarhia castes and mainly East African backgrounds; Sikhs of the Nam Dhari tradition whose belief in a continuous line of living Gurus sets them apart from mainstream Sikh traditions; the Ahmadiyya, followers of Ghulam Mirza Ahmad of Qadian whom other Muslims do not regard as fellow Muslims; the Ravidasi congregation of 'untouchable' castes (*chuhra, chamar*); and the local Baha'i. The local movement thus combines two rather unequal sets of parties: on the one hand, the most established Christian churches, each with its tradition of colonial missionization and its perceived social responsibility for the joint welfare of all in the post-migration 'multi-ethnic society'; on the other hand, notably those segments of religious opinion which are branded heterodox by the traditions from which they once seceded. They are thus likely to be more receptive to an understanding of faith which suggests, in a characteristic phrase, that 'the Lamps are many, but the Light is One'.

Certainly, their followers appear rather less worried about the doctrinal difficulties that Interfaith activities raise for many Christians. Thus, the spiritual leader of the Ahmadiyya *community* explained that the 'movement believes that all religious leaders, whatever their faith, were chosen by God' (*The Gazette*, 20 November 1987, 8). Another striking endorsement of Interfaith as a philosophy was given to me by a Nam Dhari in his early twenties:

'Hasn't God created the whole Universe? – Well, obviously, and if you think about it, there's probably other life forms in the Universe, – I mean, we don't know, but it's not *beyond* God, is it. And wouldn't they worship a God that's fashioned after their own kind? And wouldn't God be perfectly happy with that?'

Doctrinal difficulties seem far more pronounced among the Christian Southallians who partake in Interfaith activities. To many of their fellow religionists, they may appear to compromise the essential truth claim of Salvation. Thus, an Evangelical young woman once commented to me upon the Nam Dhari using the apse of a local church for their devotions: 'I think it's dead wrong', this Anglican in her early twenties explained, 'you can't say Christ is the Saviour, and then say that other religions are just as true. I mean, if you're a Christian, you can't say that.' At a more exalted level of doctrinal argument, these difficulties appear in finer language, but they are tangible none the less. Roman Catholics, for instance, are exhorted, by the relevant Papal missive 'Nostra Aetate' of 1965,

> *prudently* and lovingly, through dialogue and collaboration with the followers of other religions, *and in witness to Christian faith and life* to acknowledge, preserve and promote the spiritual and moral goods found among these people, as well as the values in their society and culture.
>
> *(Westminster Interfaith Programme 1990, 2–3, my italics)*

Yet the duty of witness, as here recalled, is a clear reminder of the Christian aim of evangelization. Even episcopal support for Interfaith activities is powerless in the face of orthodox constructions of Scripture. The dilemma was cast into clear relief at the licensing of a new curate in the very church that hosts the Nam Dhari worshippers. Anglican ritual prescribed the following exchanges, no matter how incongruous they appeared to the representatives of other faiths invited to attend:

AREA DEAN: Jesus said, I have been given all authority in Heaven and Earth. Go then, to all peoples everywhere and make them my disciples: Baptise them ... and teach them to obey everything I have commanded you ...

BISHOP: Will you joyfully sacrifice your own pleasure and ambition to bring Christ's gospel to all people?

PRIESTS: I will with God's help.

BISHOP: Will you, the people of this church, share in the work of evangelism? Will you do all in your power so to witness to the living Christ that others may find fellowship with him?

PEOPLE: We will do this with God's help.   *(St George's 1989, 6)*

The continued extraction of such sacred vows helps to clarify that what outsiders may term 'doctrinal' problems are, to insiders, problems of conscience. That matters of conscience may be involved in the creation of a new *community* of believers across faiths, is acknowledged explicitly even by its organizers. Thus the local Interfaith Programme administered by Roman Catholics proposed to run a 'School of Faith' with the aim:

> to explore and study Faith under all its aspects and in all its relations ... In today's world, ... is there an issue more topical, more important, more urgent, that people of faith can take up together *with the freedom of their conscience* and in the shared *peace of their minds and hearts*, than Faith itself?
>
> *(Westminster Interfaith 1989 a, 3, my italics)*

How far the believer can go in embracing another religious tradition is a matter, in this reading, of conscience rather than doctrine. Yet while this individualist approach may make little of doctrinal orthodoxy for its own sake, it must burden the now autonomous believer with judgements of conscience that require scrupulous self-questioning. In the event, even the term 'School of Faith' had to be abandoned for the pale and noncommittal title of an 'Interfaith Awareness Programme' (Westminster Interfaith 1989b, 1).

Matters of conscience, however, need not arise in the pointedly pluralist activities that characterize Interfaith as a tendency. They often appeal to concerns common to 'people of faith' and validated by a wider, and not necessarily theist, public. Among such themes are environmental concerns, biblically phrased as 'Stewardship of the Earth', feminist strands of thought interpreted as 'Woman's Role in God's Plans', and of course political and humanitarian issues such as racism, Apartheid, and poverty in Inner Cities or the Third World. Such a focus on 'issues' serves cross-religious *community*-building in two complementary ways. On the one hand, it strengthens the impression that all religions converge on a shared judgement; on the other, it can acknowledge that the paths to this judgement are distinct to each spiritual tradition. A good example of this complementarity can be seen in an anti-Apartheid leaflet well received by Southallians of the Interfaith *community*:

Hinduism teaches that the Divine is revealed in all people. It rejects Apartheid because it does not recognize the infinite worth of everyone.

Buddhism seeks liberation from suffering by eliminating greed, hatred and delusion. The tragic folly of Apartheid exploitation and oppression is a paradigm of these three roots against which Buddhists struggle.

Sikhism teaches that the Creator is in the created and the created in the Creator. The one true God is within all. Apartheid denies this fundamental principle in practice, and Sikhs are therefore opposed to Apartheid.

Judaism has a strong sense of the evils of racism. Jews have long suffered racist persecution, reaching an obscene climax in the Nazi attempt at genocide. Jews are fundamentally opposed to Apartheid racism with its fascist affinities and practices.

Christianity recognizes that all human beings are made in the image of God. It follows Jesus Christ who identified himself with the poor, oppressed and needy … Christians therefore work and witness against Apartheid.

Islam teaches the equality of all people and demands that equality, justice and mercy be practised … Muslims must 'enjoin what is right and forbid what is wrong' so Islam deplores Apartheid and supports those who struggle against its oppression.   *(Multi-Faith Committee 1989, 7)*

Such appeals to substantive convergence evade the problems of doctrine and conscience that would otherwise stand in the way of forging an Interfaith religious *community*.

Perhaps the most characteristically religious discourse in 'bringing together the people of faith' is that which relies upon symbolic forms shared across doctrinal divides. Interfaith worship often integrates the sharing of food, the handling of devotional objects from other religions, and the ceremonial lighting of candles. Doctrinal limitations apply even to these symbols, of course: Christians may share in the consecrated *prasad* consumed by Hindus and Sikhs; yet they may not in turn share their own consecrated host or wine; Hindus devoted to symbolic worship of the flame (*arti*) do not consider it equivalent to a merely decorative candle. Yet the symbolism of light is singularly accessible across faiths, perhaps because it reflects the ambiguity of 'faith' as the common bond among the Interfaith community. Most of its members are enjoined to profess a substantive 'faith in', yet wish also to acknowledge 'faith as such' as their point of convergence. Likewise, doctrinally orthodox interpretations often equate the light with a named Divinity worshipped in a particular tradition; yet Interfaith congregations can easily see in the shared symbolic form a symbol of Divinity as such.

Developments such as these recall Cohen's (1985) insight that in 'the symbolic construction of community', symbolic forms are often used because of, rather than in spite of, the ambiguity and polyvalence of their meanings to different constituencies. Thoughtful Interfaith activists are fully aware of these ambiguities; yet they are seldom stressed or criticized as such. To do so would indeed run counter to the very object of Interfaith activities, to construct a community of all 'people of faith' that stretches across religious divides.

At first sight, Southall's Interfaith initiatives may appear insufficiently radical in some ways and insufficiently representative in others, to counterbalance the emphasis on religious *communities* that prevails in town. Yet, like the socialist and feminist networks, these minority groupings insert their activities at crucial junctures in the *community* culture surrounding them. Socialists and feminists provided the language in which ethnic ideas of *community* were pitched against political ones; Interfaith networks provide the language in which ideas of religious *community* are questioned in two separate ways. The first of these raises the possibility of one religious *community* composed by all who believe. The second pitches the idea of mutually independent religious *communities* against that of a 'multicultural *community*' of Southallians united in an attitude of 'equal respect for all religious traditions'. This latter contestation about the meaning of *community* appears most tangible and influential in Southallians' views about the religious education of the young.

Contesting religious *community*: convergence, encompassment, and 'multicultural' equality

The contestation of religious meanings attached to the word *community* entails not only questions of faith, but also matters of state. In Britain, religious worship has for long played a role in state education, and English law has, since the introduction of universal schooling, obliged all publicly financed schools to hold daily plenary assemblies of a religious nature. These usually comprise various announcements and admonitions, the singing of a religious or other edifying hymn, and an act of worship according to the teachings of the Church of England or, in denominational schools, the Roman Catholic church or the Jewish faith. In Southall, school assemblies began, over the 1970s, to develop a format derived from the Multi-faith variant of Interfaith ideas. A local pupil described the usual form as it had taken shape over the years: 'Most days, they read us a parable from some religion. Like, very often it's a Buddhist parable, and sometimes a parable from the Bible, or on Guru Nanak's birthday it's a parable from the Guru Granth, or on Holi it's a parable from the Ramayana.' Any acts of prayer were read out in English, with the instruction to 'close your eyes and be silent as we pray'.

One may remark, incidentally, on the effortless use of the word 'parable', probably glimpsed from teachers intent on showing the 'holy stories' of all religions as being generically the same; one may also note the preference extended to Buddhism, a religion with no local constituency but a favourite point of reference for many Interfaith activists from intrinsically theist traditions. Yet this pragmatic solution to holding religious assemblies in schools attended by a 'multi-cultural' variety of students had never, to my knowledge, been questioned. It accorded well, in fact, with the religious expectations of Southall youth. For one thing, and as I have detailed on pages 147–8, young Southallians socialize quite freely across religious *community* boundaries, and our survey respondents overwhelmingly disapproved of single-faith schools. Even if the relevant law had permitted the splitting-up of daily assemblies on religious *community* lines, it would be surprising to see even 10 per cent of local youngsters approving of such a separation.

The context which makes sense of their views, however, is wider. Local youths are raised in a milieu in which different religious *communities* do not only co-exist side by side, but appear to converge in a number of ways. Some of these moments of convergence are orientated on Christian templates, and I shall briefly refer to domestic celebrations at Christmas time, an emphasis on worship on Sundays, and the homogenizing effect of discussing religious tenets in English. Other moments of convergence, more consciously perceived among Southall youth, concern the comparability of religious injunctions and, most importantly perhaps, the idea that different religious teachings might converge upon the same ultimate 'truth'.

Some of the practices on which Southallians of different religions have come to converge have been described elsewhere (Baumann 1992). Many Sikh and Hindu families have adopted celebrations of Christmas; beside the sending of Christmas cards, these often involve seasonal decorations in the home, Christmas parties at schools and offices, and the exchange, on Christmas Day, of wrapped presents among family and friends. Some of these practices are especially for the benefit of children, and I have hesitated to ascribe to them too explicit a religious significance. Suffice it here to say that Hindu and Sikh celebrations of the Christian occasion present a tangible example of a convergence by two traditions upon practices originating with a third.

A less conspicuous moment of convergence, but one which may indeed subtly alter established religious conceptions, is shared congregational worship on Sundays. Southall's four Sikh gurdwaras and two Hindu mandirs all attract large numbers of believers for acts of worship on Sunday, and one may hear complaints that individual worship on other days of the week is in decline. 'Back home you go to the temple when you feel like it', a member of a mandir committee once told me, 'only here, people think that Sunday is Temple Day, and the rest of the week is not'. Such convergences of practices, and perhaps even conceptions, are also implied in standardized English-language glosses which have become commonplace. Religious festivals are most readily glossed in phrases such as: 'Diwali is our Christmas' by Hindu and Sikh Southallians, and 'Eid is our Easter' by their Muslim neighbours. Larson even heard a little Muslim girl wishing for 'Eid eggs'. (Larson 1989, 72). There is, I think, more of conceptual substance in this engaging pun than meets the eye: the English language clearly serves as a point of convergence as much as Christian conventions of Sunday worship or Christmas celebrations do. It is absolutely commonplace to hear young Sikhs speak of the Ten Gurus as 'our gods' or, on the Judaeo-Christian as well as

Muslim model, 'our prophets'. An Imam, a Gyanni and a Pandit are like-wise referred to as readily as 'our priest' or 'their priest'. What may be most interesting about such linguistic convergences is what they imply in more general and cognitive terms. They lend plausibility to the common-sense view that different religions are comparable to each other and, more than that, are transformations of the same basic structure. Given the meta-vocabulary that convergent translations create, each religion has its own peculiar Diwali or Easter, prophets and priests, and its own inventory of a limited set of rules and injunctions. On certain injunctions, of course, they agree: 'It doesn't matter', as a young Sikh explained, 'what religion you're from: it's wrong to kill, and it's wrong to steal things, and you must have some respect.'

With regard to other injunctions, religions can be seen to permutate the same few basic possibilities: 'You see, the Muslims aren't allowed to drink, but they can smoke, and we [the Sikhs] can't smoke, but we can drink. So it's the same thing, only different, innit?' Or: 'The Muslims don't eat pork, and the Sikhs don't eat beef, and the Hindus don't eat meat at all.' The picture of religious variety that emerges from these and the many other comparisons easily offered by schoolchildren and teenagers is effortlessly pluralist: all religions converge upon one matrix of defining features and are thus not only comparable but homologous; and each defines its peculiarity by selecting one or another of a limited common stock of injunctions, be they on diet or fasting, days of devotion, marital or funerary procedures. If young Southallians were trained as anthropologists of religion, their first choice of paradigm might well be a morphological variety of structuralism. Religious injunctions, at any rate, are compared quite spontaneously as mere transformations of the same basic structure. This belief in a convergence of all religions upon approaching the same tenets can go even further, as the following inter-view excerpt may show:

Q.:   So that [i.e. multi-faith worship at school] doesn't bother you?
HURSH: No; all religions say the same few things.
Q.:   Really? What do they say? Can you –
HURSH: They say: God exists. And he is the creator. And secondly, be good; and then if you are good, you'll have it good, either while you're alive or maybe later.
Q.:   But don't they mean different things when they say God is the Creator?
HURSH: Well yes, God has a different character in each. Like the Muslim God is a very strict God and wants submission. The Christian God is a more kind God and giving and ... and for the Hindus, God is not like a father or a person, but an entity, like Brahma, you know, an entity.

Q.: And the Sikh God?

HURSH: That's not really so clear, because apart from God they believe in their Gurus, and sometimes they think that these are Gods. But that's quite wrong.

Admittedly, it is not quite usual to find young Southallians who are so articulate in their recognition of convergences. My interlocutor, Hursh, was a young man of exceptional intelligence, raised as a Hindu, and preparing to study physics and philosophy after leaving school. I shall return to the exchange below. Yet however far young Southallians may pursue their observations, all but the most restrictively raised acquire a strong sense of 'different religions' being 'about the same thing'. This accords well with the results of our survey quoted above (table 10). Asked to distinguish 'what divides adults' and 'what divides youth' in Southall, the divide of religion was thought more important for adults than for youth.

Yet no degree of convergence observed, or indeed endorsed, by the young can remove the question of religious *community* from the arena of cultural contestation. Most parents in Southall, and certainly not South Asians alone, tend to view religious enculturation as the pivot of *community* enculturation, at least so far as their children are concerned. That religion continues to function as the local *community* marker *par excellence* was brought home to me, fortuitously, during the last year of my fieldwork. The catalyst was a botched attempt to reform English law.

One part of a new 'Education Act (1988)' stipulated that daily school assemblies were to contain 'an act of worship ... of a mainly Christian nature'. The, almost proverbially English, pragmatism of the Southall solution was thus, in effect, declared illegal. True, schools with large minority intakes could apply to opt out of the Christian bias enshrined in the law; but the understandable furore about a newly passed legal prescription of Christian hegemony rendered school assemblies a matter of ethnic and community politics. A condensed example of this contestation could be seen in a one-day conference attended by some thirty Southallians, of which I shall offer a short Case Summary here.

Case Summary: Southallians' models for school assemblies

The one-day conference was sponsored and hosted by the Borough council, which assembled local politicians, civil servants, school teachers, and the representatives of local temples and mosques to deliberate upon their response to the new law. Few of the participants were aware of actual daily practice as it had evolved in Southall schools over the past decade or two. It was assumed without question that daily assemblies had to entail acts of active prayer by at least some of the students assembled, and much of the meeting's energy was thus directed to developing 'models' of how school assemblies should or could be organized. Below, I offer a diagram (figure 2) which summarizes the choices for daily school assemblies that participants came up with or implied in the course of their discussions. As the diagram shows, the thirty or so Southallians identified and supported five 'models' for school assemblies, be they for each faith by itself or for all faiths together. Notably, one further option, namely that school assemblies should be altogether secular, was denied any local support. The suggestion, put forward by an education officer of Afro-Caribbean background, was given short shrift by the assembled Southallians. The civic discourse of secularism was effectively countered by the discourse of multi-culturalism, equally civic in origin: 'minorities' and 'minority cultures', it was said, had to be 'represented' in schools, and they were, for this purpose, equated with religions.

To examine the options put forth, they can be arranged in a sequence from the most particularist, orientated on single-faith assemblies for each religious *community*, to the most pluralist, orientated on Interfaith practices. Thus, Option 1 favours a separate assembly for the adherents of each religion, to be held every day or at least on some days. The argument was phrased with a strong reference to the bond between parents and children: 'Without separate assemblies, we will lose our children', and indeed, 'now that we can have separate assemblies, we will get our children back into the community'. The devotional education of the young, their purity of faith, and their continued commitment to a *community* defined on the basis of religion represented the major rationales for this particularist option.

Figure 2   Southallians' models for school assemblies

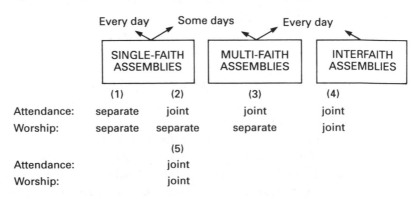

A slightly less particularist model, here called Option 2, envisaged a rota of religiously specific assemblies which should be attended by children of all faiths. Active participation in prayer should be reserved for pupils of the 'host community' on that day, and some insisted that prayers should be spoken in the relevant 'community languages', that is, Punjabi, Hindi, and Urdu or Arabic. In this way, authenticity of religious practice could be combined with a joint attendance which should ensure equal 'representation' for all, as well as an attitude of 'mutual respect'. This option enjoyed almost as much favour as the first, not least perhaps because it could appeal to the civic values of multi-culturalism and the 'representation' of all 'minorities' by means of a rota.

The third option envisaged a multi-faith assembly for all and thus more or less reflected the status quo in Southall schools. Prayers in any one religious tradition should be accompanied by a respectful silence on the part of those brought up in another tradition. This option, strongly orientated toward the values of mutual respect, could be implemented every day, or else as an addition to the single-faith assemblies of Options 1 or 2. It was regarded as a compromise, which entailed the usual drawback of failing to satisfy the advocates at either end of the spectrum.

A full and mutual participation by all children in the prayers of all others constituted the final two options envisaged by Southallians. One, numbered 4 in figure 2, reflects the Interfaith position, a fully joint act of worship, regardless of the traditions to which pupils or prayers belong. It was formulated in direct opposition to the particularist Option 1. While this first option had been justified as a means of retaining, or even regaining, the youngest generation for their parents' religious *community*, the proponent of this Interfaith option passionately disowned the *community* discourse:

We have already lost our children. Your kids are lost already! We have lost the precious time to put controls on our kids. If you want to keep your children, go back [to the subcontinent]! Here, they are lost from the community. They are all in one big society now. All are together in English society. If we now introduce separate groups again, we are condemning our own society!

The assembly's reaction was, for the most part, stunned silence. In the course of the later debate, speakers often returned to this passionate plea, in order to profile their own ideas as more in tune with 'what the community wants'. Yet, surprisingly, joint attendance as well as joint active worship reappeared later in an Option 5, which suggested single-faith assemblies characterized by indiscriminate cross-participation. Though again intended as a compromise, the option failed to draw much support.

Four points might be noted from this brief exposition. An obvious one is the sheer variety of options put forth by a mere thirty or so Southallians. It ranges from the most exclusive particularism to the most inclusive endorsement of partaking in the prayers of all other religions. Secondly, the data have shown the pivotal role that many parents, though certainly not all, continue to assign to religion as a means of anchoring their children in their *community*. Thirdly, a striking feature of the entire day's discussion was the unquestioned assumption that single-faith assemblies and even single-faith acts of worship were possible at all. The deliberations proceeded as if all children were either Sikh, Hindu, Muslim, or Christian; and indeed as if no one had ever heard about Sikhs worshipping in Mandirs or the ambiguities associated with the congregations of Nam Dhari, Ahmadiyya, Ravidasi or, for that matter, Jehovah's Witnesses. The participants were not, of course, unaware of these. Yet the contestation as played out, in this context, was about the claims of religious *communities*. Classificatory anomalies would have endangered the very premises of the dominant discourse, such as they appeared in the more particularist options.

Lastly, perhaps the most striking feature of the discussion was the absence, throughout the day, of any exclusivist truth claims. Even the proponents of particularist assemblies limited their argument to the civic discourse of multi-culturalism in which each *community* was to be 'represented' and none was to be 'made to feel second-class'. Assuredly, the assembly was not a representative sample of Southallians. Yet it included men well known for their confirmed religious convictions and personal forthrightness. Even these spoke in a tone of value-free and pluralist multi-culturalism, as if everyone believed all religions to be equally legitimate and indeed equally true. Recalling the data I collected in contexts other than public debate, it is most unlikely that many of the discussants believed this all of the time. It is not uncommon, at least in private, to cast doubt on the legitimacy of a major religion or, more commonly, a minor subdivision or 'sect'. Furthermore, the organizers of the conference had, of course, followed their mailing list which favoured the members of elected temple committees, rather than the, often itinerant, Holy Men (*sant, guru, pir*) who, on their visits to Southall, re-inspire exclusivist paths to religious truths and contend for followers among those in search of authoritative statements.

Yet, throughout the day, the only reference to religious truths came from a former member of a Sikh gurdwara committee who was aged about seventy and by far the oldest participant. He did not share the other participants' effortless command both of English and of the consciously multi-culturalist turns of speech. Contrary at least to my expectations, he declared himself in favour of both Interfaith and of separate but fully cross-participatory assemblies. In discussing his rationale, I shall leave the confines of this brief case summary.

In calling for children to participate indiscriminately in each others' worship, the aged participant exclaimed: 'I am not more educated man. All I know is One God, One God, One God. *Sat sri akal!* – One God!'

At first sight, this emphatic statement may appear as the most condensed endorsement of religious convergence: the faiths and prayers of all religions converge upon the same ultimate Truth. Yet the truth of this very convergence is encapsulated in the Punjabi words '*sat sri akal*', the central axiom of Sikh orthodoxy from Guru Nanak's writings onwards. Other religions and new practices such as interfaith worship are claimcd, thus, to follow from the very truth on which Sikhism is predicated. The Sikh faith, in other words, is not one set of convictions that needs to be articulated with other sets, but a body of truths that encompasses all other approaches to God, however comprehensive or incomplete.

I have already made use of the notion of encompassment and described it as an intellectual strategy favoured by Hindu Southallians in dealing with the boundary toward Sikhs, especially those of lower castes. As a cognitive strategy, though, it is of course not limited to people raised as Hindus. On the contrary, in discussing specifically religious notions of difference, it combines very usefully with the recognition of convergences. The two dynamics of perceiving convergence and claiming encompassment may indeed reinforce each other, as I have argued elsewhere (Baumann 1994). A telling example is also contained in the young Hindu Southallian's analysis of convergence given above (p. 180). I resume the quotation where, there, I left off:

[HURSH: That's not really so clear, because apart from God they believe in their Gurus, and sometimes they think that these are Gods. But that's quite wrong.]
Q.:   But doesn't this interfaith produce a mish-mash of religions?
HURSH: I suppose it does. But I find that – quite sensible, really. I believe that Jesus is another reincarnation of Brahma, and Guru Nanak is, too. Only Mohammed is not, because he never said he was divine, and Gobind Singh and the other Gurus, – the same thing: Gurus are not Gods, and they never said they were.

What appeared, at first sight, as an unreserved endorsement of religious convergence, has turned, with a minimum of argumentative effort, into a claim of encompassment. Not only does the speaker adjudicate other people's comprehension of their own doctrines, but he explicitly encompasses the founders of two other religions as reincarnations of Brahma, the divine 'entity' of his own faith.

The belief in convergence *with* the 'Other' and the claim to encompassment *of* the 'Other' appear thus as two faces of the same coin. What one dynamic grants, the other claims back. Thus is tolerance of, and more than that, civic equality with the 'Other' reconciled with an over-arching, selectively encompassing 'own' claim to truth. Both of these dynamics, beliefs in convergence and claims to encompassment, can co-exist in the same social arena and indeed the same informants' minds. Under conditions which favour an observable convergence of practices, Southallians are able to postulate a convergence of conceptions among all religions and, at the same time, to claim that their own encompasses the truths of all others. I have given other examples, taken from Muslim and Christian thinking, elsewhere (Baumann 1994) and need not dwell on them here.

In the present context, claims to encompassment are of interest as one of two answers to the recognition of cross-religious convergences. To recognize these convergences, as many younger Southallians do, throws into question the boundaries between religious *communities*: they can be made to appear merely contingent or, more threateningly, superficial. Claims to encompassment avert this danger. In saying that the tradition of one's own religious *community* encompasses the truths of other faiths, one has, paradoxically perhaps, reconfirmed the boundary around one's own. It has been rendered, not so much permeable or relative, as subtly and self-confirmingly expansive.

A second strategy of dealing with religious convergences, or in their absence even with religious difference, is that more commonly pursued in public discussions, including the one I have summarized. It uses the idioms of multi-culturalism, making appeal to the formulaic 'unity in diversity' or the more moralist 'equal respect', and transfers these, orig-inally secular and civic, postulates to religious diversity. In this way, too, the boundedness of religious *communities* as defined by doctrinal markers can be reasserted by implication. What is worth noting, however, is that such indirect reassertions are deemed necessary in the culture of Southallians. If Southall culture relied on the dominant discourse alone, reaffirmations would not be required. What I have argued, instead, is that Southallians' dual discursive competence turns ideas of *culture* and *community*, be they defined on ethnic, political or religious criteria, into matters of cultural contestation. *Communities* are not self-evident collectives, in Southall as probably elsewhere, and *cultures* are not merely the reifiable heritages that the dominant discourse stresses so exclusively.

7

Conclusion

Summary of the argument
The *community* patterning of the demotic discourse
The local persistence of the dominant discourse
The relationship between dominant and demotic discourse
The question of rights

Summary of the argument

There is a discourse that has come to dominate the representation, descriptive as well as political, of people singled out as ethnic minorities. This dominant discourse equates ethnic categories with social groups under the name 'community', and it identifies each community with a reified culture. Chapter 2 has traced how this discourse has been able to achieve hegemony. It is conceptually simple, lends itself to highly flexible applications in both common-sense and policy contexts, and shows an enormous ideological plasticity. Wishing to describe Southallians living in a plural society, rather than reifying their cultures, I could not take this discourse at face value. Instead, chapter 3 asked what, if anything, might constitute the shared culture of Southallians. The answers were ambiguous. Southallians appeared most readily to agree on deprecating their town: it was a place to move out of, and moving out locally was considered moving up socially. This seemed to make sense in the light of economic commonalities that reached across ethnic boundaries. Yet these boundaries were accentuated over decades of *community*-building and had come to dominate the political processes in town. Lacking its own comprehensively civic institutions, the town appeared as a mosaic of separate *communities*, vying with each other for badly needed public resources.

Applying the dominant discourse locally, Southallians most commonly divided their town into five seemingly self-evident *communi-*

ties of *culture*. Chapter 4 therefore reviewed these five *communities* as they were locally recognized, and in so doing followed the assumptions of the dominant discourse. Yet there was already evidence that the equation between *community* and a reified *culture* could, in certain contexts, be disengaged by Southallians themselves. Chapter 5 therefore reviewed each *community* once again.

Disengaging the dominant equation of *culture* with ethnic or religious *community* tended to take a different form in each. Among the Sikh *community*, there were strong dynamics of forging new *communities* of caste; among Hindu Southallians, by contrast, one could observe claims of a Hindu *culture* encompassing people and ideas of other *communities*. Muslim Southallians were clearly aware that the local *community* of believers was divided into a variety of contending *cultures*. Among the *community* of Afro-Caribbeans, one could identify several approaches explicitly aimed at 'finding', and thus consciously creating a new common *culture*, while white Southallians, usually equivocal about their *community* status, cultivated a minority consciousness without explicit reference to a *community culture* and attempted identifications with the *cultures* of surrounding *communities*. All these renegotiations of *culture* and *community* form part of what anthropologists conceive culture to be in the first place: a process of making and remaking collective sense of changing social facts, rather than some reified possession that, in a phrase coined by Yabsley, treats it as the 'tagged and tied luggage of isolated groups' (Yabsley 1990, 135).

In tandem with this first and dominant discourse of culture as the possession of ethnic or religious communities, there thus appeared evidence of a second discourse, which I have called the demotic. Southallians engaged in one or the other, depending upon their judgements of context and purpose. Given this dual discursive competence, the meanings and interrelations of *culture* and *community* could be seen as matters of social contention and, in the anthropological sense, cultural contestation. These contestations were centrally concerned with reaffirming or redefining the meaning of *community*. Examples could be seen in the construction of an *Asian community* with its *Asian culture* by the young; the critique of *Asian culture* by socialist and feminist Southallians who proposed a unified 'Black *community*' instead; and in the redefinition of religious *community* advanced by Southall's Interfaith networks. I have shown these redefinitions debated by Southallians at large and described how these debates contest the very meaning or meanings of culture and community. Several questions arise from the data. The first must ask why, and how far, the demotic discourse might differ from one *community* to another. The second asks why the demotic discourse of culture as process and *community* as creative project does not, in Southallians' eyes, invalidate the dominant discourse altogether. This will allow for a clearer view of the empirical limits of the demotic discourse. Finally, the findings will be related to the question of community, as opposed to civil, rights.

The *community* patterning of the demotic discourse
Different Southall *communities* appear to favour different ways of dissolving the dominant equation between 'culture' and ethnic or religious community. This observation should not be overstated, and I have deliberately spoken of patterning only. The strategy of encompassment, to name an example, appears privileged among Hindu Southallians, but it is open also to Sikhs or, for that matter, to pan-Africanists speaking of an African-Caribbean *community*. Not to acknowledge these overlaps would be a denial of personal agency, as well as a reintroduction of the dominant discourse by the back door. Yet the data indicate unequivocally that 'patterning' is not too strong a word. To account for this observation, one may consider two reasons. Firstly, I shall argue that members of each *community* are indeed able to draw upon some shared values and compatible versions of their history that distinguish them from selected others. Secondly, I shall propose that *community* boundaries reflect perceived structural positions in the post-migration environment. This helps to account for the simultaneity of Southallians perpetuating pre-migration *communities* and at the same time consciously creating new, post-migration cultures.

The shared heritage that each ethnic *community* equates with its *culture* differs, of course, from one to the other. To many South Asian Southallians, the *culture* of their respective *communities* is predicated upon its religious heritage and the historical dynamics on the Indian subcontinent. To many Afro-Caribbean Southallians, it is predicated on a history of exploitation shared across islands and, in the pan-Africanist version, among all people of African descent. For many Irish as well as English Southallians, the dominant equation evokes a past life in culturally homogeneous local *communities* now 'lost'. Given that members of each *community* thus predicate their equation of *culture* and *community* on different perceived heritages, it becomes more plausible that the equation validated in such different ways should also be dissociated in different ways in each.

A second reason for this patterning may be seen in the perceived structural position of each *community* in the shared, but highly competitive arena of Southall. Different *communities* continue, by and large, to occupy different positions in the demographic, economic, political, and social fabric of town. Southallians' own assessments of these differences are likely to have a direct bearing on their choice between the dominant discourse and the demotic one: a *community* thought unified by structural advantages or disadvantages is more likely to be endorsed as the possessor of a reified *culture*. Conversely, as Southallians judge that their *community*'s structural position is becoming more differentiated, the equation between their *culture* and their *community* is reformulated, and new *communities* are acknowledged or created. The class distinction of East African migrants is a case in point. The new equation is not, however, predicated on a simple class definition of *culture*, but subtly articulated with the idiom of caste, long validated as a *culture* marker in South Asian heritages.

The converse process makes equal sense. As structural positions are thought, by Southallians, to show less differentiation, the equation of *community* and *culture* is reformulated to be more inclusive. A clear case in point is the incipient endorsement of an *Asian community* among the young. It is commonly predicated on a shared conviction that all 'Asians' are equally subject to racial discrimination and thus find themselves in the same structural position. To render this new collective plausible as a *community*, it is necessary to identify it with a shared *culture*, that is, an *Asian culture* which sets aside the heritages of religion and caste as *culture* markers, and proceeds to construct new cultural commonalities that span these distinctions. The popularity of Bhangra music can be understood in this context as providing a symbolic and expressive focus of a new *Asian culture* in Britain.

The variety of co-existing, and sometimes contending, definitions of *communities* as *cultures* thus feeds on both a shared historical heritage and a more-or-less consensual assessment of a shared structural position. The example of newly forged *communities*, be they on a large scale such as the Afro-Caribbean or Asian, or on a small one such as the Ramgarhia or the Ravidasi, raises the second analytical question, namely why Southallians should not simply drop the dominant equation of culture with ethnic community. After all, the variety of *community* definitions would appear to offer strong evidence that *communities* are processually constructed, rather than found as the ready-made social correlates of consistent and bounded *cultures*.

The local persistence of the dominant discourse

At first sight, it appears paradoxical that even the proponents of admittedly new *communities* continue, in chosen contexts, to profess the dominant equation and sometimes indeed apply it to their creations. The
seeming paradox has several explanations that mutually reinforce each
other. For one, the equation of *culture* with *community*, and especially
ethnic and religious *communities*, is the hallmark of the dominant
discourse, that is, the discourse favoured by dominant institutions and
agents. For so-called immigrants and ethnic minorities, it represents the
currency within which they must deal with the political and media estab-
lishments on both the national and the local level. Southallians hear
national parties and governments and nationwide media speaking of
them, and adjudicating their claims, in the language of ethnic communities distinguishable by reified cultures. On the local level, too, the claims
for public resources are adjudicated community by community, and what
defines a community is its culture. The dominant discourse represents the
hegemonic language within which Southallians must explain themselves
and legitimate their claims.

A second explanation may, to some extent, be seen in the mere fact of
migration. Southallians raised abroad would not be the first migrants to
show signs of a 'cultural conservatism' which maintains traditions,
conventions and proprieties long cast to the winds back home. I am
reluctant to place too much weight on this reason, not least since I have
never been to the Punjab, East Africa, or the Caribbean. Admittedly,
when a reader tells me that 'publicly endorsing caste endogamy is
becoming unacceptable for many people [in India]', I am reminded of the
young Punjabi Southallian who, returning from his first trip 'back India',
remarked how 'much more modern' he had found conventions there.
Migrants do, of course, remove themselves from the cultural process
itself and may then seek refuge in reifying that cultural process into a
cultural heritage of their ethnic or religious *community*. Such 'cultural
conservatism' may thus contribute toward maintaining the dominant
discourse as a local one. One should be wary, however, of postulating
pseudo-psychological mechanisms and dynamics thought to apply to
migrants because they migrated. The different approaches to *culture* in
the Afro-Caribbean *community*, and the contestations over *community*
among Southallians at large have reflected plenty of voices that show no
trace of a quasi-'natural' 'cultural conservatism' ascribable to former
migrants. This psychologizing topos is, at any rate, rather selective in
what it wishes to explain. Migrant or not, the very process of encultur-

ating children necessitates a certain amount of reification of the collective heritage one wishes them to reproduce or at least learn about. As Berger and Luckmann (1967) have stressed from the outset of this debate, 'reification is a modality of consciousness, more precisely, [...] a modality of man's objectification of the human world' (Berger and Luckmann 1967, 106-7). To reify ideas is a propensity embedded in the objectivation of social life, observable among sociologists and native populations no less than among former migrants.

The least tribalist way to explain why Southallians do what they do, still seems to me to lie in what other Southallians do. If one *community* finds that playing the dominant game of reified *cultures* will gain it resources and respect, any other *community* would be foolish to opt out of the dominant rules. There is, usually, little point in engaging the demotic discourse when facing resource competition predicated on the dominant one. Yet there are also internal reasons why Southallians speaking of their *communities* engage the dominant discourse with ease and conviction.

In serving a *community*, be it an old or a new one, two idioms are used concurrently. One is phrased in the language of conservation, and its usefulness stands to reason. An appeal to build upon a heritage older than one's own efforts establishes traditional legitimacy. Even the development of a new *community* is facilitated by appeal to a heritage, especially when it can be reified. Should this not be plausible, then the *community* heritage needs to be portrayed as having been dormant, latent, or unjustly neglected. New *communities* often claim to fulfil potentials that have been extant for a long time. The prior existence of that *community* potential legitimates as continuity what, to the outsider, must appear as a new departure. The legitimation by fulfilling a past potential is complemented by a second legitimation which invokes a future potential. Thus, the dynamic and innovatory aspects can be expressed as '*community* building' and '*community* development'. The two idioms, none the less, must be balanced consistently, so that an appeal can be made at once to the legitimacy of tradition and the legitimacy of future purpose.

Yet different *communities* often face different heritages to appeal to or indeed overcome. The confirmation of a unitary Afro-Caribbean or indeed pan-Africanist *community* may be highly plausible on the strength of a shared heritage of exploitation and oppression; the unification of an Asian *community*, by contrast, must first overcome the divisions between old and new, more inclusive or more exclusive, religious, caste, and congregational *community* heritages. Southall's South Asian *communities* may fuse what was distinct on the subcontinent, or differentiate what seemed unitary there. To render visible a shared heritage behind these old or recent divisions requires an alternative writing of history. A good example, observed in 1989, may be seen in reviving the memory of an *all-Asian* anticolonial hero. I have described how ideas of an *Asian community* have, even among the young, to contend with the divisions of religion and caste, as well national loyalties. The new *Asian* unity is orientated, first and foremost among the young, upon a legitimacy of the future. Yet to be convincing, it also requires a legitimacy of the past.

Most heroes of anti-colonialism and the struggle for independence are, of course, identified with Pakistani or Indian nationalism, or with Muslim, Sikh, or Hindu heritages. One remarkable exception, however, entered young Southallians' purview in the late 1980s. A Punjabi named Uddam Singh had survived the infamous Amritsar massacre of 1919, in which some 350 unarmed civilians were killed by British troops under the command of General, later Sir, Michael O'Dwyer. Recasting his name as Ram Mohammed Singh Azaad to reflect the joint Hindu, Muslim, and Sikh aspiration toward freedom (*azaad*), Uddam determined to alert the British public to the injustice of British rule by assassinating O'Dwyer. He resolved, moreover, not to do so in a secret ambush, but at a public election meeting in Westminster, so that his own public trial and his execution, in July 1940, would fuel and inspire the cause. Uddam Singh thus provides a symbolic means by which the aspirations toward an *Asian community* can build upon a legitimacy of the past. This traditional legitimacy of the anti-colonial cause can now strengthen and complement the widely accepted future legitimacy of an *Asian community* united in the face of racist discrimination in Britain.

Just as the appeals to past legitimacy are constructed differently within each *community*, so the appeal to future legitimacy shows patterned differences. Across the board, its principal catalyst is the fear of racist discrimination and the perceived need to resist it as a newly united *community*. This fear, none the less, appears unevenly distributed across the recognized local ethnic *communities*. Many adult South Asian Southallians trust that discrimination can be overcome by means other than forming one comprehensive *Asian community*. They tend to agree, conversely, that Afro-Caribbeans suffer the most intense racist discrimination, and most Afro-Caribbeans can see in '*community* building' their best chance of countering it. Irish Southallians present the most equivocal case in this regard. Very few of them embrace the option of becoming a politically recognized ethnic community to better their life-chances, and most of them fear that it will make matters worse. This is so despite a cultural heritage that can plausibly be seen as a shared history of colonial oppression and united rebellion. Yet this Irish Republican heritage is widely associated with the Provisional IRA, and its public endorsement is not merely discredited by people in Britain, but curbed by an Emergency Legislation unique in Western Europe. The complexity of the case shows the discretion with which past heritages are, and sometimes must be, assumed or set aside in the constant re-creation of culture.

The weighing of legitimacies of the past and those of the future must thus differ from one *community* to another, and from one time and place to another. This consideration provides a further reason for both the ethnographic questions I have asked: it makes it clearer why the demotic discourse should be patterned differently in different *communities*, and it throws a further light on the persistence of the dominant discourse among Southallians who engage the demotic as well.

What defines Southallians' culture is thus not that they replace the dominant discourse with the demotic one at all times. Rather, Southall culture entails a dual discursive competence, embracing the dominant as well as the demotic, and it is the dominant that emphasizes the conservation of existing *communities* and the demotic that allows Southallians to re-conceive *community* boundaries and contest the meaning of *culture*. These contestations, however, tend to stop short of taking one final step: the word *culture* remains restricted, in many contexts, to its reified meaning. This observation, implicit in much of the data of the previous chapter, poses the question of how the two discourses relate to each other.

The relationship between dominant and demotic discourse
The demotic discourse, which allows Southallians to create new *communities* as well as to subdivide or fuse existing ones, is not an autonomous opposite, or independent alternative, to the dominant one. It is used to undermine the dominant one whenever Southallians, pursuing their aims as they see them, judge it useful in any one context. Yet it does not make the dominant discourse lose its salience: it would hardly be dominant, after all, if Southallians could 'switch it off' altogether.

The very existence of a demotic discourse which separates *culture* and *community* and reconsiders their meanings, is a reaction, arising in a plethora of different contexts, to the dominant one. It represents an alternative discourse, but not an independent one. This general observation becomes most tangible when one surveys the use of the word *culture* among Southallians. In the parlance of most Southallians, the meaning of *culture* is not nearly as negotiable as the meaning of *community*. *Culture* is still largely reserved to describing the stable heritage about which, for the sake of which, or indeed against which, one negotiates change. There are numerous exceptions to this observation, and one need only recall data gathered among Afro-Caribbean and white Southallians, as well as, among children, the twelve-year old who saw *culture* as 'new things made that there haven't been made'. There are further exceptions, of course, among Southallians with strong cross-*community* commitments. Yet in putting my argument with the due qualifications, I shall regard all these as exceptions.

Most Southallians are in most contexts hesitant to use the word *culture* in its de-essentialized sense, even when they do engage the demotic discourse and debate what *community* might mean. Cultural change, that is, culture in its de-essentialized anthropological meaning, is not denied of course. Yet the process of culture-making is more often called 'developing the *community*', '*community* building', or 'changing the *community*'. Most leadership of, social service for, and even membership in, a *community* are made to appear as servicing the reified *culture* of that *community*. Indeed, most Southallians I know are as happy to call themselves 'members' of a *culture* as they are to be counted members of one or another *community*. Even when *culture* is questioned, as for instance by socialist and feminist Southallians, the word is very often used to describe the reified and stable heritage that manifests the existence of a recognizable *community*. Why should this be ?

There is nothing wrong, of course, with Southallians' conception of *culture*. Anthropologists have no copyright on the term, and Southallians have every right to use it in whatever ways they find useful. But their usage often differs from that of anthropologists, and the difference needs to be accounted for. It is remarkable, after all, that so many Southallians should reserve their concept of *culture* to designate a seemingly immutable object amidst all their creative processes of changing *community* allegiances, *community* formations, and *community* loyalties. Two explanations I have mentioned already. The difference between most Southallians' and most social scientists' conceptions of culture may have something to do with a post-immigration 'cultural conservatism', or they may simply result from the need to reify *culture* in order to enculturate the young, especially in a culturally plural milieu. More important, however, appears to me the imbalance between the two discourses themselves. The word 'culture' is 'occupied', in and by the dominant discourse, to mean a reified entity.

The same could be said, at first sight, about 'community'. Yet the word has a far more tangible and commonsensical meaning than the abstract 'culture'. Often enough in the dominant discourse *about* ethnic minorities, it does entail insinuations of ethnic or religious otherness and even exclusion; but it also retains its place in common-sense parlance where, in Gilroy's words, it 'signifies ... mutuality, cooperation, identification and symbiosis' (Gilroy 1987, 234). This dual signification is, I take it, precisely why Williams (1976) regarded it as problematic, sociologists have shunned it, and Ignatieff (1992) called it a dishonest word. What this dual significance allows for, however, is to reassess what collectives Southallians apply the word to. The same is not true of the word 'culture'.

What tangible referents it associates are seemingly tangible 'bodies' of tradition and custom, readily subject to reification. In the dominant discourse, this reified understanding of culture is given a privileged place: it defines what counts as a community. If Southallians were to use *culture* as an idea equally negotiable and processual as *community*, their usage would threaten to deprive *communities* of their very *raison d'être* as the dominant discourse has fixed it. A *community*, however new or old, that cannot point to a *culture* which it stands for, serves or owns, risks losing that part of its legitimacy that is orientated on the past. Such are the dictates, and such the hegemony, of the dominant discourse.

This reasoning must sound rather abstract, not least because it attempts to explain what is *not* done, rather than what is. It fits well, however, with the more concrete observations of the dominant discourse in use. To sketch these in briefly, let me return to the first observations about Southall as a town.

What most Southallians share in common, across all observable *community* boundaries, is the wish to move both 'out and up', and the competition for scarce public resources that *community leaders* vie for on behalf of each *community*. This happens in an arena called 'town' but characterized by few civic institutions, little civic pride, and extraordinary levels of need. Competition is thus intense, and as the dominant rhetoric of *community* is a resource in this competition, so is a largely reified conception of *culture*. Take away competition predicated on ethnic or religious *community* criteria, and Southallians' definitions of *culture* might well come to parallel anthropologists' definitions of culture.

Yet there is little prospect of this happening. On the contrary, political practice based on the dominant discourse has elevated appeals to *community* needs and *community* rights to the level of a substitute civic resource. Drawing on Kalka's (1991) insightful ethnography, chapter 2 has mentioned how public policies can indeed create the very *communities* that are then to be recognized and served. It is only recently that such political practices have been questioned. The problems raised, however, go to the very heart of what the dominant discourse was expected to achieve.

The question of rights
One of the chief reasons for which ethnopolitical movements embraced the reification of 'their' cultures lay in their demands for a new kind of rights. These rights of *communities* were more collective in conception than the traditionally individualist civil rights, yet far more geared toward economic emancipation than generally Human Rights. Often, these new *community* rights were to make up for the effects of past discrimination. This new class of rights had been far commoner in colonial and post-colonial states than in Western democracies. In India, Beteille (1991) traces their origin to colonial policies of 'community' balance:

Caste quotas in education and employment were introduced during British rule and, in some parts of the country, all positions in certain sectors of employment and education were reserved according to caste and community. These quotas were designed more in the interest of political balance than of social equality.
(*Beteille 1991, 205–6*)

With independence, the caste quotas were retained, or rather reconceived, as a mechanism, safeguarded in the constitution itself, of promoting a more equitable distribution of opportunities across caste and putative 'ethnic' boundaries. Yet they exacted a price: 'There has been ... some limitation of individual rights, including the right to equal opportunity, in the interest of policies designed to bring about greater equality overall' (Beteille 1991, 194).

Beteille constructs the comparative dimension of his essay by following Dworkin's ([1977], 1984) distinction between equality as a right and equality as a policy, and associating the one with American individualism, the other with the more collectivist cultural foundations of the Indian Constitution. Yet in India, too, caste quotas and reservations have led to violent riots and self-immolations, and many Indians, while 'in favour of a policy of equality ... argue that the disadvantaged ought to be defined by rational economic criteria and not by caste' (Beteille 1991, 207). Furthermore, Dworkin's distinction is drawn to provide a commentary, intended for law students and thus intrinsically conservative in its assumptions, on the classic DeFunis case which contested 'reverse discrimination' (Dworkin 1984, 224–35). The idea of 'equality as a policy', as opposed to a right, has become a part of United States practice as much as it is of the Indian constitution. The question, however, is: equality of what?

The distinctions that underlie this question have been drawn most clearly by Wilson (1987) who helped to spark the current debate about 'welfare reform' in the United States. What is at stake, according to Wilson, are three different principles of equality: those of individual opportunity, group opportunity, and life-chances. Political attention to a merely individual equality of opportunity, enshrined in the 'Great Society' project, proved insufficient since it could not remove the accumulated effects of group discrimination in the past (Wilson 1987, 146). Following the principle of equal group opportunities, 'people have been formally categorized ... on the basis of race or ethnicity [...with the aim] not only to prevent discrimination, but also to ensure that minorities are adequately represented in ... employment, in public programs, and in education' (Wilson 1987, 114).

These categorizations, as basic to ethnic targeting as they are to affirmative action, are, evidently, the dominant discourse in practice. They elevate the ethnic or cultural categories recognized by one or more parties into quasi-groups, and proceed to endow these quasi-groups, now defined by reified cultures, with collective rather than individual rights. In the American case, as in the British, this predication of policies on the dominant discourse appears to have spanned the gulf between established policy makers and self-declared ethnic initiatives for well over two decades. Yet several developments appear to have undermined this consensus. Leaving to one side, for the moment, the financial crisis of the United States 'welfare system', and discounting white resentments at affirmative action, such as I have pointed to in Southall, the dominant discourse is by its very premises a barrel without a bottom. Assuming a minimum of economic purpose rationality, ethnic and cultural communities will proliferate as soon as their construction is rewarded with tangible resources. Plural societies, after all, show a plethora of cross-cutting social cleavages which can be designated 'community' cleavages at will. At the same time, community movements undergo a process of segmentation which Turner (1993) has pointed to in his critique of multi-culturalism in the United States. The competitive use of the dominant discourse may come to favour 'cultural nationalists and fetishists of *difference*, for whom *culture* reduces to ... a license for political and intellectual separatism' (Turner 1993, 414). This latter development is all the more inevitable if engagement of the dominant discourse fails to deliver the goods of equality that its established protagonists have promised. These established spokesmen are by no means all-white or, in India, all high-caste. On the contrary, the community-specific use of the dominant discourse helps the co-optation of ethnic elites, just as the social policies predicated on ethnic targeting tend to favour nascent elites within identified ethnic constituencies. Yet the 'truly disadvantaged', as Wilson (1987) calls them, tend to get least of the opportunities now apportioned along ethnic or community lines. It is with this rationale that Wilson takes up Fishkin's (1983) idea of basing policies of equality on an equality of life-chances:

The major factor that distinguishes the principle of equality of life-chances from the principles of equality of individual opportunity and equality of group opportunity is the recognition that the problems of truly disadvantaged individuals – class background, low income, a broken home, inadequate housing, poor education, or cultural or linguistic differences – may not be clearly related to the issue of previous discrimination ... Accordingly, programs based on this principle [i.e. equality of life-chances] ... would be targeted to truly disadvantaged individuals regardless of their race or ethnicity.   *(Wilson 1987, 117)*

The consensus on predicating rights and social policies on ethnic criteria seems, at first sight, to have come to the end of its twenty-year run. In retrospect, it may appear as a transient compromise between old elites who translated racist assumptions into the culturalist language of the dominant discourse, and new elites who fought for civil equality on the premise of ethnic, caste, or religious 'group' identities. Yet the matter may not be as simple as that.

In Europe, too, the dominant discourse has been found politically wanting. Here, it has come to be critiqued under the name 'multi-culturalism'. Writing of multi-culturalism in Germany, Radtke (in press) identifies its political practice as clientelist and its effects as a 'folkloric' self-ethnicization of minorities. In the Swedish case, Schierup (in press) diagnoses a process of 'enclavisation' which helps produce ethnic, sectarian or 'fundamentalist' marginalization. In Britain, where the dominant discourse united the entire political spectrum from right to left, both wings have begun to question its usefulness. This may lead to a reaffirmation of the old integrationist project (Schlesinger 1992), or it may lead to a renewed stress on social policy, as opposed to ethnic targeting. Thus, Al-Azmeh (1993) has found that 'structural and spatial segregation and social involution and ghetto formation lie at the basis of culturalism ... [as] the prevalent mode of discourse' about ethnic and religious minorities (Al-Azmeh 1993, 7), and has called for a renewed emphasis on social policies that are anti-culturalist and anti-essentialist. The options of ethnic targeting and social policy may not, in practice, have to be mutually exclusive, and Modood (1993) has argued that the effectiveness of general initiatives of social policy could be enhanced by aiming specifically at deprived and disadvantaged categories within identified ethnic communities. One might think, thus, of general social policy initiatives aimed specifically at, say, 'Muslim women' or 'Afro-Caribbean youth'. The suggestion sounds reassuring at first sight: it certainly takes leave of the dominant stylization of communities into homogeneous collectives marked by a uniform, reified culture. Yet it also risks singling out precisely those supposed 'problem groups' that the dominant discourse has pre-defined under its ethnic labels. It is, in other words, the dominant discourse rehabilitated by the back door, that is, as the ethnic *modus operandi* of a purportedly generalist social policy. It is possible that this is the best that can be done after twenty years under the hegemony of the dominant discourse. The question must indeed be faced as to how far a generalist social policy is feasible at all. To consider it, I shall focus, in turn, on policy makers, *community leaders*, and the intended or putative beneficiaries.

Policy makers in charge of public funds will certainly feel obliged to take into account such sociological factors as migratory history, linguistic disadvantage, or indeed racist patterns of discrimination. If nothing else, they distort the labour market, and they do not, in principle, raise any questions about community rights. They apply as much to the single homeless youngster migrating from Liverpool to London as to dissidents who have been granted political asylum. Yet since even Wilson (1987) concedes that 'equality of individual opportunity' has not removed the effects of past or continuing ethnic discrimination, it is hard to see how an indiscriminate pursuit of 'equality of life-chances' could do any better. Furthermore, one can expect even small numbers of homeless migrants or political refugees to develop ideas of a shared community and to lobby for social-policy resources on the collective strength of this community status. Policy-effective as the term has been for the past twenty years, it will not simply be abandoned by those who need to claim scarce public resources.

'Community leaders', likewise, will not lightly discard the dominant discourse which they have been raised upon, and sometimes raised by. Any switch from ethnic targeting to a generalist social policy has to take into account what is there already, historically and, just as importantly, locally. At the local level, I see no insurmountable obstacles to social policy taking leave of the dominant discourse. Most of the *community leaders* I spoke to in Southall were proudest, not of the municipal grants that benefited their own *community*, but of the case-work that filled most of their spare time. It would be naive, and I say this because I thought so before I went to live in Southall, to think of case-work as tampering with symptoms. For *community leaders*, at least at the local level, it is the morally most demanding, and the affectively most rewarding, public activity they know. Yet the higher claims to leadership and spokesmanship reach toward the national level, the more will *community leaders* have to rely upon the legitimation that only the dominant discourse can confer on their judgements and views.

Thirdly, and probably most importantly, the people whom anthropologists study and local *leaders* try to serve, are themselves often beholden to ethnic and cultural reifications when they discuss the uses of social policies and civic or collective rights. It would be desirable however, for public debates to take a more informed account of the views, conceptions, and, in the anthropological sense, the culture of the intended beneficiaries.

Few, if any, Southallians deny the legitimacy of ethnic or cultural considerations in the making and remaking of laws. All Southallians I know, whatever their ethnic labels, think it right that there is a 'Race Relations Act' which punishes racist discrimination, and most recognize that such discrimination is powerful in the job market, though not necessarily the housing market. Such differences need to be taken into account. Similarly, all but two Southallians whom I spoke to about the Rushdie Affair favoured extending the blasphemy law to protect all religions in Britain, and the two exceptions wanted to see it abolished altogether, much as the highest legal authority in Britain has done since 1979. There is thus no question of Southallians denying the legitimacy of ethnic and cultural considerations *per se*. But they are usually supported because they may enhance civil equality. The critical point is often reached when it comes to the allocation of public resources on categorical collective criteria.

I have mentioned resentments about job advertisements that specify a particular ethnic minority status, as they played a role in the 'Black or

Asian?' controversy. Further problems arise when the dominant discourse is used, in a particular local or national form, to determine considerations of collective need. It stands to reason that, with limited resources, a distribution 'community by community' will, in time, develop two unintended effects. One is the growth of patronage and clientelism, which may contribute to political corruption or 'only', but just as dangerously, the mere perception of unfair advantage. The other is that it pitches different perceived communities against each other in competition and rivalry. As it was expressed above, 'we're tied to each other back to back, and we're struggling for fuck's sake to get free.' Effective public policies will want to end this waste of energies used up in back-to-back struggling, one community pitched against another. But policy makers, like *community leaders*, cannot count on support unless they understand the people they wish to serve. These people are far more sophisticated in their ways of thinking about, and dealing with, cultural, community, and ethnic difference than they have been made out to be. This is a point of direct concern to the practice of ethnicity studies in general and community studies in particular.

As the debate intensifies between the advocates of community rights and the protagonists of social policies based on civil rights, community studies are certain to be questioned about their assumptions. In reducing the culture of former migrants to an epiphenomenon of their reified ethnicity, many community studies have laid themselves open to charges of 'culturalism'. With many, indeed, the charge will stick, and some have turned out to be nothing better than academically disguised charters for new communities in the image of the dominant discourse. Yet these failings are not inherent in the genre as such. One can certainly limit one's study to, let us say, 'Sikhs in Middletown' without reducing all their actions and words to a symptom of 'Sikhness'. Neither does such a study have to treat ethnicity as if it were the same phenomenon in all situations. Wallman (1979) has stressed how ethnicity in the workplace can be constructed quite differently from ethnicity in a residential context. Furthermore, even in a residential context such as the Southallian, people may go far beyond the dominant discourse to construct the boundaries, and indeed the meanings, of culture, community, and ethnic identity. These discourses need to be distinguished and contextualized, and I can see no way of doing this other than through intensive field-work, the hallmark of community studies, and a consistent revalidation of culture as an analytical concept. Lutz and Abu-Lughod (1990) are, I think, right that 'for many, ... the term [culture] seems to connote ...

fundamentally different, essentialized, and homogeneous social units' (1990, 9). Yet this is a result of ethnographers reflecting the reifications they find, instead of analysing them. Even when focusing on an analysis of discourses, rather than reified cultures, the idea of culture remains essential in order to locate the articulation of the different discursive competences we find.

This task would be easy, or indeed unnecessary, if as Keesing has argued, cultural essentialism were just the result of anthropologists constructing some 'radical alterity – a culturally constructed Other radically different from Us' (1994, 310). But it is not only anthropologists who 'deal with' what they call 'other cultures'. Many of our informants also do so, and we need to find out why, when, and how the people we study may reify in some contexts what in others they are aware of creating themselves. By the same token, it may well appear convincing that:

the notion of an authentic culture as an autonomous internally coherent universe no longer seems tenable, except perhaps as a 'useful fiction' or a revealing distortion.   *(Rosaldo 1989, 217)*

Yet the fact remains that Southallians, and probably other people elsewhere, subscribe to this useful fiction some of the time, and disown it at other times. They are thus not dupes of the dominant discourse. But neither are they post-modernist champions of a cult which worships 'hybridity' or 'border zones' for their own sakes. The search for unbounded 'borderlands' and supra-cultural indeterminacies may indeed lead us back to a slightly more *risqué* re-run of an infatuation with the exotic. Southallians, by contrast, develop their discursive competences in close connection with the social facts of everyday life, and they cultivate fine judgements of when to use what discourse in which situation. There is plenty for community studies to do in exploring such 'multi-cultural' cultures at the local level and in pitching their sophistication against the simple choices proffered in policy debates. The Southall data clearly show that there is no idea as important for understanding social life as the concept of culture.

References

Anon. 1988. 'Dominion and the African Caribbean Community'. Typescript, 4 pp., circulated in Southall

Afro-Caribbean Focus and Beyond. 1987. *Up Front*. Brochure, privately printed

Al-Azmeh, A. 1993. *Islams and Modernities*. London: Verso

Anderson, Elijah. 1990. *Streetwise. Race, Class, and Change in an Urban Community*. Chicago: The University of Chicago Press

Asad, Talal. 1990. 'Multiculturalism and British Identity in the Wake of the Rushdie Affair', *Politics and Society*, 18, 4, 455–80

Aurora, Gurdip Singh. 1967. *The New Frontiersmen*. Bombay: Popular Prakashan

Ballard, Catherine. 1979. 'Conflict, Continuity and Change. Second-generation South Asians', in Verity Saifullah Khan (ed.), *Minority Families in Britain. Support and Stress*. London: Macmillan, pp. 109–29

Ballard, Roger. 1972. 'Family Organisation amongst the Sikhs in Britain', *New Community*, 2, 1, 12–33

1990. 'Migration and Kinship: The Differential Effect of Marriage Rules on the Processes of Punjabi Migration to Britain', in C. Clarke, C. Peoch, and S. Vertovec et al. (eds.): *South Asians Overseas*. Cambridge: Cambridge University Press, pp. 219–49

Banton, Michael. 1983. *Racial and Ethnic Competition*. Cambridge: Cambridge University Press

Barth, Fredrik (ed.). 1969. *Ethnic Groups and Boundaries. The Social Organization of Culture Difference*. London: George Allen & Unwin

1994. 'A Personal View of Present Tasks and Priorities in Cultural and Social Anthropology', in Robert Borofsky (ed.), *Assessing Cultural Anthropology*. New York: McGraw-Hill, pp. 349–61

Baumann, Gerd. 1990. 'The Re-Invention of *Bhangra*: Social Change and Aesthetic Shifts in a Punjabi Music in Britain', *The World of Music* (Berlin), 2, 81–98

1992. 'Ritual Implicates "Others": Rereading Durkheim in a Plural Society', in Daniel de Coppet (ed.), *Understanding Rituals*. London and New York: Routledge, pp. 97–116

1994. '"The Lamps are Many but the Light is One"? Processes of Syncretization in a Multi-ethnic Suburb of London', in Goran Aijmer (ed.),

Syncretism and the Commerce of Symbols. Gothenburg: University of Gothenburg Press, pp. 1–18

Berger, Peter and Thomas Luckmann. 1967. *The Social Construction of Reality. A Treatise in the Sociology of Knowledge*. Harmondsworth: Penguin Books

Beteille, André. 1991. *Society and Politics in India: Essays in a Comparative Perspective*. London and Atlantic Highlands, NJ: The Athlone Press

Bhachu, Parminder. 1985. *Twice Migrants. East African Sikh Settlers in Britain*. London: Tavistock

Bourdieu, Pierre and Jean-Claude Passeron. 1977. *Reproduction in Education, Society and Culture*. London: Sage Publications

1984. *Distinction. A Social Critique of the Judgment of Taste*. London: Routledge & Kegan Paul

Brah, Autar. 1987. 'Women of South Asian Origin in Britain: Issues and Concerns', *South Asia Research*, 1, 1, 39–54

Burghart, Richard (ed.). 1987. *Hinduism in Great Britain: The Perpetuation of Religion in an Alien Cultural Milieu*. London: Tavistock

Clayton, Jacquie. 1988. 'The Southall Detached Youth Project Annual Report. 1987–88.' Unpublished typescript

Clifford, James. 1988. *The Predicament of Culture. Twentieth-Century Ethnography, Literature, and Art*. Cambridge, MA: Harvard University Press

Cohen, Anthony. 1985. *The Symbolic Construction of Community*. Manchester: Manchester University Press

Comaroff, John and Jean Comaroff. 1992. *Ethnography and the Historical Imagination*. Boulder, CO: Westview Press

Comitas, L. and D. Lowenthal (eds). 1973. *Work and Family Life – West Indian Perspectives*. New York: Anchor Books

Crompton, Yorke. 1971. *Hinduism*. London: Ward Lock Educational

Dewan, Veeno. 1988. 'Upcoming: Cobra', *Ghazal and Beat* 4, March 1988, 8 Southall, Middx.: Derbar Publishers

Dominion. 1989. *Annual Report of the Dominion Centre. 1988–89*. Xerograph, 18 pp. Southall: Dominion Centre

Dummett, Ann. 1984. *A Portrait of English Racism*. London: CARAF Publications

Dumont, Louis. 1980. *Homo Hierarchicus. The Caste System and its Implications*. Augmented English translation. Chicago: Chicago University Press

Dworkin, Ronald. [1977] 1984. *Taking Rights Seriously*. London: Duckworth

Ealing. 1982. *The 1981 Census: Ward and Borough Profiles*. London: London Borough of Ealing Town Planning Division, Technical Services Group

Education Reform Act (1988). London: Her Majesty's Stationery Office

Fischer, Michael. 1986. 'Ethnicity and the Post-Modern Arts of Memory', in James Clifford and George Marcus (eds.), *Writing Culture. The Poetics and Politics of Ethnography*. Berkeley: University of California Press, pp. 194–233

Fisher, George. 1983. 'Language in Political Context: The Case of West Indians in Britain', *Oxford Review of Education*, 9, 2, 123–31

Fitzherbert, K. 1967. *West Indian Children in London*. London: G. Bell & Sons

Fishkin, J. 1983. *Justice, Equal Opportunity, and the Family*. New Haven, CT: Yale University Press

Fox, Richard. 1985. *Lions of the Punjab. Culture in the Making*. Berkeley: University of California Press

Fuller, C. J. 1992. *The Camphor Flame. Popular Hinduism and Society in India*. Princeton, NJ: Princeton University Press

Genovese, Eugene D. 1974. *Roll Jordan Roll. The World the Slaves Made*. New York: Pantheon Books

Ghazal and Beat. 1988a. 'Growing Up with Kuljit Bhamra' *Ghazal and Beat* 4, March 1988, 14. Southall, Middx.: Derbar Publishers

  1988b. 'London Promoters', *Ghazal and Beat* 8, August 1988, 13–14. Southall, Middx.: Derbar Publishers

Gillespie, Marie. 1989. 'Technology and Tradition: Audio-Visual Culture among South Asian Families in West London', *Cultural Studies*, 3, 2, 226–40

  1995. *Television, Ethnicity and Cultural Change*. London: Routledge

Gilroy, Paul. 1987. *There Ain't No Black in the Union Jack. The Cultural Politics of Race and Nation*. London: Routledge

  1992. 'The End of Antiracism', in J. Donald and A. Rattansi (eds.), *'Race', Culture and Difference*. London: Sage Publications in association with The Open University

Goody, Jack. 1968. 'Introduction', in Jack Goody (ed.), *Literacy in Traditional Societies*. Cambridge: Cambridge University Press

Goody, Jack and Ian Watt. 1963. 'The Consequences of Literacy', in *Comparative Studies in Society and History*, 5, 3, 304–45. Reprinted in Goody (ed.) 1968, 27–68

Grant, E. 1989. Review of 'Omega Rising: Woman of Rastafari', *Spare Rib*, 204, 32

Gupta, Akhil and James Ferguson. 1992. 'Beyond "Culture": Space, Identity, and the Politics of Difference', *Cultural Anthropology*, 7, 1, 6–23

Haaland, Gunnar. 1969. 'Economic Determinants in Ethnic Processes', in Fredrik Barth (ed.), *Ethnic Groups and Boundaries. The Social Organization of Culture Difference*. London: George Allen & Unwin, pp. 58–73

Halliday, Fred. 1992. *Arabs in Exile: Yemeni Migrants in Urban Britain*. London: I.B. Taurus & Co

Hawkes, Barbara. 1990a. 'Southall: An Ethnography of Change', BSc dissertation in Sociology, Department of Human Sciences, Brunel, The University of West London

Hawkes, Barbara. 1990b. Appendix to 1990a

Hechter, M. and Gumperz, J. J. 1982. 'Afterword 1', in C. Fried (ed.), *Minorities: Community and Identity*. Berlin: Springer-Verlag, pp. 208–9

Henriques, F. 1949. 'West Indian Family Organisation', *American Journal of Sociology*, 55, 1, 30–7

Herskovits, M. J. 1947. *Trinidad Village*. New York: Alfred Knopf

Hillery, G. A. Jr. 1955. 'Definitions of Community: Areas of Agreement', *Rural Sociology*, 20

Hiro, Dilip. 1971. *Black British White British*. London: Eyre & Spottiswoode

Hundleby, Richard. 1987. 'A Place for Everyone … (*sic*). A Report on Afro-

Caribbean Cultural Provisions in Southall, based on a Case Study and its Contextualisation', Research Report, 40 pp. Dept. of Human Sciences, Brunel, The University of West London

IBRG. 1989. Haringay Irish in Britain Representative Group, Annual Report for. 1988–1989. London Borough of Harringay: typescript

Ignatieff, Michael. 1992. 'Why "Community" is a Dishonest Word'. *The Observer*, 3 May 1992, editorial page

Jabal, Themba. 1987. 'Black Unity and a Lost Identity in a Multi-racial Society'. *Up Front*. Southall: Afro-Caribbean Focus and Beyond, p. 8

James, W. 1986. 'A Long Way from Home: On Black Identity in Britain', *Immigrants and Minorities*, 5, 3, 258–84

Jones, S. 1988. *Black Culture, White Youth: The Reggae Tradition from JA to UK*. London: Macmillan Education

Jones, Trevor. 1993. *Britain's Ethnic Minorities. An Analysis of the Labour Force Survey*. London: Policy Studies Institute

Kalka, Iris. 1991. 'Striking a Bargain. Political Radicalism in a Middle-Class London Borough', in Pnina Werbner and Muhammad Anwar (eds.), *Black and Ethnic Leaderships in Britain. The Cultural Dimensions of Political Action*. London: Routledge, pp. 203–25

Kandre, P. 1967. 'Autonomy and Integration of Social Systems: The Iu Mien (Yao) Mountain Population and their Neighbours', in P. Kunstadter (ed.), *Southeast Asian Tribes, Minorities, and Nations*. Princeton, NJ: Princeton University Press

Kapferer, Bruce. 1988. *Legends of People, Myths of State: Violence, Intolerance and Political Culture in Sri Lanka and Australia*. Washington, DC: Smithsonian Institution Press

Katz, J.H. 1978. *White Awareness Handbook for Anti-Racism Training*. Norman, OK: University of Oklahoma Press

Keesing, Roger. 1994. 'Theories of Culture Revisited', in Robert Borofsky (ed.), *Assessing Cultural Anthropology*. New York: McGraw-Hill, pp. 301–10

Khalsi, Sewa Singh. 1992. *The Evolution of a Sikh Community in Britain. Religious and Social Change among the Sikhs of Leeds and Bradford*. Leeds: University of Leeds Community Religions Project Monograph Series no. 4

Khilnani, Sunil. 1990. 'For Want of an Authority', review of MacLeod 1989. *The Times Literary Supplement*, London, 19–25 January 1990, 68

Kingston Group. 1985. *Festivals of the Faiths*. Kingston, Surrey: Kingston Group for Racial Understanding and Equality

Kirwan, Paul. 1965. *Southall. A Brief History*. London: London Borough of Ealing Library Service. Second impression 1980

Kogon, Eugen. [1946] 1974. *Der SS-Staat. Das System der deutschen Konzentrationslager*. Munich: KindlerVerlag

Larson, Heidi. 1989. 'Asian Children – British Childhood.' PhD thesis, Department of Anthropology, The University of California, Berkeley

Lowie, Robert. 1927. *The Origin of the State*. New York: Russell and Russell

Lutz, Catherine and Lila Abu-Lughod (eds.) 1990. *Language and the Politics of Emotion*. Cambridge: Cambridge University Press

McCann, May. 1985. 'The Past in the Present: Some Aspects of the Politics of

Music in Northern Ireland.' PhD thesis, Department of Social Anthropology, The Queen's University of Belfast

Macfarlane, Alan. 1977. 'History, Anthropology and the Study of Communities', *Social History*, 5, May, 631–52

McGarry, Teresa. 1990. 'A Study of "The Irish" in Southall.' BSc dissertation in Sociology, 2 vols., Department of Human Sciences, Brunel, The University of West London

McLeod, W. H. 1974. 'Ahluwalias and Ramgarhias: Two Sikh Castes', *South Asia*, 4, 78–90

1989. *Who is a Sikh? The Problem of Sikh Identity*. Oxford: Clarendon Press

Mannheim, Karl. 1982. 'The Problem of Generations', in Chris Jenks (ed.), *The Sociology of Childhood. Essential Readings*. London: Batsford Academic and Educational Press, 256–69

Matthews, D. M. 1953. *Crisis of the West Indian Family*. Port of Spain (Trinidad): University College of the West Indies, Caribbean Affairs Series

Mitchell, J. Clyde. 1956. *The Kalela Dance: Aspects of Social Relationships Among Urban Africans in Northern Rhodesia*. Rhodes-Livingstone Papers, no. 27. Manchester: Manchester University Press

Modood, Tariq. 1988. 'Who's Defining Who?' *New Society*, 4 March 1988, 4–5

1993. 'Re-Thinking Racial Disadvantage in a Context of Pluralism.' Paper presented to the Commission on Social Justice, London

Morris, H. S. 1968. *The Indians in Uganda*. London: Weidenfeld & Nicolson

Multi-Faith Committee. 1989. 'Apartheid – A Religious Response.' Folded pamphlet. London: The Multi-Faith Committee, Anti-Apartheid Movement

Murphy, Dervla. 1987. *Tales from Two Cities. Travels of Another Sort*. London: John Murray. Reprinted 1989, Harmondsworth: Penguin Books

Nash, Manning. 1989. *The Cauldron of Ethnicity in the Modern World*. Chicago: University of Chicago Press

Parry, Jonathan. 1979. *Caste and Kinship in Kangra*. London: Routledge & Kegan Paul

Pettigrew, Joyce. 1975. *Robber Noblemen*. London: Routledge & Kegan Paul

Phoenix, Ann. 1988. 'Narrow Definitions of Culture: The Case of Early Motherhood', in S. Westwood and P. Bhachu (eds.), *Enterprising Women. Ethnicity, Economy, and Gender Relations*. London: Routledge

Poulter, Sebastian. 1986. *English Law and Ethnic Minority Customs*. London: Butterworths

Pryce, Ken. 1979. *Endless Pressure. A Study of West Indian Life-Styles in Bristol*. Bristol: Bristol Classical Press

Pullé, Stanislaus. 1974. *Police Immigrant Relations in Ealing*. London: Runnymede Trust for Ealing Community Relations Council

Radtke, Frank-Olaf. In press. 'The Construction of Ethnic Minorities and the Ethnicisation of Social Conflict in the Discourse of Multi-Culturalism', in J. Rex and B. Dury (eds.), *Ethnic Mobilisation in Europe in the 1990s*. London: Avebury

Reeves, Frank. 1983. *British Racial Discourse. A Study of British Political Discourse about Race and Race-Related Matters*. Cambridge: Cambridge University Press

Robinson, Vaughan. 1986. *Transients, Settlers and Refugees: Asians in Britain.* Oxford: Clarendon Press

Rosaldo, Renato. 1989. *Culture and Truth: The Remaking of Social Analysis.* Boston, MA: Beacon Press

Rose, H.A. 1911–19. *A Glossary of the Tribes and Castes of the Punjab and North-West Frontier Province.* Lahore: Government Publications

Rothschild, Joseph. 1981. *Ethnopolitics: A Conceptual Framework.* New York: Columbia University Press

Sahgal, Gita. 1990. 'Fundamentalism and the Multi-Culturalist Fallacy', in *Against the Grain. A Celebration of Survival and Struggle.* Southall: Southall Black Sisters Collective, pp. 16–24

Sahlins, Marshall. 1994. 'Goodbye to Tristes Tropes: Ethnography in the Context of Modern World History', in Robert Borofsky (ed.), *Assessing Cultural Anthropology.* New York: McGraw-Hill, pp. 377–94

Said, Edward. 1978. *Orientalism.* London: Routledge & Kegan Paul

Schierup, Carl-Ulrik. In press: '"Culture" or "Agency"? Ethnic Mobilization in the "Swedish Model"', in J. Rex and B. Dury (eds.), *Ethnic Mobilisation in Europe in the 1990s.* London: Avebury

Schlesinger, Arthur M. 1992. *The Disuniting of America: Reflections on a Multicultural Society.* New York: Norton

Schneider, David. 1969. 'Kinship, Nationality and Religion in American Culture', in Robert Spencer (ed.), *Forms of Symbolic Action.* Proceedings of the 1969 Annual Spring Meeting of the American Ethnological Society. Seattle: University of Washington Press for AES, pp. 116–25

Schneider, David. 1980. *American Kinship. A Cultural Account.* Second edition. Chicago: University of Chicago Press

Smith, Anthony. 1986. *The Ethnic Origins of Nations.* Oxford: Basil Blackwell

Southall Black Sisters. 1986. Southall Black Sisters Annual Report. Typescript

Southall Musical Enterprises. 1987. 'Report (S.C.C.P./3), February. 1987.' Typescript, 12 pp

SR and IRR. 1981. *Southall. The Birth of a Black Community.* Campaign Against Racism and Fascism. London: Southall Rights and Institute of Race Relations

St George's. 1988. 'Confirmation Service for Southall … on Wednesday 11th May. 1988.' Order of proceedings, typescript

   1989. 'Licensing of the Revd. Jay Kothare as Senior Curate on 20th July. 1989.' Order of proceedings, typescript

Tambs-Lyche, Harald. 1980. *London Patidars. A Case Study in Urban Ethnicity.* London: Routledge & Kegan Paul

Taylor, J. H. 1976. *The Half-Way Generation. A Study of Asian Youths in Newcastle upon Tyne.* Windsor: National Foundation for Educational Research

Tönnies, Ferdinand. [1887] 1967. *Community and Society.* New York: Harper Torchbooks

Turner, Terence. 1993. 'Anthropology and Multiculturalism: What is Anthropology That Multiculturalists Should Be Mindful of It?' *Cultural Anthropology*, 8, 4, 411–29

Tylor, Edward Burnett. [1871] 1958. *Primitive Culture.* New York: Harper Torchbooks

Usharbudh, Pandit and Yorke Crompton. 1982. *Hinduism: Some Basic Facts.* London: The Hindu Centre

van den Berghe, Pierre L. 1975. 'Ethnicity and Class in Highland Peru', in Leo Despres (ed.), *Ethnicity and Resource Competition in Plural Societies.* The Hague: Mouton, pp. 71–85

van Dijk, Teun. 1991. *Racism and the Press. Critical Studies in Racism and Migration.* London: Routledge

van der Veer, Peter. 1994. 'The Foreign Hand: Orientalist Discourse in Sociology and Communalism', in Carol Breckenridge and Peter van der Veer, *Orientalism and the Postcolonial Predicament.* Philadelphia: University of Pennsylvania Press, pp. 23–44

Vayda, Andrew. 1994. 'Actions, Variations and Change: The Emerging Anti-Essentialist View in Anthropology', in Robert Borofsky (ed.), *Assessing Cultural Anthropology.* New York: McGraw-Hill, pp. 320–9

Vertovec, Steven. 1992. 'Community and Congregation in London Hindu Temples: Divergent Trends', *New Community*, 18, 2, 251–64

In press: 'Hindus in Trinidad and Britain: Ethnic Religion, Reification, and the Politics of Public Space', in Peter van der Veer (ed.), *Nation and Migration: The Politics of Space in the South Asian Diaspora.* Philadelphia: University of Pennsylvania Press

Wahhab, Iqbal. 1989. *Muslims in Britain. Profile of a Community.* London: Runnymede Trust

Wallman, Sandra (ed.). 1979. *Ethnicity at Work.* London: Macmillan

1982. *Living in South London. Perspectives on Battersea 1871–1981.* Aldershot: Gower for the London School of Economics and Political Science

Weber, Max. 1978. *Economy and Society. An Outline of Interpretive Sociology,* ed. Guenther Roth and Claus Wittich. Berkeley: University of California Press

Werbner, Pnina and Muhammad Anwar (eds.). 1991. *Black and Ethnic Leaderships. The Cultural Dimension of Political Action.* London: Routledge

Westminster Interfaith Programme. 1988a. Newsletter to friends, dated March 1988. Typescript

1988b. Newsletter to friends, dated June 1988. Typescript

1989a. Newsletter to friends, dated June 1989. Typescript

1989b. Newsletter to friends, dated December 1989. Typescript

1990. 'Twenty-Five Years of Nostra Aetate: A Multifaith Celebration.' Order of proceedings

Williams, Raymond. 1976. *Keywords. A Vocabulary of Culture and Society.* London: Fontana

Wilson, William J. 1987. *The Truly Disadvantaged. The Inner City, the Underclass, and Public Policy.* Chicago: The University of Chicago Press

Yabsley, Hazel. 1990. 'Proximity. Processes of Ethnicity and Community Explored in Southall.' BSc dissertation in Sociology and Social Anthropology, 4 vols., Brunel, The University of West London

Young, Michael and Peter Willmott. 1957. *Family and Kinship in East London.* Harmondsworth: Penguin Books

Index

Cambridge Studies in Social and Cultural Anthropology

Editors: ERNEST GELLNER, JACK GOODY, STEPHEN GUDEMAN,
MICHAEL HERZFELD, JONATHAN PARRY

*available in paperback